SETTING THE SPIRITUAL CLOCK

WORSHIP AND WITNESS

The Worship and Witness series seeks to foster a rich, interdisciplinary conversation on the theology and practice of public worship, a conversation that will be integrative and expansive. Integrative, in that scholars and practitioners from a wide range of disciplines and ecclesial contexts will contribute studies that engage church and academy. Expansive, in that the series will engage voices from the global church and foreground crucial areas of inquiry for the vitality of public worship in the twenty-first century.

The Worship and Witness series demonstrates and cultivates the interaction of topics in worship studies with a range of crucial questions, topics, and insights drawn from other fields. These include the traditional disciplines of theology, history, and pastoral ministry—as well as cultural studies, political theology, spirituality, and music and the arts. The series focus will thus bridge church worship practices and the vital witness these practices nourish.

We are pleased that you have chosen to join us in this conversation, and we look forward to sharing this learning journey with you.

Series Editors:
John D. Witvliet
Noel Snyder
Maria Cornou

"Paul Louis Metzger has once again demonstrated an amicable and coherent way that evangelical fervor can be married to Catholic timekeeping. This marriage is not only designed for long-term use but is actually exciting! The secular calendar is neither ignored nor glamorized. I loved what he wrote about the celebration of Black History Month in Lent and the need to retreat from American exceptionalism on the Fourth of July. Marian feasts are treated with reverence, but the 95 Theses of Martin Luther also get rehabilitated. *Setting the Spiritual Clock* is a handbook to a liturgical life receptive to profoundly ecumenical insights. Christian unity seems much more palpable in the light of its lucid but simple provocations."

—PETER J. CASARELLA
Professor of Theology, Duke Divinity School

"A delightful walk through the entire Christian year. At once devotional and practical, this book is a useful guide for pastors, worship leaders, and faithful Christians of all traditions. Warmly recommended!"

—TIMOTHY GEORGE
Distinguished Professor, Beeson Divinity School of Samford University, and general editor of the 28-volume *Reformation Commentary on Scripture*

"Over the past twenty to thirty years in evangelical circles there has been a renewed interest in the central place of practice in the Christian life. We are not just thinking things but embodied creatures who 'know' as much through what we do as through what we think. This recognition has been reinforced in an existential way by the rootlessness we are experiencing. The current upheaval in our world is leaving us disoriented in so many areas, leading us to search for ways to ground our lives. In this book Paul Louis Metzger not only makes the theoretical case for the liturgical year as a central element in Christian formation, but he also takes the next logical step and offers practical resources. Through a series of meditations grounded in the liturgical cycle he encourages us to enter into the pattern of renewing the Christian narrative in community. Rather than simply advocating for the place of practice, he offers communities ways to foster attentiveness to the Christian story throughout the seasons. May this book enrich churches in recovering, in practical ways, the vital gift of the liturgical year!"

—PETER ROBINSON
Academic Dean and Professor of Proclamation, Worship and Ministry, Wycliffe College, University of Toronto

"This is a gem of a book. A gem because it is rare: part devotion, part reflective essay, a combination of deep biblical and theological wisdom, wise conversation partners, and cultural engagement. And also a gem because its content deserves to be mined and treasured as we seek to follow Jesus in this complex cultural and political moment. Constructively building on other recent efforts to retrieve the liturgical calendar as a part of the re-formation of our Christian imaginations, faithful engagement with this book will surely help its readers orient their lives around the Son in this secular, pluralistic age."

—KRISTEN DEEDE JOHNSON
Dean and Vice President of Academic Affairs,
Professor of Theology and Christian Formation, Western Theological Seminary

"In the face of a hypermodernity that increasingly corrodes Christian identity and community, the church needs to reclaim an understanding of time (and place) that is rooted in the life and person of Jesus Christ. We need to reset our clocks to Jesus' time, and Paul Louis Metzger's book helps us to do just that. Filled with wise meditations throughout the Christian year, this book is a sure guide for Christian pastors, churches, and families."

—JOEL SCANDRETT
Assistant Professor of Historical Theology, Trinity School for Ministry

"Though confessionally evangelical in its orientation, *Setting the Spiritual Clock* invites readers rooted in variegated Christian traditions to take seriously the formational power of biblical stories deeply woven in the liturgical calendar of the Christian church. Journeying through the seasons of the Christian calendar, the author masterfully guides readers to discern the transformative presence of Christ's Easter glory breaking through the 'secular eclipse' that reigning cultural narratives often generate. Wrestling with the currents of the post-Christendom era, with a particular concern for increasing secularization, Metzger offers a timely response redeeming Christian narratives in a culturally meaningful way."

—DAVID SANG-EHIL HAN
Dean of the Faculty, Vice President for Academics,
and Professor of Theology and Pentecostal Spirituality, Pentecostal Theological Seminary

SETTING THE SPIRITUAL CLOCK

Sacred Time Breaking Through the Secular Eclipse

Paul Louis Metzger

CASCADE *Books* • Eugene, Oregon

SETTING THE SPIRITUAL CLOCK
Sacred Time Breaking Through the Secular Eclipse

Worship and Witness Series

Copyright © 2020 Paul Louis Metzger. All rights reserved. Except for brief quotations in critical publications or reviews, no part of this book may be reproduced in any manner without prior written permission from the publisher. Write: Permissions, Wipf and Stock Publishers, 199 W. 8th Ave., Suite 3, Eugene, OR 97401.

Cascade Books
An Imprint of Wipf and Stock Publishers
199 W. 8th Ave., Suite 3
Eugene, OR 97401

www.wipfandstock.com

PAPERBACK ISBN: 978-1-7252-5870-9
HARDCOVER ISBN: 978-1-7252-5871-6
EBOOK ISBN: 978-1-7252-5872-3

Cataloguing-in-Publication data:

Names: Metzger, Paul Louis, author.

Title: Book title : Setting the spiritual clock / Paul Louis Metzger.

Description: Eugene, OR: Cascade Books, 2020 | Includes bibliographical references and index.

Identifiers: ISBN 978-1-7252-5870-9 (paperback) | ISBN 978-1-7252-5871-6 (hardcover) | ISBN 978-1-7252-5872-3 (ebook)

Subjects: LCSH: Church year. | Theology, Spiritual. | Liturgy.

Classification: BV30 .M50 2020 (print) | BV30 (ebook)

NOVEMBER 3, 2020

Except where otherwise indicated, Scripture quotations are from the ESV© Bible (The Holy Bible, English Standard Version©), copyright © 2001 by Crossway, a publishing ministry of Good News Publishers. Used by permission. All rights reserved.

Scriptures marked KJV are taken from the King James Version (KJV): King James Version, public domain.

Scripture quotations marked (NIV) are taken from the Holy Bible, New International Version®, NIV®. Copyright © 1973, 1978, 1984, 2011 by Biblica, Inc.™ Used by permission of Zondervan. All rights reserved worldwide. www.zondervan.com. The "NIV" and "New International Version" are trademarks registered in the United States Patent and Trademark Office by Biblica, Inc.™

To worship leaders who foster church family communion,
To my sister Nancy and brother Todd,
"Blest be the tie that binds our hearts in Christian love."

CONTENTS

Timely Acknowledgments | xi

Introduction: Checkbooks, Calendars, and What We Cherish | 1

I ADVENT: JESUS IS COMING! | 15
   Jesus Is Coming! Are We Waiting for Him? | 17
   Looking for Jesus in the Least Likely of Places—Bethlehem | 19
   "Joy to the World!" But Why? | 22
   God's Peace Defies Circumstances | 25

II CHRISTMASTIDE: JESUS IS BORN! | 29
   Christmas Day Is Finally Here! What's the Big Deal? | 31
   Christmas Day Is Over, But Jesus' Life Has Only Just Begun! | 34
   Remember Hanukkah—Celebrate Religious Liberty | 36
   New Year's Eve and Day: Foolish Feasting or Joyful Solemnity? | 40
   Mother Mary Stands at the Crossroads of the New Year | 43

III EPIPHANYTIDE: GOD IS WITH US! | 47
   Epiphany: What We Worship Is Quite Revealing | 49
   Epiphany, Baptismal Theophany, and Jesus' Life as a Rich Tapestry | 52
   Epiphanytide: Seeing Jesus Is Believing and Following | 56
   Epiphanytide: Jesus' Signs Aim at Faith, Not Fanfare | 60
   Jesus' Baby Dedication Reveals the New World Order | 63
   Transfiguration: Transitioning to Lent and Later | 66

IV LENT: DIE TO SELF TO GAIN JESUS! | 71
   Ash Wednesday: Lament Indifferent Faith | 73
   Lent and Black History Month: Liturgies
      of Lament and Celebration | 77
   Forty Days of Lenten Purpose | 80

Esther's Fast, Purim, Lent, and International Women's Day | 83
What Did God Give Up for Lent? | 87
Lent: Giving Up Vice to Gain the Savior | 90
Lenten Extravagance | 92

V HOLY WEEK: JESUS DIES TO BRING NEW LIFE! | 97
Palm Sunday, Holy Week, and Holy War | 99
Maundy Thursday: Jesus' Last Stand Is Everlasting | 103
Don't Pass Over the Passover on Good Friday | 107
Holy Saturday: Wholly in the Dark? | 110

VI EASTERTIDE: JESUS IS RISEN! | 115
Easter: New Creation and Vocation in the Promised Land | 117
Thank God It's Divine Mercy Sunday | 121
We See Jesus When Breaking Bread Together | 124
Jesus' Resurrection Doesn't Depend on Faith, But Deepens It | 127
Sometimes Doubt Is Devotion | 130
Post-Resurrection Appearances—Faith Resuscitation | 132
A Mother's Day Tribute: The Pierced Heart | 134
On Memorial Days, Honor the Dead, Not Religious Propaganda | 137
The Ascension: Jesus Has Some Serious Hang Time | 140
Ascension and Pentecost: Above the Fray Yet on the Ground | 143
Pentecost Sunday: Happy Birthday to the Missional Church! | 146

VII ORDINARY TIME: FOLLOW JESUS IN THE SPIRIT TO THE END! | 151
The Trinity Is Not Just for Trinity Sunday, But the Whole Year | 154
Corpus Christi Sunday: Discerning Christ's Real Presence | 157
What Would Father's Day Be Like for Jesus? | 161
A Fourth of July Reflection: Taking Exception to American Exceptionalism | 164
May Jesus Order Our Steps During Ordinary Time | 168
Jesus Acts Extraordinarily During Ordinary Time | 172
Chronos Governs the Day. May *Kairos* Govern Our Lives | 175
Conquer Inordinate Desire During Ordinary Time | 178
Mary's Assumption: An Unassuming Heart and Honor | 181
Mary's Dormition: Worth Losing Sleep? | 185
The Church Calendar Reorders Us: Communal Past and Present | 188
Mark Your Calendars Daily for Christ's Return | 191
Pray for Creation Care Today | 195
"Let There Be Light!"—Don't Take It Lightly | 199

Honor God's Temple of Creation | 203
Confess to God and Fellow Humans—But Plants? | 207
How Godlike Are Humans Functioning on Earth? | 211
Care for the Creation: Feasting with St. Francis and St. Kateri | 215
The Christian Life: Pilgrimage through the Years | 218
Honor Disability Awareness Sunday and the Differently Abled | 222
All Sinners' Day | 226
Who Will You Be on Halloween—A Repentant Monk? | 228
All Saints' Sunday | 230
Alive on Earth and in the Afterlife | 233
Purgation of Souls and Spotless Sheep, Not Goats | 236
Dealing with Unmet Expectations of Jesus at Life's End | 241
Celebrate Christ the King, Not Secular Creep | 244

Conclusion: Out of Joint and Time? Reset the Spiritual Clock | 248

Appendix: How to Read This Book | 251

Bibliography | 257
Scripture Index | 277
Name Index | 285
Subject Index | 287

TIMELY ACKNOWLEDGMENTS

THIS VOLUME ON THE church calendar is all about time. In fact, we are all about time, as humans are temporal beings. We account for matters across time and during our time period. In the United States, we are often focused or fixated on beginning and ending meetings on time. If we are alert, we ask ourselves whether meetings, such as church services we attended, were timely or momentous.

We live in unprecedented times requiring momentous responses, including worship gatherings. As this book goes to print, the novel coronavirus speeds us up or slows us down depending on the context. There is an immediate and urgent need for medical supplies and a vaccine. We cannot produce and transport resources quickly enough. This life-threatening virus is no respecter of geographical, economic, ethnic, religious, ideological, or generational boundaries. It spreads incredibly fast, just as it shuts down fast-growing economies and our personal lives. Welcome to the new normal.

Churches, other religious bodies, civic authorities, businesses, and individuals are working alongside courageous healthcare professionals to provide relief. Spiritual care must accompany physical care, and so while practicing physical distancing, worship services are operating remotely thanks to online technologies. While not ideal in many cases, it is necessary presently.

Just think: the Christian church has met weekly throughout all the seasons of the church year since Pentecost, just weeks after the Alpha and Omega rose from the dead more than twenty centuries ago. The church has endured countless challenges from natural disasters and persecution to internal strife throughout the ages. The restrictions on public gatherings due to the virus is one of countless ordeals the church has faced. Perhaps we who are Christians living and worshiping in countries that provide religious liberty have a new level of appreciation and passion for coming together in open assembly before the virus spread and after the virus draws its last breath.

Timely Acknowledgments

No matter our context, no matter whether we worship in public openly and freely, we can find inspiration from the church throughout history and the church across the globe. The universal reality of the church in time and across space encourages us: we are not alone as God's people respond to this pandemic in the present hour, or to another such crisis of global proportions in the months and years ahead. Like the church at large, we look to the Ancient of Days. Further to hymn master Isaac Watts's reminder, the same God who has been our help in ages past and hope for years to come provides shelter and solace in the face of our various trials, including plagues and pandemics. This ageless God is our eternal home.

Many of us belong to church families or homes. I dedicate this book to worship leaders in these church homes here and abroad in their fight to foster communal intimacy in their congregations as best they can amid required physical distancing. May God grant them strength and creativity. May the church calendar be a rich resource to the communities of faith they serve. May it shape the pattern of our lives no matter when this global pandemic comes to an end and no matter how long the new normal lasts. May all of us realize that God's timetable does not follow the secular calendar. No matter what happens during this or that trying season, may we all take to heart our participation in God's eternal story, which the liturgical calendar features from Jesus' first advent to his second coming.

Many thanks to Rodney Clapp, my editor at Cascade Books. This is the second book I have had the privilege of writing in collaboration with Rodney, the first being *Exploring Ecclesiology* (Brazos, 2009), coauthored with Brad Harper. Rodney has influenced my thought over the years, as a thinker and writer who conceives the Christian faith in robust ecclesial terms. I am also grateful for Brad, whose own ecclesial vision and passion helps shape the work we do together as professors at Multnomah University and Seminary, and as directors of The Institute for Cultural Engagement: New Wine, New Wineskins. I also wish to thank Lynnette Boyer and Clint Birkeland for their collegiality and stellar editorial assistance in the completion of this project. Their collaboration and keen appreciation for the importance of the church calendar in ecclesial life have been most timely. Research Librarian Suzanne Smith at Multnomah University and Mariko Metzger closer to home came to our aid in seeking to submit the manuscript before Christ's second coming—Suzanne with providing access to sources during the coronavirus shutdown and Mariko with formatting footnotes. A hearty thanks to them as well, and to brother Matt Farlow for indexing. It just goes to show it takes a village to raise a theologian and a book, especially related to Christian community and ecclesiology.

Timely Acknowledgments

Speaking of ecclesiology, I am grateful for my students in ecclesiology courses at Multnomah Seminary and University. These students express such passionate and thoughtful care for the church and seek ways to enhance faithful witness. Our dialogues have provided nourishment and energy for this project, including Halden Doerge's insightful remark years ago in class, which I expand upon here: the secular calendar with its alternative rituals, rhythms, and cherished events often fills the temporal-liturgical void whenever congregations don't recognize the liturgical seasons of the church year. This and related musings took shape in entries at my column *Uncommon God, Common Good* at Patheos, which I later edited, expanded, and augmented for this volume.

Having noted the need for recognizing the church calendar, I wish to express my gratitude for my late parents William and Audrey Metzger, who raised me in Christian community and whose Christian imagination feasted on the liturgical calendar. My mom was a church choir director, choir member, and soloist. She loved hymn sings and my dad loved listening to her sing. Mom passed away in late February this year, joining Dad in the presence of Christ. But my parents' Christian faith, hope, and love live on here below in the hearts of many, not least of which are my older sister Nancy and younger brother Todd. My sister carries Mom's grace and gift for singing as a soloist, and together with Todd and me benefited from Mom's choir instruction and delight in diverse forms of music, from Marian Anderson to Johnny Cash. Nancy and Todd are my closest living links to my parents. That tie reminds me of Christ connecting us to the church and the church connecting us to Christ. The vital connection to my siblings is a testimony to their forbearance in putting up with the middle child, and to our parents' legacy of love, which as the apostle writes, binds everything together in perfect harmony (Col 3:14). Along with worship leaders, I dedicate this book to Todd and Nancy.

Finally, I wish to express my gratitude and appreciation to my wife Mariko and to our children, Christopher and Julianne. As time moves on, I find myself increasingly savoring the moments and memories with them and our growing family, including Christopher's wife Keyonna and daughter Jaylah. The same goes for my bond with the church, which is also a family. I desire to be mindful and live in the moment of the liturgical seasons, asking God to teach all his children to number our days (Ps 90:12).

INTRODUCTION: CHECKBOOKS, CALENDARS, AND WHAT WE CHERISH

You learn a great deal about people and what they cherish by looking at their checkbooks and calendars. This happens on an individual as well as corporate or national level. Let's consider a few examples, as it will help us delve into the importance of the church's own calendar.

On an individual level, you find out what people prioritize, including food, clothing, and other necessities, favorite charities, work, entertainment, exercise, and rest. At the close of the secular calendar year, people are often scrambling to write checks for tax-deductible gifts. At the beginning of the new year, the same people (quite possibly you and me!) are making New Year's resolutions that they may keep for a time, but quite likely falter to maintain and eventually forget. I've been there more than once.

On a corporate or national level, you find out what a community or populace finds most important for its identity based on the dates it remembers regularly. Our secular calendars often list these key dates. In the United States, where I live, a calendar may list key events, national holidays, and historically significant political and cultural heroes. According to the National Archives, you will find the following listed as "federal holidays": New Year's Day, the Birthday of Martin Luther King, Jr., Washington's Birthday (now often referred to as Presidents' Day), Memorial Day, Independence Day, Labor Day, Columbus Day, Veterans Day, Thanksgiving Day, and Christmas Day.[1] According to one US Senate document, Inauguration Day is included in the list, making it eleven.[2]

Whether US citizens think seriously about the selection of holidays, or simply look at them as possible occasions to relax, Congress's intent in choosing these dates was to emphasize dimensions of the country's heritage that have shaped our identity as Americans. According to that same

1. National Archives, "2019 Federal Holidays."
2. Stathis, "Federal Holidays."

Setting the Spiritual Clock

US Senate document, each selection of a national holiday "emphasizes particular aspects of the American heritage that molded the United States as a people and a nation."[3] The selection process can be quite painstaking, as the document suggests. For example, the recognition of Dr. King's birthday as a federal public holiday was the result of an arduous fifteen-year struggle.[4] The aim was to highlight his contribution to the civil rights movement.

You learn a great deal about what is important to American society based on what is recognized as a federal public holiday. *As with national monuments, the federal calendar reflects the nation's liturgy.* "Liturgy"? Why would I use a religious term to discuss a secular subject? One reason is that the word originates in a broader social context. Another reason is that national liturgies often transcend or surpass the bounds of statehood to project transcendent or all-encompassing narratives and invite or demand total allegiance (minus perhaps private religious sentiments).

It's important to give more context to the first reason for the use of the word *liturgy* in discussing the federal calendar. *Liturgy* is derived from the Greek composite word *leitourgía* (from the combination of Greek words for "pertaining to the people"—*leitós/láos* and "work"—*érgon*), which meant in its original setting a public duty performed by a citizen in respect to the state or "common welfare of the people." In the Septuagint, the word and its equivalent were adapted to refer almost entirely to Israel's chief end of worship and public duties of the priestly line in the tabernacle or temple. The New Testament picks up on this idea when we find in Hebrews 8:6 Jesus performing a surpassing liturgy or "ministry" (*leitourgías*) as the great high priest or "liturgist" of the New Covenant Law (Heb 8:1–6). The writer declares: "But as it is, Christ has obtained a ministry that is as much more excellent than the old as the covenant he mediates is better, since it is enacted on better promises" (Heb 8:6). The word *liturgy* came to refer to the entire scope of Christian ritual and service in public worship in contradistinction to private meditation, prayer, and devotion.[5] Adolf Adam refers to the Christian liturgical year as "the commemorative celebration, throughout a calendar year, of the saving deeds God accomplished in Jesus Christ."[6] Lev Gillet (a "Monk of the Eastern Church") views the church's liturgical year

---

3. Stathis, "Federal Holidays."

4. Rothman, "MLK Day."

5. Catholic University of America, "Liturgy," *New Catholic Encyclopedia*, 727–29; Fortescue, "Liturgy," *Catholic Encyclopedia*; Cross and Livingston, eds., "Liturgy," 994.

6. Adam, *The Liturgical Year*, vii.

Introduction: Checkbooks, Calendars, and What We Cherish

as "an abridgement of the history of salvation."[7] These are helpful, concise descriptions.

Now to return to the subject of calendar in general terms. Christmas Day is the only nationally recognized occasion that intersects with the Christian calendar. However, it should be noted that in the first two centuries of the Christian movement, the church did not prioritize Jesus' birth. Moreover, it is worth highlighting that Christmas Day also has significance for pagans and secular people alike—albeit for different reasons.

Key to a nation or religion's liturgy is sacrifice, heroism, and martyrdom. Thus, holidays like Veterans Day and Memorial Day loom large. So, too, does the birth of a people, as symbolized by the Fourth of July. While not officially constituted as federal public holidays, Mother's Day and Father's Day are intended to recognize the major contributions that parents make in the formation of the populace.

The church calendar does not officially recognize Mother's Day, though the church calendar in many ecclesial traditions does recognize Mother Mary's holy obedience and virtue as *theotokos* (God-bearer or Mother of God). The church does not officially recognize Father's Day, nor the federal holiday recognizing Washington as the founding father of this nation. However, the church does recognize Jesus—who is the author and perfecter of our faith (Heb 12:2)—as the founder of the church, which is a holy nation (see 1 Peter 2:9).

While many in our society would like to privatize religion and the church, the church and religion are not private realities or dimensions of life. Moreover, America has often operated as a church and manifests civil religion, though it has evolved considerably since the nation's birth. G. K. Chesterton once remarked that America has the soul of a church and was founded on a creed.[8]

My main concern in drawing attention to the privatizing and publicizing of religion and the church as well as the church-like features of America is not to push for a Christian theocracy. *Rather, my aim here is to highlight the respective liturgies of the church and secular state. Just like the US, the church goes through an arduous process of recognizing certain days as constitutive for molding its populace.* While there is no unanimity between East and West (or in the West itself) on a universal Christian calendar, various church traditions mark key days of the Christian year.[9]

---

7. Gillet, *The Year of Grace*, 87.
8. Mills, "The Nation."
9. Shepherd, "Church Year."

Setting the Spiritual Clock

The Christian year does not begin on January 1 or the Fourth of July, but on the first Sunday of Advent around the beginning of December. While it is common to recognize the new year in keeping with the secular calendar, we who are Christians should be sure to mark our calendars to reflect the Christian story. Stories shape our lives. Just as the children entered a new world of Narnia in C. S. Lewis's *The Lion, the Witch and the Wardrobe*,[10] so we must enter the world of the Bible and calendar events that mark the seasons of our Christian life cycle, year in and year out. Otherwise, other stories—no matter how great and lofty as those of grassroots movements, great individuals or nations are—will eclipse the Christian narrative. *This book is a sustained attempt to set our spiritual clocks according to the liturgical or church calendar, which circles the glorious Son as he breaks through the secular eclipse.*

We will return to the subject of setting the spiritual clock and secular eclipse shortly. In the meantime, it is important to highlight the approach this volume takes to featuring the church calendar in comparison with some other works that are vital contributions to the liturgical year:

- Cindy Crosby, ed., *Ancient Christian Devotional Lectionary Cycle A–C* (InterVarsity, 2007–2011). Crosby's volumes highlight readings from the church fathers in their engagement of Scripture in keeping with the liturgical cycles of the year. While certainly sensitive to church history, *Setting the Spiritual Clock* is more synthetic. It provides a biblical-theological-historical-cultural engagement of the Christian calendar.

- Hoyt L. Hickman with Don E. Saliers, Laurence Hull Stookey, and James F. White, *The New Handbook of the Christian Year*, 2d ed. (Abingdon, 1992). Hickman and colleagues provide a detailed guide for use in services from across the ecclesial spectrum. *Setting the Spiritual Clock* provides a devotional guide for meditation and preparation for biblical exposition on themes pertinent to the church calendar rather than an aid for worship services in various Christian traditions throughout the year.

- Mark Oakley, ed., *A Good Year* (SPCK, 2016). Oakley's edited volume is a collection of seven articles addressing the significance of holy seasons throughout the church year. *Setting the Spiritual Clock* gives more detailed consideration to particular days, including those that occur during Ordinary Time, throughout the ecclesial year.

- Kendra Tierney, *The Catholic All Year Compendium: Liturgical Living for Real Life* (Ignatius, 2018). Tierney's book aims to aid Catholics in

10. Lewis, *The Lion*.

Introduction: Checkbooks, Calendars, and What We Cherish

living into the church calendar in concrete and practical ways. While *Setting the Spiritual Clock* can certainly aid Catholic readers, it has in mind a more general Christian audience.

- Robert E. Webber, *Ancient-Future Time: Forming Spirituality through the Christian Year* (Baker, 2004). Webber has done perhaps more than anyone in evangelical circles to relay the undying significance and relevance of the ancient church's wisdom. Through chapters dedicated to various important seasons in the church calendar, Webber enlightens the reader to the import of ordering their spiritual lives in keeping with the liturgical year. *Setting the Spiritual Clock* takes to heart Webber's fresh explorations of the ancient church for the future of faith, though in a more devotional manner befitting weekly devotionals.

Mention of these resources suggest that this volume will be ecumenical in scope, although situated with an eye trained on my evangelical theological and cultural context. The evangelical tradition of which I am a card-carrying member is often Biblicist and anti-historical/traditional, as well as anti-ecumenical in orientation. It tends to look down on liturgical churches as being stale, detached from people's daily lives, and unbiblical. It behooves the careful critic and faithful disciple to ask what it means to be "biblical," and whether there are ways of being biblical in a variety of ways in diverse ecclesial and cultural contexts, including forms of liturgical expression. Moreover, just as it is problematic to discount Scripture as authoritative, so it is disturbing when we claim to filter everything through Scripture, when, in fact, the situation is far more complex.[11]

As an example of such complexity, if you were to look carefully at any given church fellowship, you will find that there are various extra-biblical traditions and rituals as well as rites of passage and authority structures that shape that body of believers. They include: where the pulpit, Lord's Table, or piano/organ/drum kit is placed; what kind of art is displayed or technology is used; whether a church sings hymns or praise choruses and how many songs are performed in a given service; if and when there is confirmation; who can vote on church matters—"members" or laity in general; and who actually governs the church. Here we need to account for those situations where instead of finding "extra-biblical" traditions, we find unbiblical traditions. May it be duly noted that it is not always the pastor, elders, and/or congregation who govern a church based on godly wisdom, but rather an

---

11. The point is not to be less biblical but more biblical, as well as theologically grounded. Regarding the need for laying deep theological foundations for a given tradition or movement's liturgy, see Senn, *New Creation*.

individual who has longevity, is most affluent, has more formal education, or has greater influence or prestige in the broader community.

Going further, "Low-Church" Christian traditions (including many evangelical communities) have liturgies, just like "High-Church" traditions. They may not follow the Christian calendar, perform the Eucharist/Lord's Supper every Sunday, or clothe their pastors in priestly robes, but they worship in song and in proclamation of the Word of God, offer prayers, and honor Christmas, Easter, and possibly a few other days in the church calendar. Apart from the association with the word *ecumenical* that suggests (to some evangelicals) "watering down" doctrinal distinctives for some vague sense of Christian unity, Christian Scripture exhorts us to pursue unity with the whole Christian community (see John 17, for example). This is the best sense of "ecumenical," as it conveys the passionate pursuit of visible unity with the entire body of Christ here on earth.[12]

While the evangelical community has much to offer the larger church with our emphasis on personal relationship with Jesus in evangelism and devotions, commitment to the rigorous study and exposition of Scripture in many contexts, as well as grassroots activism, we have much to learn from the larger Christian communion.[13] The church did not begin when each of us came to know Jesus personally. It precedes us and the evangelical movement, and it extends beyond us in the world today. While holding true to the vital aspects of our evangelical Protestant tradition, we should be open and desirous of learning and benefiting from the riches of other ecclesial traditions, when there is no sense of biblical compromise. Moreover, these traditions often help safeguard against "secular creep" in our worship services, given their aim of filling the Christian calendar with attention to the time- and world-altering reality of Jesus Christ. Apart from its clear Catholic orientation, what Protestant evangelical cannot give a hearty "Amen" to the following statement regarding the liturgical calendar?

> Many holy men and women through the ages, however, have set their internal clock to the liturgical calendar and have found their lives reshaped in the process—for the purpose of the liturgical calendar is to orient our days around the person of Jesus. This process begins with Sunday worship, which is the cornerstone of the whole liturgical calendar. We celebrate Mass each Sunday—rather than on the Jewish Saturday—in recognition

---

12. Brad Harper and I pursued this evangelical and ecumenical balance in *Exploring Ecclesiology*.

13. See for example the balanced treatment of how evangelicals benefit (and can be benefited by) the larger church community in Braaten and Jenson, eds., *In One Body*, 55–56.

Introduction: Checkbooks, Calendars, and What We Cherish

that when Jesus resurrected on Easter Sunday He began the renewal of the whole world and the universe was fundamentally changed (see Catechism of the Catholic Church, No. 1193). As the liturgical poet John Keble, a great friend of Blessed John Henry Newman, exclaimed in his poem "Easter Day," Easter sheds "light on all the year," making Sundays "more glorious break, / An Easter Day in every week." Sunday worship reveals to us the nature of the world in which we live.[14]

May evangelical Christians join with Christians of various ecclesial traditions across the globe in welcoming Jesus' Easter Day shedding light on every day and night throughout the year, not just Sundays, but also every moment of the seemingly secular work week. There can be no such thing as a "Sunday-only" Christian.

Here we now return to the theme of setting the spiritual clock. Hans Frei wrote about *The Eclipse of Biblical Narrative* in modern thought, whereby the reader evaluates or judges the biblical text in view of attempted historical reconstructions rather than approaches the text as rendering the history it narrates, as in pre-modern interpretation.[15] *Something similar happened in the modern period with the removal or erosion of the sacred liturgy in the broader societal imagination. In its place we find secular liturgies that often cloud or eclipse Jesus' Easter glory in the Christian imagination.* Sacred liturgy involved molding Christians as a virtuous community with a teleological or eschatological orientation involving perfection through our union with Christ.[16] In contrast, today we often find the autonomous individual free of all temporal and spatial boundaries. Where community does exist, liturgy is often the projection of an autonomous human agent in loose association with other such individual agents, or the imposition of a hegemonic force of individual tyranny or collectivist derivation, including the nation state.

One example of a secular liturgy eclipsing sacred space and time is the shopping mall. The shopping mall is a secular worship center involving liturgy and ritual founded upon a deity of sorts. The hidden force known as the invisible hand of the market controls the individual producers, retailers, and consumers. Apart from the opening and closing hours, the worshiping customer is led to shop without a sense of time given the absence of clocks in stores. In place of Classical Theism's spaceless and timeless God, the Market is seemingly omnipresent and timeless. An abundance of mirrors makes up for the absence of clocks. Those mirrors parallel in parasitical form icons

---

14. Heady, "What Is the Liturgical Calendar?"
15. Frei, *Eclipse*.
16. Along these lines, refer to MacIntyre, *After Virtue*.

of the Trinity and great saints who inspire us and serve as windows into the divine reality. In their place, mirrors provide opportunity for self-worship as we fixate on ourselves. There's no sense of belonging to something holy and transcendent and that inspires us to pursue the path of virtue. In the place of tradition and teleology involving human virtue, we pursue boundless freedom and maximum pleasure, comfort, health, and wealth—in other words, the American Dream. Given the predominance of this way of being, we might well ask: how often do our worship services at church reflect a shopping mall experience that fixates on fickle individual religious consumer preferences of praise, and purchases of fleeting happiness and frivolous religious goods or products through our giving?

This is a far cry from the biblical narrative and its inherent liturgical practices. Take for example the pilgrimage feasts that helped to orient and bind the Jewish community. Three times a year the people of Israel were commanded to journey to Jerusalem to honor God and offer costly sacrifices at the Temple:

> According to the Torah, God commanded the Israelites: "Three times a year shall all your men appear before the LORD your God in the place that God will choose [referring presumably to the Temple in Jerusalem], on the festivals of Pesah (Passover), Shavuot (the Feast of Weeks), and Sukkot (the Festival of Booths). They shall not appear empty handed. Each shall bring his own gift, appropriate to the blessing which the Lord your God has given you" (Deuteronomy 16:16)....
>
> The pilgrimage festivals created an opportunity for the Jewish community to reaffirm their communal commitment to the covenant with God, strengthen the self-identification of the nation as a religious community, and entrench the sanctity of Jerusalem and the place where the Temple stood in the religious consciousness of the people. These festivals are at their core a community-building experience.[17]

The tradition of pilgrimage three times a year reflected a teleological orientation in a historical vein, as God promised to deliver his people and lead them into the Promised Land. The tradition centered in this teleological paradigm fostered a vibrant community.

Jesus was raised in a home that honored his Jewish heritage and its various feasts and festivals. From his earliest days through childhood to adulthood, Jesus practiced the Jewish tradition and participated in its community-building experiences, including the pilgrimage feasts. Such

17. Kohn, "Pilgrimage Festivals?"

Introduction: Checkbooks, Calendars, and What We Cherish

tradition involved teleology and eschatology. Each of the pilgrimage feasts shaped the Jewish people as a missional movement that obeyed God's Law to cultivate virtuous love of God and neighbor and prepared them for worship in the Messianic age when they would dwell in the Promised Land of rest. Certainly, as we will find in the entries on Holy Week, Jesus remembered the Passover and understood himself to be the focal point of bringing healing through his suffering to Israel and the nations. If Jesus did not find these liturgical celebrations to be dead tradition, but essential to his spiritual practice and mission,[18] shouldn't we do the same and honor the Christian calendar when it reflects and extends the biblical story?

Now some may object and claim that Christianity is not about special days. Certainly, we are not to allow others to judge us spiritually based on observing festivals and Sabbaths. Instead, we are to put ourselves under the judgment of Christ to whom the substance of spirituality belongs. He is our Sabbath rest and the substance of the various biblical images in salvation history. As Paul wrote to the church in Colossae, "Therefore let no one pass judgment on you in questions of food and drink, or with regard to a festival or a new moon or a Sabbath. These are a shadow of the things to come, but the substance belongs to Christ" (Col 2:16–17). With Paul's point in mind, I would hate to see us allow other calendars, such as that of a great nation, to cast their shadows on Jesus and his church's life. Jesus and his church must alone mark the seasons of the church calendar year, as well as mold our souls.

Again, we are not to allow others to judge us based on whether we observe certain festivals and the Sabbath. The substance belongs to Christ (Col 2:17), who is Lord of the Sabbath (Matt 12:8) and the one to whom the festivals like Passover point. He is our Passover lamb (1 Cor 5:7). As the focal point of the biblical pageantry and liturgy, Jesus should inspire and shape our liturgical expression.

As Lord of the Sabbath, Jesus did not allow certain Sabbath practices to stand in the way of caring for others in need. He told the religious establishment: "The Sabbath was made for man, not man for the Sabbath. So, the Son of Man is lord even of the Sabbath" (Mark 2:27–28). But that does not mean Jesus did away with liturgy. He reframed the church's liturgy to circle around his Father through him in the Spirit. So the writer of the Epistle to the Hebrews exhorts his readers who considered abandoning Christ to return to their Jewish traditions: "And let us consider how to stir up one another to love and good works, not neglecting to meet together, as is the habit of some, but encouraging one another, and all the more as you see the Day

---

18. See for example Burge, *Jesus and Jewish Festivals*.

drawing near" (Heb 10:24–25). Many of the initial recipients of this epistle had their hearts, imaginations, and habits in the wrong place. The author appealed to them to reconsider: How could they go back to the old way of life centered in a temple that would soon disappear when Jesus, according to Hebrews 8, ministers as the royal priest in the heavenly temple of the New Covenant? Hebrews does not call for removing liturgy but reframing it in and through Jesus as the center of worship.

Instead of trying to do away with liturgy, we should think again. Liturgy, including the church calendar, involves a communal response to the sacred.[19] We cannot get away from liturgy and the way we shape and structure existence according to certain patterns and rhythms centered in what we find to be our ultimate concern. *God wired us to be liturgical beings (homo liturgicus), and so we will either repeat God's liturgical norms or create our own, including calendars.*

The question is not whether we have a liturgy, but what kind of liturgy we have, express, and embody. The shopping mall example above was not a one-off exception to the rule, but one example among a multitude of others. James K. A. Smith puts it this way in his discussion of humans as liturgical beings:

> Recovering religion as ritual is not just another way to domesticate it or explain it away. Rather, the point is to appreciate the enchantment of our rhythms, the incarnation of devotion, the way rituals are a last tether to sacramentality that tell us something about ourselves. Even if a secular age is increasingly willing to throw overboard an array of beliefs and norms we associate with religion—precisely *because* we associate them with religion—we are a long way from giving up on ritual. It's not that we're a-religious; we just inhabit different liturgies. Our penchant for finding grooves for our longings and hopes

---

19. Mircea Eliade refers to the sacred as that which "always manifests itself as a reality of a wholly different order from 'natural' realities." *Sacred and Profane*, 10. Eliade refers to the revelation or "*act of manifestation* of the sacred" as "hierophany." Eliade refers to "the incarnation of God in Jesus Christ" as "the supreme hierophany," 11. Drawing from Rudolf Otto, Eliade highlights "the numinous," which the religious person (*homo religious*) experiences. This experience involves an overwhelming sense of "awe-inspiring mystery" (*mysterium tremendum*) and "fascinating mystery" (*mysterium fascinans*), 9–10. Theologically and liturgically speaking, God who is wholly different or "wholly other" according to Otto (see Eliade, *Sacred and Profane*, 9) becomes one with us as the incarnate Christ. Jesus is the manifestation of the sacred in history. The Spirit awakens us to experience Jesus as this manifestation of the sacred. The liturgical calendar reflects his sacred incarnate glory as it encircles him.

Introduction: Checkbooks, Calendars, and What We Cherish

is a backhanded witness to our enduring nature as worshipers. *Homo religiosis* is fundamentally *homo liturgicus*.[20]

As liturgical beings, what rituals will shape our existence and worship of God? While immediacy and individual experience in worship have their place, without the historical and global church context in mind, we lose our moorings. We must account for the biblical reality that we arise in a concrete historical and larger social context and are proceeding toward a particular end, namely the Promised Land to which Jesus leads us. Otherwise, the American Dream of upward mobility from New Year's to July 4 to Black Friday can easily displace the faith once and for all delivered to the saints, and which culminates in the Christian calendar with Christ the King Sunday at the close of the church year. Allow the biblical and ecclesial panorama involving the great cloud of witnesses throughout salvation history to inspire us as we pursue "the founder and perfecter of our faith" to the finish line (see Heb 12:1–2).

Like humans generally, Christians are seasonal beings. Our rhythms follow the seasons and cycles of life. The Christian liturgical seasons are Advent, Christmastide, Epiphanytide (which overlaps with the first phase of Ordinary Time), Lent, Easter Triduum, Eastertide, and Ordinary Time (second phase). This book traces these seasons, except in the case of the Easter Triduum, which begins on Maundy Thursday evening and ends on Easter evening. In its place, we feature Holy Week, which runs from Palm Sunday through Holy Saturday. Easter Sunday will appear under Eastertide (which officially begins at sunset on the eve of Easter). It is also worth noting that this volume extends Epiphanytide to last until Lent, reserving the discussion of Ordinary Time to its second phase. As noted above, in the traditional liturgical calendar, Epiphanytide overlaps with the first phase of Ordinary Time. Together they close at Lent. *An appendix is provided to help the reader navigate the essays in this volume in accordance with the liturgical seasons and days of observance, as many may wish to do. Others may choose to read the book from front to back at their own leisure. Either approach is fine.*

The reader will find a section dedicated to each specified liturgical season. Each section will begin with an introductory reflection followed by a series of entries pertaining to that season. The introduction to each section will orient the reader to what follows as well as highlight the book's central focus articulated earlier: namely, to set our spiritual clocks according to the Christian calendar, which circles the radiant Son as he breaks through the secular eclipse. Just as a total or partial eclipse may reset a species' internal

---

20. Smith, "Homo Liturgicus." See also his work *Desiring*.

clock,[21] so secularity resets our orientation to the world. Perhaps what is even more perplexing is that we are often unaware of this secular reset.[22] While it is incumbent upon Christians to engage the surrounding culture in an irenic, dialogical, and nonsectarian manner, we must also make sure that as the church we focus our imaginations on the glorious Christ, around which the liturgical calendar rotates, as he breaks through the secular eclipse. As Robert Webber makes clear in reflecting on Christian time's shaping of spirituality, "it is of utmost importance that we begin with Christ, who is the source of our spirituality and the one who gives meaning to time. Without

---

21. See for example the discussion of how eclipses impact the "internal clocks" of various species of animals and plants in Zirker, *Total Eclipses of the Sun*, 184–87. It has been debated whether humans rely "more on social cues than light to set their body clocks." Smolensky and Lamberg, *The Body Clock Guide*, 33. However, regardless of the nature-nurture issue, eclipses of natural or cultural-ideological varieties do indeed impact our imaginations and orientation to the world.

22. In his work on Charles Taylor's *A Secular Age*, James K. A. Smith highlights three ways in which secularity has been understood to shape people's lives. First, it splits reality into two spheres: the sacred, religious, spiritual vs. the mundane, nonreligious, earthly (Secular1). Second, it splits society into two domains: the public as nonreligious and private as religious (Secular2). Third, secularity champions pluralism over exclusivism. The Christian faith is one option among many from which to choose (Secular3). Adding to this challenge, religious belief is not the easiest option to accept (another way to put it may be that the Christian faith is not the most user-friendly product or cheapest brand). Ultimately, secularism leaves us with an all-or-nothing scenario. While Christians may inadvertently accept the first and second options and reject the third due to adherence to the claim that Jesus is Lord, secularism's desired reach is total. Contrary to the "secularization theory" that involves the "subtraction story," the modern world is far more than the subtraction of God and faith. It is a substitution that eclipses religion. It takes its place as "exclusive humanism." See Smith, *How (Not) to Be Secular*, 20–22, 142–43. It is worth noting here that for Taylor exclusive humanism does not ultimately jettison Christianity with its deletion of religious content. Secularism presupposes and co-opts Christianity and presents itself as an all-encompassing framework from beginning to end. See for example Taylor's discussion of "subtraction stories" in *A Secular Age*, 22, 26–27. Having noted Taylor and Smith's engagement of the concept of secularism, it is worth pointing to Hugh Whelchel's commentary on what he sees as the hodgepodge adoption of the first two aspects of secularism and rejection of the third in Christian circles. Such an eclectic or piecemeal adoption gives rise to "private religious time" in the contemporary Christian imagination: "This explains one of the most significant problems in the current evangelical church. An overwhelming number of Christians today completely embrace Secular1 and Secular2 above, while many more struggle with Secular3 because of the exclusive claims of Christianity. They live schizophrenic lives, existing as a secularist at work and in the public square, but then as a religious believer in their private lives. They seem unaware of the Apostle Paul's charge to do *everything* to the glory of God (1 Cor 10:31) because they are caught up in this sacred-secular divide. As a result, the gospel becomes only a bus ticket to heaven and, except for some private religious time, has minimal effect on how many Christians live their lives." Whelchel, "Sacred-Secular Divide."

Introduction: Checkbooks, Calendars, and What We Cherish

Christ there could be no Christian time. It is Christ who determines the Christian year, and it is through the practice of Christian-year spirituality that Christ is formed within us."[23]

It is important to pause at this point in the effort to strike the right balance on cherishing the sacred in the Christian community in the context of our secular age. The aim in contending against what I refer to as the "secular eclipse" or "secular creep" in Christian worship (including the church calendar) is not sectarian. This book simply seeks to make certain that the Savior rather than a secularist paradigm shapes our narrative, imagination, and sense of time in the church.[24] Without this orientation, we will not survive as authentically and distinctively Christian in our secular, pluralistic age. With this mind-set and heart-set, we will thrive.[25] That said, it is essential to authentic Christian witness that we pursue genuine and meaningful dialogue with the broader community. The Bible encourages and exhorts us to be prepared always to enter into conversation and make a cogent and compelling case for our Christian faith as an alternative way of life while engaging others in an inquisitive and charitable manner (1 Pet 3:15). This perspective and posture are needed now more than ever, since we cannot presume that faith is axiomatic for the broader society. As Charles Taylor shows, ours is a secular age, where Christian belief is no longer a given.[26]

Having attempted to orient the reader to the balance to strike concerning the sacred and secular, it is important to note other features that help situate the readership in terms of what they can expect to find in the ensuing pages. In addition to tracing the seasons of the church calendar, this volume features special occasions, such as Jesus' birthday at Christmas, the church's anniversary celebration on Pentecost, and certain deaths. Deaths? Yes, in addition to remembering Jesus' death on Good Friday, the church

---

23. Webber, *Ancient-Future Time*, 24.

24. Webber laments the secularization of worship, most notably in "the typical evangelical calendar." He draws attention to various national and local special days filling the evangelical calendar and writes, "This strange mixture of the patriotic, sentimental, and promotional shows how far removed we are from a Christian concept of time." Webber, *Ancient-Future Faith*, 111.

25. Webber's Ancient-Future series claims that the ancient church arose in a pluralistic society that bears striking similarities to our present-day context. The Christian community must draw from the ancient Christian narrative and practices if it is to flourish in our postmodern world. A recent article noting the move among Christians of various stripes, including evangelicals, to immerse themselves in liturgical practices is Tara Isabella Burton's "Christianity Gets Weird."

26. Taylor, *A Secular Age*. The following statement strikes a good balance: "The point is not to be sectarian or to try to put ourselves at odds with non-Christians. The point is to keep God's story at the center of our lives and calendar." Claiborne et al., *Common Prayer*, 15.

honors saints on the occasions of their passings, since it is understood that they have passed into their eternal glory. We have paid tribute to a few of these saints as representatives of the great cloud of witnesses. There is no way a book of this size with its intended focus could account for every day in the church calendar, or every day honoring a saint. Similarly, this book does not account for the three-year church calendar cycle from A to C, nor the various scriptural readings associated with those particular years in the cycle. Rather, the aim is to provide an overview with an emphasis placed on the Son of God breaking through the secular eclipse whereby we celebrate sacred time. In general, the various sections comprise a series of essays that account for each week of the church calendar, though there will at times be more than one entry, as in the case of Holy Week.

Mention was made of saints above and the dates in the church calendar that honor their passing. My own saintly mother recently entered her eternal rest. On February 23, 2020, my mom passed away peacefully. From now on, I will take to heart in a renewed way her birthday on August 28 and her death on February 23. Mom used to remind me of my deceased grandparents' birthdays. They were alive to Mom, as was my father who passed away several years before her. Mom cherished them. It never got old to honor their birthdays, just like we never get tired of celebrating the birthdays or anniversaries of living loved ones. In fact, we love going to the shopping mall or florist to purchase a gift for them. We would never say of cherished children or beloved spouses that we celebrated their lives at their births or our marriages on our wedding days, so there's no need to express our love and appreciation in future years. The same goes for Jesus' birthday or resurrection from the dead, or the church's anniversary (Pentecost). If we love him and his people, we will remember them. Remembrance is one of the ways we keep our love alive, as in honoring them on special days with festive parties, feasts, and gifts.

As I stated at the outset of this introduction, you learn a lot about people and what they cherish by looking at their checkbooks and calendars. What might others learn about what and who we love if they were to look at our checkbooks and calendars on any given Sunday and on Christian holidays and landmarks throughout the year?

I

Advent: Jesus Is Coming!

Advent is about Jesus coming to earth. Ultimately, Advent is about Jesus moving history forward—not backward—toward its climax when he comes again. And yet, ironically, the contemporary version of the "Christmas season" has creeped backward into the autumn, not because of an attraction to Christ but because it is good for business.

It is little wonder that business sensibilities shape people's senses during the Christmas holiday season. Gordon Bigelow argues that the market ideology is the dominant narrative that shapes our psyche today, thereby eclipsing the biblical story in the minds of many. He writes:

> Economics, as channeled by its popular avatars in media and politics, is the cosmology and the theodicy of our contemporary culture. More than religion itself, more than literature, more than cable television, it is economics that offers the dominant creation narrative of our society, depicting the relation of each of us to the universe we inhabit, the relation of human beings to God. And the story it tells is a marvelous one. In it an enormous multitude of strangers, all individuals, all striving alone, are nevertheless all bound together in a beautiful and natural pattern of existence: the market. This understanding of markets—not as artifacts of human civilization but as phenomena of nature—now serves as the unquestioned foundation of nearly all political and social debate.[1]

The Christian calendar instructs us that the market does not dictate value. Advent is not ultimately about futuristic projections of Christmas

---

1. Bigelow, "Let There Be Markets," 33.

I—Advent: Jesus Is Coming!

sales that require extending the season backward into the autumn to grow the profits. Rather Advent is about the prophecies concerning the Messiah's emergence or visitation on the stage of history.

Nor is Advent about our visiting nostalgic white Christmas scenes reminiscent of a Thomas Kinkade painting and Hallmark card, or binge watching cherished classic Christmas season films. No, Advent is about traveling to Bethlehem with Mary and Joseph to experience the uncommon joy and peace wrapped in swaddling clothes. His joyful and peaceful presence blankets and shelters us so that we do not succumb to the fleeting happiness of holiday good cheer or falter under the heavy-handed and violent order that political establishments so often enforce. Thus, it is no surprise or coincidence that the four Advent candles are "Prophecy" for hope, "Bethlehem" for faith, "Shepherd" for joy, and "Angel" for peace. To these four lighted themes, we now turn.

JESUS IS COMING! ARE WE WAITING FOR HIM?

The Christian calendar year begins today with the first Sunday of Advent. Advent's Latin root means "coming" or "arrival," and signifies Jesus' coming to earth. In addition to celebrating Jesus' appearance at his first advent, we await his second advent, when he will judge the nations and reconcile all things to God.

Often, the first week of Advent draws attention to the prophetic expectation of the Messiah's appearance. The first candle of the Advent wreath is often referred to as the Prophecy Candle or Prophet's Candle. It symbolizes hope related to those who first spoke of the Messiah's coming into the world.

Matthew's Gospel references various texts from the Hebrew Scriptures that the New Testament community believed were prophetic utterances fulfilled in Jesus (read Matt 1:23 and 2:6). From the Gospel of Matthew's perspective, the New Testament community is not alone in anticipating Jesus' coming. The saints of old also longed for his appearance, a point that 1 Peter also makes (read 1 Pet 1:10–12).

The prophets did not see with their own eyes what they prophesied, nor did other saints who longed for the coming of the promised Messiah. Hebrews 11:39–40 reads of the saints of old who longed for the fulfillment of the promised inheritance in Christ, "And all these, though commended through their faith, did not receive what was promised, since God had provided something better for us, that apart from us they should not be made perfect."

I marvel at these Old Testament saints for their tenacity, resilience, and patience. The same goes for the New Testament saints who were undergoing extreme suffering, even persecution. Such was the context of 1 Peter and Hebrews. Like the saints of old, they were awaiting the fulfillment of the ages, when the Messiah will make all things new.

I—Advent: Jesus Is Coming!

We wait for Jesus' appearing today. Or do we? In view of the seemingly eternal delay, have we moved on to entertain other "messiahs," other plans, and other hopes? The times in which we live make it increasingly difficult to wait. In our quick fix and instant gratification culture, it is getting increasingly taxing by the day to wait. High-speed Internet can easily lead to high-speed spirituality, where everything is now. Thus, it is even more important that we slow down and reframe our imaginations in honor of Jesus' story. We should ask ourselves, no matter our background or context: When Jesus returns to earth, will he find long-suffering faith, or only casual religious browsers surfing the web at a high speed?

The Advent season helps us reframe our imaginations and expectations. As with the church throughout the centuries, as well as with the Hebrew saints of old who longed for the Messiah's appearance, we anticipate the long-awaited deliverer and live now in view of his coming.

The author of Hebrews would tell us the best is yet to come, as he encourages his readers to wait patiently and encourage one another—and all the more—in the communion of the saints as the day of Jesus' reappearing advances (Heb 10:24–25). But can we wait? Moreover, if we do wait rather than look elsewhere for satisfaction, how will we make the most of our time?[2]

We wait by being industrious and active in participating in Jesus' mission through his Spirit. Jesus will consummate his kingdom when he returns, but we are participants in that kingdom which he inaugurated during his first advent. Thus, the Lord is already here, as we actively wait by living out his will here and now to love God with all our hearts and our neighbors as ourselves, just as he taught and modeled for us. So, we await his coming by living for him, even by living for others. Advent is a time to remember and reenact Jesus' story. Come, Lord Jesus, come!

---

2. For more on the theme of waiting at Advent, see Newman, *Waiting for Christ*.

LOOKING FOR JESUS IN THE LEAST LIKELY OF PLACES—BETHLEHEM

Today marks the second Sunday of Advent. As with all four Sundays of Advent, today celebrates Jesus' arrival in the world. Many churches use Advent wreaths to mark the occasion. Often, the candle marking the second Sunday is called the "Bethlehem Candle." The emphasis is on faith and notes Mary and Joseph's sojourn to Bethlehem.

No doubt, people who casually engaged the Scriptures would have expected the Messiah to come from Jerusalem. After all, Jerusalem was the capital city. But those who knew their Scriptures well would have realized that the Messiah was destined to come from Bethlehem. Matthew 2:6 points this out, as the Gospel quotes a portion of Micah 5:2. Micah 5:2 reads, "But you, O Bethlehem Ephrathah, who are too little to be among the clans of Judah, from you shall come forth for me one who is to be ruler in Israel, whose coming forth is from of old, from ancient days" (Mic 5:2).

Bethlehem had a special place in Israel's history. King David was born and raised there. However, it was an ordinary place lacking great significance by all other accounts. It's just like God to bring significance to otherwise insignificant places or people.

God often shows up in unexpected places. Who would have thought that God would have had Samuel journey to Bethlehem to anoint a king from the line of Jesse—in fact, the youngest of Jesse's sons, David? Even the prophet Samuel, whom God sent to Jesse's household to anoint one of his sons as the king to replace Saul, was not looking with God's eye point-of-view. When he sees the eldest of Jesse's sons, he assumes immediately that this young man is the person God has chosen as king. But God speaks to Samuel and says, "Do not look on his appearance or on the height of his stature, because I have rejected him. For the LORD sees not as man sees: man looks on the outward appearance, but the LORD looks on the heart" (1 Sam 16:7).

I—Advent: Jesus Is Coming!

God's surprising choice of king did not begin there. Judah's line was chosen over Reuben's (Jacob or Israel's firstborn) and God's presumed favorite Joseph and his children, Ephraim and Manasseh. When Israel blessed his sons, he said of Judah: "The scepter shall not depart from Judah, nor the ruler's staff from between his feet, until tribute comes to him; and to him shall be the obedience of the peoples" (Gen 49:10). Later in the story, we find that God chooses Ruth, a refugee from Moab, and Boaz of Bethlehem (see Ruth 2:4) in Judah to be the ancestors of the Messiah. They are the parents of Obed, who is the grandfather of David. Add to that the equally striking truth that Boaz was the son of Rahab, the prostitute from Jericho who responded in faith to God. Matthew's genealogy of Jesus includes the following: "and Salmon the father of Boaz by Rahab, and Boaz the father of Obed by Ruth, and Obed the father of Jesse, and Jesse the father of David the king" (Matt 1:5–6). One can go so far back as to consider the surprising truth that God chooses a slave people, not Egypt, to be the chosen people. Israel was chosen based on their ancestor Abraham, who was himself a Gentile like all the other people of the earth until he was circumcised in response to God's call and promise by faith (see Gen 12:1–3; 15:7; see also Gen 17). The Jewish people stand by election, as do all other people who respond by faith to God's promise of the deliverer (again, see Gen 12:1–3; Gal 3:16, 29). God did not choose Egypt or Babylon or Rome, but Israel, not for its own sake, but for the sake of the world, to bring forth the Messiah. Mary and Joseph reflect God's upside-down kingdom, too, as God chooses them to be the parents of the Messiah.

God orchestrates and uses the mighty Caesar Augustus's census to orchestrate his plan (Luke 2:1–7). No one in his or her right mind would have expected the Messiah to arise from Bethlehem, that is, unless they accounted for the prophetic word (see Mic 5:2). Instead, the peoples of the earth will look to Jerusalem or to Rome or Washington. They can move (or claim to move) capitals from places like Tel Aviv to Jerusalem. But ultimately, it is not Zion that marks the presence of God, but Jesus. Just as he is the living Torah, so he is the Temple or place where God dwells (Bethel). Jesus is God with us, Immanuel (Matt 1:23).

God shows up in the least likely of places—places like Bethlehem, a town where many Palestinians live today, including Christians. In fact, Bethlehem has been recognized as "the most heavily Christian city in Palestine," even though many American evangelical Christians do not appear to account for their brothers and sisters' existence.[3] All too often, foreign policy, including evangelical support for the recognition of Jerusalem as the

---

3. Allen-Ebrahimian, "Evangelicals Side with Israel."

Looking for Jesus in the Least Likely of Places—Bethlehem

capital city of Israel, seems to overshadow Christian policy for Christian Zionists.[4]

God will continue to show up in the least likely of places and faces, faces like Mary and Joseph, and Palestinian Christians in Bethlehem and elsewhere, too. Philip Brooks beautifully brought this point home in "O Little Town of Bethlehem."[5] Brooks went back and forth between the past and present and brought worshipers today into the narrative with his use of the first-person plural. Unlike those who would focus only on the first and second comings, Brooks saw Jesus as continually coming to be present in our midst. One commentator on the hymn compares it favorably with those unfortunate songs that teach that "God was present in the birth and manifestation at Bethlehem and will be present again at the end of time, but that humanity languishes in the vast interim between a theology that betrays the sacramentality of God's gift throughout time and the incarnation of the risen Christ in humanity as a whole and the church as the elected remnant reflecting that humanity."[6] Brooks's own congregation in Philadelphia, which would have sung this song in 1867, experienced social upheaval similar to the time in which Jesus was born.[7] Brooks made sure that they would not languish in their worship. God was with them in their plight, just as much as he was with Mary and Joseph and the people of Bethlehem, and just as he is with those in Bethlehem, Philadelphia, and elsewhere today.

Governments will rise and fall, capitals will move to and fro, social turbulence will ebb and flow, but Jesus' kingdom in human hearts and lives of living faith across the region and globe will last forever. In view of his lasting presence in unsuspected places and people of faith, how then will you and I seek to discern God's presence today?

---

4. Fisher, "The Jerusalem Issue."
5. Brooks, "O Little Town of Bethlehem," #21–22.
6. Connell, *Eternity Today*, 136–37.
7. Connell, *Eternity Today*, 137–38.

"JOY TO THE WORLD!" BUT WHY?

Today is the third Sunday of Advent. The candle on the Advent wreath marking the occasion signifies joy. But why? Perhaps it has something to do with this candle being called the "Shepherd's Candle." After all, the candle signifies the shepherds' joy at the news of the Lord Jesus' birth.

How striking it is that God's angel and heavenly host go first to these humble and hungry shepherds, according to Luke's Gospel. No matter how striking, it should not be surprising, if you are an avid reader of Luke's work. As is evident from Luke's account of the Beatitudes, God blesses the poor, the hungry, and those who weep, and fills those with joy who align themselves with Jesus the Messiah (Luke 6:20–23). The birth narrative in Luke 2 manifests these same themes.

The shepherds went from being filled with fear to being filled with joy at the appearance of the angel who announced Jesus' birth to them. In fact, the angel exhorted them not to fear and assured them that he brought them "good news of great joy" (Luke 2:10). If these shepherds had been afraid and then filled with joy at the angel's appearance and announcement, just think how they must have felt when a heavenly multitude appeared with the angel and declared the good news of the Messiah's birth (read Luke 2:8–14).

If I had been one of these shepherds, I might have been paralyzed by awe. But somehow or other, the shepherds had enough composure and wits about them to act upon the angel's announcement. Upon hearing the angel's report and then the declaration of the heavenly host, the shepherds went with haste to see the baby. Then they shared with anyone who would listen that the Messiah had been born in Bethlehem. The shepherds marveled, glorifying and praising God for all they had seen and heard (read Luke 2:15–20).

In between the wonderment of those who heard the shepherds' report and the shepherds' ongoing amazement, we find Mary treasuring and pondering all that she herself witnessed (Luke 2:19). Perhaps Mary remembered

"Joy to the World!" But Why?

what she herself uttered when an angel announced to her that she would be the mother of the Messiah (ponder her words in Luke 1:46–55). Just as Mary had been chosen to be the mother of the Messiah, so, too, these shepherds were the first people on record to greet the Messiah and his parents. Who would have thought that Mary or the shepherds would have been chosen? But as Mary declared earlier, he exalts those of "humble estate" (Luke 1:52). God brings down the mighty and proud, including the rulers and the rich, and raises up those who are weak and of no account by the established order's standards (Luke 1:51–53).

Joel Green puts the shepherds in their literary and historical context, showing that it is no coincidence that Luke's Gospel would highlight them. Here's Green:

> Shepherds in an agrarian society may have small landholdings, but these would be inadequate to meet the demands of their own families, the needs of their own agricultural pursuits, and the burden of taxation. As a result, they may hire themselves out to work for wages. There were, then, peasants, located toward the bottom of the scale of power and privilege. That they are here cast in this dress is unmistakable, for the same contrast introduced in Mary's son—the enthroned versus the lowly (1:52)—is represented here: Augustus the Emperor and Quirinius [Governor] on the one hand (2:1–2), the shepherds on the other.[8]

Luke wanted to bring home this stark contrast to his readers. Does it come home to us today? If we are not careful, we can turn Luke's Gospel account into a Hallmark card that goes on the shelf, and then gets discarded after Christmas Day has passed. To guard against that possibility, let's let Mary and the shepherds guide us on how to respond. What did they do? Mary treasured and pondered all that occurred. The shepherds got up and went to see the child. Then they went away praising God and making the good news known to everyone they encountered.

What did Mary treasure and ponder? What did the shepherds declare? Perhaps it was a sense of wonder over God exalting the weak, the lowly, and seemingly insignificant. What do we treasure, ponder, and declare? The angelic host and the author Luke (a doctor by trade) think and talk differently than the world system, which elevates the rich and powerful. The angels' and this angelic doctor's highlight reel of events surrounding the Messiah's birth include lowly shepherds and this blessed maiden of little account by most standards. In contrast to the world system both then and now, the angelic host discerned God's heart. They knew that Mary, her husband Joseph,

---

8. Green, *The Gospel of Luke*, 130–31.

I—Advent: Jesus Is Coming!

and these shepherds are the ones whom God has chosen, with whom he is pleased, and upon whom his favor rests (Luke 2:14).

So, what will you and I declare this third Sunday of Advent, when we light the third candle—a candle of joy? What serves as the basis for the joy with which we celebrate this Advent season? The joy that Mary and the shepherds experienced was not a temporary aura of Christmas lights that come down after the holidays, nor Christmas wrap that gets thrown away (sometimes with the presents) not long after Christmas Day. Rather, the joy is the result of "the glory of the Lord" that "shone around them" (2:9). This joy is in response to the baby born in the manger, whose eternal reign will remove the haughty and oppressive and lift the humble and oppressed, like the shepherds of old. Those who are "shepherds" today make haste with joy to Bethlehem to see the wondrous child and declare his birth.

GOD'S PEACE DEFIES CIRCUMSTANCES

Today marks the fourth Sunday of Advent. The fourth candle on the Advent wreath is often called the Angel's Candle and is taken to signify peace in keeping with the angelic host's declaration: "Glory to God in the highest, and on earth peace among those with whom he is pleased!" (Luke 2:14). Glory and peace go together in Luke's Gospel. Luke 2:14 states, "Glory to God in the highest, and on earth peace among those with whom he is pleased!" Paul Minear sees a direct connection between the glory and peace here: "The more glory the more peace, and the more peace the more glory."[9]

It's not any kind of glory and any kind of peace, though. So, how do we discern the signs of God's glory and peace? For starters, Luke's Gospel grounds the connection in Jesus. Elsewhere in Luke's Gospel, the resurrected Jesus appears to his disciples and declares, "Peace to you" (Luke 24:36). Before proceeding further, it is worth noting the fundamental connection between Luke 2 and the rest of the Gospel. All too often, we take a biblical text out of its immediate context and apply it generally. Just as there is a fundamental connection between glory and peace, so there is a fundamental connection between the birth narrative and the whole of Luke's Gospel: "The infancy narrative can be seen as a true introduction to some of the main themes of the Gospel proper, and no analysis of Lukan theology should neglect it."[10] This should not come as too much of a surprise, since all four canonical Gospels focus on the single life of Jesus. Thus, glory, peace, as well as joy will surface in relation to Jesus elsewhere (see Luke 10:20; 15:7, 10, 20–24; 24:36: Luke connects joy, peace, and heaven with the gospel of Jesus' kingdom).

There was not much godly peace or shalom and glory at the time of Jesus' birth. After all, the "Pax Romana" or Peace of Rome and its own form

---

9. Minear, *To Heal and To Reveal*, 50.

10. Brown, *The Birth of the Messiah*, 242. See also Minear's landmark discussion of this theme: "Luke's Use of Birth Stories," 112.

I—Advent: Jesus Is Coming!

of glory blanketed the known world in war and bloodshed. How else could Rome impose its rule on various lands whose people longed for independence and freedom? Adrian Goldsworthy maintains that the "Pax Romana" or "Roman Peace" was

> the famous peace and prosperity brought by the Roman Empire at its height in the first and second centuries AD. Yet the Romans were conquerors, imperialists who took by force a vast empire stretching from the Euphrates to the Atlantic coast. Ruthless, Romans won peace not through coexistence but through dominance; millions died and were enslaved during the creation of their empire.[11]

Rome was quick to put down any rebellions, often with the assistance of regional powers, who were subject to Rome and helped to extinguish many forms of resistance. Thus, it should not come as a surprise that news of Jesus' birth filled many inhabitants of the land with anxiety. The report that the King of the Jews had been born troubled Herod—Rome's puppet king in Judea—and all Jerusalem with him (read Matt 2:1–3).

Matthew's account goes on to reveal that Herod had all male children two years and younger in Bethlehem and the vicinity killed as a result (Matt 2:16–18). Matthew's Gospel also makes known that Jesus escaped death because an angel appeared and told Joseph to take his wife and child and flee to Egypt to avoid Herod's wrath (Matt 2:13–15). In view of the preceding account of Herod and the wise men (which no doubt took place a while after Jesus' birth), as well as the *Pax Romana*, it might come across as a bit surprising and ironic that God's angels would proclaim peace to the shepherds tending their flocks the night of Jesus' birth (Luke 2:13–14).

Even the occasion for Jesus' birth was anything but peaceful. Caesar Augustus, the Roman Emperor, had ordered a census of the known world in order to impose taxes on his subjects throughout the empire to enrich Rome and strengthen his military's grip on the nations. So, Joseph and Mary had to return to their ancestral town of King David to be accounted for, even though Mary was ready to give birth to Jesus (Luke 2:1–7). I doubt Joseph and Mary experienced much peace along the way, as they sojourned hurriedly among other travelers on their way to their ancestral homes to be registered. Joseph and Mary even had to take shelter among farm animals and place their newborn son in a manger because there was no room for them in the inn (Luke 2:7).

---

11. See the summary statement at the Yale University Press webpage for Goldsworthy, *Pax Romana*.

God's Peace Defies Circumstances

Peaceful circumstances? Hardly! But Joseph and Mary did experience God's peace in the face of their overwhelming ordeal. After all, they knew God was leading them and that there is no better place than to be in the center of God's will. So, the angelic host's declaration to the shepherds about peace being among those on whom God's favor rests no doubt would have resonated with Jesus' parents (Luke 2:14).

Let's take a closer look at the declaration. It does not simply account for God's peace for his favored subjects, but also God's exalted and glorious status: "Glory to God in the highest, and on earth peace among those with whom he is pleased!" (Luke 2:14) God reigns over all empires and nations. While it was taken as a given in Rome that Caesar was a god, the Bible begs to differ. While no ruler reigns apart from God's will, that does not mean everything an emperor or king does meets with God's favor. Certainly, God orchestrated plans and events so the census would lead Joseph and Mary to the predestined place of the Messiah's birth—Bethlehem, the city of David (Matt 2:3–6; cf. Mic 5:2–3). Caesar had no idea. Herod only found out as a result of the wise men's appearance and inquiry, and because of the scholarly report that the Messiah would be born in Bethlehem. Try as he might to kill the Christ, Herod could not outwit God, who reigns in the highest!

Circumstances cannot and will not get the better of God, or his Messiah. As the Hallelujah Chorus proclaims, "He shall reign forever!" Seemingly invincible and immortal Caesars come and go, as do their puppet kings like Herod, but God and Messiah Jesus will rule forevermore.

As mentioned at the outset of this essay, the fourth Sunday of Advent focuses on the angels' declaration of peace on earth (Luke 2:14). What bearing does this declaration have on us here and now? As you go about taking care of last-minute Christmas shopping and preparing for Christmas festivities, or as you sit alone viewing anxious news reports across the globe, know that God's glorious peace does not come about through normal means. Nor does God's favor rest on supra-ordinary types. Rather, God's peace and glory come to us through this baby lying in a manger in the face of imperial oppression old and new.

We may miss Jesus and his glorious peace in the midst of the holiday festivities and stresses, or those with whom he will be found, like the lowly shepherds who made their way to greet Jesus upon hearing the angelic host declare his birth (Luke 2:8–21). The angels did not go to Rome to declare the news to Caesar (as far as we know), nor to Herod in Jerusalem, but to the remote and forgotten ones like those in Bethlehem.

We will miss Jesus at Christmas, even if we place nativity sets in public places or replace "X" with Christ in greeting cards and signs, if we do not associate with his kind of people. We need to put Christ back in our

I—Advent: Jesus Is Coming!

hearts and in our interaction with the innless and homeless, the refugees and immigrants, those the system marginalizes, no matter their religion or pedigree, to experience God's glorious peace.

The more God's glory is revealed in Jesus the humbler we become and the more we associate with those who are lowly. When such is the case, the more peace we will experience, since God's peace is just. It is shalom. The more peace we experience the more we witness God's humble glory. This same glorious peace falls on shepherds tending their flocks by night. Empires will come and go, and with them their turbulent rule. But Jesus' peaceful and glorious kingdom will reign in human hearts and across the known and unknown world someday. He will reign forever! Take heart. Experience peace in view of him and his kingdom rule this day.

II

Christmastide: Jesus Is Born!

As noted in the brief introduction to Advent, the Christmas season has creeped backward into the autumn with the secular calendar rather than proceed forward in view of Advent with Jesus coming/coming again. Perhaps the creep backward sheds light on why Christmas ends abruptly on Christmas Day. The continuation of Christmas is not good for "after Christmas" sales. One Anglican article put it this way:

> The observation of a prolonged festive Christmas celebration continued through the middle ages and the early modern era, but, at least in America, has all but faded away in a blur of post-Christmas shopping, gift returning, and diet/exercise resolution planning.[1]

The sudden halt to Christmas on December 25 is a far cry from Christmastide, which extends Christmas to twelve or forty days, as the case may be. Such an abrupt end to Christmas might suggest mistakenly to some that Jesus and the Christian life are stillborn. What a far cry from the story and biblical pageantry reflected in Christmastide!

The Christian liturgical season does not end with Christmas Day and the new birth. Instead, it's about the process of growth and development, including obedience, as the various events and occasions during Christmastide make clear. Not only does Christmastide celebrate "The Nativity of Our Lord Jesus Christ" (December 25), but also Christmastide celebrates saints and martyrs like Stephen, deacon and first martyr (December 26), John, apostle and evangelist (December 27), the Holy Innocents who were slain

---

1. French, "Christmastide." Works on the Christmas season include Keller, *Hidden Christmas* and Tickle, *Christmastide*.

II—Christmastide: Jesus Is Born!

by Herod in his search for the Christ child (December 28), Thomas Becket, Archbishop of Canterbury and martyr (December 29), and the circumcision of the Lord in fulfillment of the Law on January 1, a day which also honors Mary as Jesus' Mother. As we look back to such events in biblical and ecclesial history, especially Jesus' determination to be born for our sake and his circumcision involving his parents' obedience to God, they move us forward to go with him on life's journey, just as he is God with us.

CHRISTMAS DAY IS FINALLY HERE! WHAT'S THE BIG DEAL?

The Advent Season is all about preparing for Jesus' coming. A great deal of anticipation and hope mark the season. Is the build-up worth it? Do all the great expectations find fulfillment on Christmas Day?

The answer depends on the expectations wrapped up in the question. Ironically perhaps to many, the New Testament does not wrap up all expectations for the Messiah in Jesus' birth. In fact, only two of the four canonical Gospels about Jesus' life feature birth narratives (Matthew and Luke). Yet, all four canonical Gospels (Matthew, Mark, Luke and John) feature passion, death, and resurrection narratives. Moreover, the church fathers of the first two centuries did not place focus on Jesus' birth or Christmas Day. According to Anglican priest and historian Andrew McGowan,

> The extrabiblical evidence from the first and second century is equally spare: There is no mention of birth celebrations in the writings of early Christian writers such as Irenaeus (c. 130–200) or Tertullian (c. 160–225). Origen of Alexandria (c. 165–264) goes so far as to mock Roman celebrations of birth anniversaries, dismissing them as "pagan" practices—a strong indication that Jesus' birth was not marked with similar festivities at that place and time. As far as we can tell, Christmas was not celebrated at all at this point.[2]

Such lack of consideration should cause us to reconsider the amount of attention we award to Jesus' birth on Christmas Day, or at least the way we attend to his advent (i.e., coming) into the world. The following statement by the United States Conference of Catholic Bishops helps orient our attention in the right direction:

---

2. McGowan, "December 25."

II—Christmastide: Jesus Is Born!

> Beginning the Church's liturgical year, Advent (from, "advenire" in Latin or "to come to") is the season encompassing the four Sundays (and weekdays) leading up to the celebration of Christmas.
>
> The Advent season is a time of preparation that directs our hearts and minds to Christ's second coming at the end of time and also to the anniversary of the Lord's birth on Christmas. The final days of Advent, from December 17 to December 24, focus particularly on our preparation for the celebrations of the Nativity of our Lord (Christmas).[3]

In keeping with this statement, our great expectations for Jesus should not find fulfillment on Christmas Day, but at his second coming to which the Advent season ultimately points. Such expectations must also involve Jesus' aim in coming into the world to bring salvation. Matthew's Gospel account puts the matter succinctly in the angel's announcement to Joseph that Mary will be the mother of the Messiah by the Holy Spirit: "She will bear a son, and you shall call his name Jesus, for he will save his people from their sins" (Matt 1:21).

Salvation is the focus of the biblical narrative. So, we must guard against fixing our gaze solely or primarily on Jesus' birth. Having said that, such focus should not be taken to suggest that the birth lacks significance. Indeed, it matters greatly. If he had not assumed our humanity (i.e., become incarnate), he could not have healed us. Jesus assumed our humanity in order to redeem us. Or as Gregory of Nazianzus would put it, "The unassumed is the unhealed." Again, "He has not assumed what he has not healed; but that which is united to his Godhead is also saved."[4]

So now, what's the big deal about Jesus' birth? Only our salvation involving Jesus' full humanity, and our full humanity, too. Jesus as the Christ could not have healed our humanity if he did not share in it fully from birth to death. There is no sense in the canonical Gospels that the divine Christ adopts the man Jesus at his baptism, and then leaves him prior to his passion and death. No, Mary gives birth to the eternal Son of God (*theotokos*) who would die for the sins of the world (see John 1:29; 1 John 2:2). In Paul's words, "God sent forth his Son, born of woman." The same Spirit through whom Mary conceived Jesus enters our hearts (Gal 4:4–7) so that we can become children of God and heirs. In the estimation of the New Testament community, only in this way could we become sons, daughters, and heirs, no longer being slaves to sin.

---

3. US Conference of Catholic Bishops, "Advent Season."
4. Nazianzus, *On God and Christ*, 158.

Christmas Day Is Finally Here! What's the Big Deal?

So, if Paul's and the canonical Gospel writers' perspectives and emphases shape your and my expectations for Christmas, then very good. However, if we expect and demand that we will experience ultimate bliss as we celebrate Jesus' birth today, then we will be greatly disappointed and disillusioned. As a result, many are ready to throw out the baby with the dirty, distorted, and deceptive expectations of joy free of sorrow, pain, and the struggle with sin. But God never made such promises to take away these burdens now. Rather, he promises to be with us so that he can bear these burdens with and for us (read Matt 1:23; 11:28–30) and, in the end, to bring ultimate redemption to us. In fact, Jesus' birth in a manger under Rome's oppressive rule and his early life under threat by Herod's murderous pursuit should tell us that God does not promise to give us our best life now. After all, Advent does not simply point to Jesus' first coming at his birth, which multitudes of Christians celebrate today, but also to his second coming at the close of history.

Today, we will open presents and watch people open them. We will throw away torn wrapping paper and consider returning some of the gifts due to style or size. But don't throw away or return the baby Jesus due to false or unfulfilled expectations. The best is yet to come.

CHRISTMAS DAY IS OVER, BUT JESUS' LIFE HAS ONLY JUST BEGUN!

If we operate by way of the secular calendar, Christmas is over—except for "after Christmas" sales and returns, as well as Christmas dinner leftovers. But for the Christian calendar, Jesus' life at Christmastide is far from over; it has only just begun! Far from being an afterglow or an afterthought, the New Testament and liturgical accounts of Jesus' early days of life give us reasons for hope amid post-Christmas blues.

Christmastide, as the Christmas season is called, lasts forty days—from Christmas Eve to February 2 with the Presentation of the Child Jesus in the Temple, according to the traditional liturgical calendar.[5] Thus, on this dating, Christmas did not end with the passing of December 25 or even after the Twelve Days of Christmas, which range from December 25 to January 6 with the Feast of Epiphany.[6]

Now for those suspicious of traditional church liturgy, but who are still quite taken with the New Testament portrayal, take to heart the appearance of Jesus in the Temple for his presentation. I doubt Simeon and Anna had traveled to Bethlehem to see the baby Jesus on his birthday, which we associate today with December 25.[7] According to the church calendar, their Christmas cheer began on the equivalent of February 2, as they witnessed the presentation of the baby Jesus in the Temple on the fortieth day after his birth (see Luke 2:22–38; see also Lev 12:1–8 and Exod 13:12–15; this is

---

5. For a treatment of the season, including the various Christian feasts considered part of Christmastide in the older, traditional Catholic calendar, see Cunningham, "Christmastide." See also Filz, "Does Christmas End on Epiphany?" For the Orthodox account, refer to Greek Orthodox Diocese, "Presentation of Christ." Another resource for the Orthodox tradition is Aslanoff, ed., *The Incarnate God*.

6. See Tait and Woodruff, "Real 12 Days of Christmas."

7. See McGowan, "December 25."

Christmas Day Is Over, But Jesus' Life Has Only Just Begun!

the time of Mary's purification and the redemption of Jesus as the firstborn son).

Simeon and Anna had been waiting long and hard for the appearance of the Messiah, who was and is the glory of Israel and light to the Gentiles. Anna was well-advanced in years, and a widow for much of her life. She stayed constantly in the Temple, worshiping, fasting, as well as praying daily and nightly. Upon encountering the baby Jesus and his parents, Anna spoke about him to everyone around her in the Temple awaiting Jerusalem's deliverance (Luke 2:38). For his own part, Simeon was led by the Spirit into the Temple where the Spirit's long-awaited promise to him was fulfilled (that is, Simeon would not see death until seeing the Messiah). There Simeon beheld Jesus, lifted him in his arms, and cried out, saying, "Lord, now you are letting your servant depart in peace, according to your word; for my eyes have seen your salvation that you have prepared in the presence of all peoples, a light for revelation to the Gentiles, and for glory to your people Israel" (Luke 2:29–32). Who knows how hard life had been for these two saints? The passing of loved ones, the coming of old age, the oppressive weight of Roman rule . . . but no matter the adversity, they never lost hope.

I have been told that January is always a horrible month for depression, even suicide. Reasons include unfulfilled expectations from Christmas, fears in the new year, credit card bills filled with payments due from Christmas shopping, and the less frequent hours of daylight as well as poor weather in many places.

There are many reasons for depression, including physiological ones, and many practical ways to address it.[8] Spiritual meditation can also help. As we who are followers of Jesus cherish Luke 2 and Christmastide, we will take energizing comfort from the fact that Jesus is with us in the midst of our trials and looming darkness. So, no matter if you take down the Christmas tree today, tomorrow or sometime next month, know that Jesus is our salvation. He is our light and our glory throughout late December, the hard month of January and beyond, not simply on Christmas Day.

---

8. Borchard, "5 Ways to Survive."

REMEMBER HANUKKAH—
CELEBRATE RELIGIOUS LIBERTY

Edward Gibbon famously remarked: "The various modes of worship which prevailed in the Roman world were all considered by the people as equally true; by the philosopher as equally false; and by the magistrate as equally useful. And thus toleration produced not only mutual indulgence, but even religious concord."[9] I do not think the Roman Empire owned the copyright on this view of religion. It has triumphed in many eras. However, dissenting views have arisen throughout history.

Take, for example, the story of the Maccabees and their Judean followers, whose courage and conviction serve as inspiration for the eight-day Jewish holiday known as Hanukkah, which is celebrated in December every year (and which was once a Christian celebration, too). According to the traditional account recorded in the first Book of Maccabees,[10] the Maccabean family and their followers refused to succumb to the tyrannical demands of the Syrian king Antiochus IV, who sought to force them to worship the Greek God Zeus and partake in pagan sacrifices. Beginning in 167 BCE and culminating in 164 BCE with the capture, cleansing, and rededication of the second Temple in Jerusalem, the Maccabees and their small band of soldiers fought for religious liberty and against what we might call today the commodification of their religion. The chief symbol of Hanukkah

---

9. Gibbon, *Decline and Fall*, 1:22.

10. Philip Jenkins challenges the traditional account, claiming that there is "quite a wide gulf separating historical reality from later religious myths." Later, Jenkins writes, "Mainly, this was not so much a straightforward revolt of Jews against pagan Greeks. Rather, it was a vicious civil war between Jewish factions, who hotly debated how far they could and should accommodate Gentile ways and ideas." And again, "It greatly behooved later writers to write the history of the revolt in pious terms, to show that those Maccabee ancestors had indeed been fighting a holy war rather than merely seizing power in a putsch." Jenkins, "Hanukkah and National Myths." For an expanded treatment of the complex historical backdrop to Hanukkah, see Jenkins, *Crucible of Faith*.

is the menorah, which is an eight-branched candelabra. The eight branches signify the miraculous intervention of God: the one drop of oil remaining in a jar at the Temple's reclamation burned for eight days in the menorah, when it should have burned only for one.

It has been argued that Antiochus IV or Antiochus Epiphanies was surprised that the Jewish people should take such offense at his attempts of adapting and syncretizing religious traditions in service to his rule, in keeping with Gibbon's claim noted at the outset of this piece. According to R. Kendall Soulen, Antiochus likely maintained that Israel's God was simply a tribal name for the transcendent and all-encompassing nameless deity of imperial rule.[11] Little did Antiochus truly grasp that for the monotheistic Maccabees the God whom the Jewish people knew and worshiped as the LORD—the name for the God of the Covenant made with the Patriarchs and revealed to Moses at the burning bush—was the Almighty God above heaven and earth, who would not allow his name or his named people to be commodified by tyrants. As with Moses and Pharaoh, the Maccabees declared that Antiochus should cease and desist.[12]

Regardless of one's perspective on the historical veracity of the first Book of Maccabees (refer to the footnote above concerning Philip Jenkins's analysis), it is indeed the case that throughout much of their history, the Jewish people have sought to navigate those religious, cultural, and political forces that would deprive them of their religious and cultural identity and liberty. Some have gone so far as to claim that Christmas in the United States has posed a threat to Judaism, and thus Hanukkah has been elevated to greater prominence as a Jewish religious holiday than would be historically warranted given that it is relatively late and intertestamental in its origin, unlike Passover or Succoth.[13] Regardless of the historical triggers for its emergence as a cherished holiday, it serves to counter forces that would weaken the Jewish heritage:

---

11. See Soulen, "'Go Tell Pharaoh,'" 51–52.

12. See Soulen's entire essay, "'Go Tell Pharaoh.'"

13. For critical reflection on this argument and Hanukkah's significance in the Jewish community in the United States, see Emma Green, "Hanukkah, Why?" Green writes: "So why, in America, has Hanukkah taken on outsized significance? Because it serves a particular purpose: an opportunity to negotiate the twin, competing pressures of ethnic tension and assimilation. As the Rowan University historian Dianne Ashton writes in her book, *Hanukkah in America*, 'Hanukkah's strongest American advocates seem to have been those who felt the complexities of American Jewish life most acutely.'" For the original source, see Ashton, *Hanukkah in America*. For a treatment of Hanukkah in more general terms, refer here: Augustyn et al., "Hanukkah."

II—Christmastide: Jesus Is Born!

> Since Hanukkah is not biblically ordained, the liturgy for the holiday is not well developed. It is actually a quite minor festival. However, it has become one of the most beloved of Jewish holidays. In an act of defiance against those in the past and in the present who would root out Jewish practice, the observance of Hanukkah has assumed a visible community aspect.[14]

Hanukkah, like many religious holidays, serves to mold a people according to the substance and form of a given spiritual tradition and story so that they and their tradition do not become eclipsed by competing narratives, whether secular or religious. Hanukkah addresses the vital concerns of religious liberty and freedom of worship. One analysis claims that the theology and themes behind Hanukkah entail the following: "Like Passover, Hanukkah is a holiday that celebrates the liberation from oppression. It also provides a strong argument in favor of freedom of worship and religion. In spite of the human action that is commemorated, never far from the surface is the theology that the liberation was possible only thanks to the miraculous support of the Divine."[15]

Going beyond singular reflection on Hanukkah, there are many reasons why people celebrate religious holidays, including Christmas and Hanukkah. Some of those reasons include ethnic, nationalist, and consumerist agendas. The following point on Hanukkah made in Green's piece noted earlier could be extended to other holidays, including those of the Christian tradition: "It's so simple, so conveniently vague, that it has been used by rabbis, advertisers, Zionists, Hebrew school teachers, and parents to promote everything from ethnic pride and nationalism to engagement in Jewish life and buying stuff."[16]

Speaking of ethnic pride and nationalism, we need to guard against those forces that bind and rebind societies in ways that favor one people group to the detriment of others. The call for religious liberty, for example, should not be taken by Christians as a rallying cry to enforce Christian hegemony in the US to the detriment of Jews, Muslims, atheists, and others. However, the solution is not the privatization and subjectification of religion, whereby it becomes merely the object of sentimental attraction of religious individuals, who should keep their convictions to themselves. On this view, the only time religion is given public credence is when it serves the GNP with the purchase of goods and services in the marketplace of

---

14. My Jewish Learning, "Hanukkah 101."

15. My Jewish Learning, "Hanukkah 101." See also the discussion of Hanukkah in Drucker, *Family Treasury*, 46.

16. Green, "Hanukkah, Why?"

commodified desire during holiday seasons, to which the quotation including "buying stuff" points.

The dominant mind-set in the US favors the democratization of religion. While it can help safeguard against religious hegemony, all too often such democratization can give rise to treating religious holidays like Hanukkah and Christmas as the equivalents of consumer products. Celebrate them, if you wish. Pick and choose and mix them together, if you like. They merely exist for fostering holiday cheer and a sense of mystery, nostalgia, or novelty. Contrary to what many Americans think, such democratization is a form of tyranny.

Today in our free market society, tyranny often takes the shape of consumer demand. This demand transforms, reshapes, and co-opts the great religious traditions so that they no longer serve to bind societies, but rather cater to other forces' agendas. Lesslie Newbigin puts the matter this way:

> Different religious traditions lose their capacity to be the binding element of societies and become instead mere options for religious consumers to select for their own private reasons, reasons which are not to be argued about. Thus "democratized," religions enter the marketplace as objects of subjective choices in much the same way as brands of toothpaste and laundry soap.[17]

As Newbigin suggests, religious traditions are better and rightly conceived as metaphysical underpinnings that serve to bind and rebind societies.

The celebration of Hanukkah with its claim to honor the LORD, whose name is not to be discarded and replaced by the leading brand deity of the month, whether Egyptian or Greek or Roman, German, American, or other, should inspire us to safeguard space for the religious and cultural minority voices whether they be Jewish, Palestinian, African American, Mexican, or other, whatever their religious tradition, rather than oppress them. We who are Christians should remember and show respect for Hanukkah during Advent and Christmastide and cherish the biblical or intertestamental Jewish holidays that often support and give rise to our own holy days like Passover/Easter and Pentecost. May we also safeguard against religious hegemony and its democratized, consumerized counterpart that for all its supposed merits can never rebind society in a manner that protects the rights of religious and nonreligious minorities and the people generally from magistrates and rulers who would use religion for their own ends to commodify the masses.

---

17. Newbigin, "Religion for the Marketplace," 152.

NEW YEAR'S EVE AND DAY: FOOLISH FEASTING OR JOYFUL SOLEMNITY?

No doubt there will be a great deal of foolish behavior on display tonight as people welcome in the New Year. For others, a joyful solemnity will mark the occasion.

For some, the solemnity includes remembrance of Jesus' circumcision. In the church calendar, obedience marks tomorrow, as various Christian communities celebrate the Feast of the Circumcision of the Lord.

The biblical background for the Feast of the Circumcision of the Lord is the account of Jesus being circumcised on the eighth day after his birth in keeping with the Mosaic Law (Luke 2:21). This was necessary for him as a physical descendent of Abraham (Gen 17:10–13) and in the quest to fulfill all righteousness and redeem those under the law (Gal 4:4–5).

I have read that the Orthodox Church celebrates the Feast of Circumcision with an all-night vigil beginning on December 31. In discussing the importance of this feast, one Orthodox site reads,

> It is truly a pity that the profound symbolism of this Feast should be "*lost*" in the "worldly tumult" of the twelve-day period between the Nativity and Theophany, and particularly on New Year's Day; and that we should lose, as well, an opportunity for us to enter more deeply into the "*circumcision made without hands*" of our Holy Baptism.[18]

At the present time, the Roman Catholic Church celebrates the Solemnity of Mary, the Mother of God, on January 1. In a discussion of the Feast of the Circumcision, a Catholic site states that

> It is to be noted also that the Blessed Virgin Mary was not forgotten in the festivities of the holy season, and the Mass in her honour was sometimes said on this day. Today, also, while in

---

18. Patapios, "Feast of the Circumcision," 2–3.

New Year's Eve and Day: Foolish Feasting or Joyful Solemnity?

both Missal and Breviary the feast bears the title "In Circumcisione Domini et Octav Nativitatis," the prayers have special reference to the Blessed Virgin, and in the Office, the responses and antiphons set forth her privileges and extol her wonderful prerogatives.[19]

More will appear on the Solemnity of Mary in the next entry. For now, I wish to emphasize that both celebrations highlight obedience. With this point in mind, it would be quite difficult to engage in debauched behavior tonight while preparing to honor the obedience of the holy family with holy feasting tomorrow.

Another feast that bears consideration at this juncture is the Feast of Fools, which was celebrated on January 1 for several centuries. A much-debated topic, the following quotation from "Feast of Fools" at *Oxford Bibliographies* serves as a good definition:

> The Feast of Fools developed in the late 12th and early 13th centuries as an elaborate and orderly liturgy for the day of the Circumcision (1 January). Celebrating the biblical principle that "God chose what is foolish in the world to shame the wise" (1 Cor. 1:27), the feast allowed low-ranking subdeacons to assume leadership roles in worship, usually reserved for the bishop or the cantor.[20]

Max Harris, the author of the piece on the "Feast of Fools," writes that "the liturgical Feast of Fools" struggled for viability in the churches. Later scholarly treatments confused the Feast with "unrelated festivities of bourgeois confraternities of fools outside the churches" that had mushroomed at the same time. Such confusion prompted "considerable misreading of the older ecclesiastical records" and contributed "to the mistaken but widespread view that the Feast of Fools was little more than a disorderly clerical revel." Harvey Cox goes so far as to write of the eventual disappearance of the Feast of Fools that

> The Feast of Fools. . .had an implicitly radical dimension. It exposed the arbitrary quality of social rank and enabled people to see that things need not always be as they are. Maybe that is

---

19. Tierney, "Feast of the Circumcision." See also Polan and Foley, "Circumcision," *New Catholic Encyclopedia*, 739–41.

20. Harris, "Feast of Fools." The article from which the quote is taken also provides a succinct historical overview and treatment of key sources. For an alternative treatment, see Maltman, "Feast of Fools," *New Catholic Encyclopedia*, 654.

why it made the power-wielders uncomfortable and eventually had to go.[21]

Regardless of one's take on the Feast of Fools, and whether one belongs to a tradition that celebrates the Feast of Circumcision, believers of every branch of the Christian family tree should at least consider these historical accounts and traditions. They have something powerful to convey on the radical nature of the Christian faith. The Lord of heaven above descended to earth, was born of the Virgin Mary, born under the Law, in the fullness of time. Jesus humbled himself in order to redeem those under the Law. He became a lowly servant, suffered and died, and rose from the dead, thereby overturning the world system of power and prestige. Christians are called to boast in the cross of Christ, which is foolishness and weakness, though it is the wisdom and power of God (1 Cor 1:18–31).

As we enter into the new year, we need to ponder in what and in whom we will boast. For example, will we boast about how much alcohol we had to drink and how foolish we acted at a New Year's party? Or will we boast in the favor of the Lord from whose joyful cup of abundant sacrifice we have occasion to drink?

---

21. Cox, *Feast of Fools*, 5.

MOTHER MARY STANDS AT THE CROSSROADS OF THE NEW YEAR

It is fitting that the Church celebrates Mary, the Mother of Jesus, on January 1. While Catholics and Protestants have been divided over the significance of Mary for the Church's life, she can and does serve as a point of connection, and not simply between the old and new year. I will develop this theme of connection in what follows.[22]

Today, the Roman Catholic Church celebrates the Solemnity of Mary, which involves honoring her as "the Holy Mother of God." While there are many feast days at Christmastide, Mary alone bears the honor of a solemnity in the Catholic Church in the days immediately following Christmas. A solemnity is chief among liturgical celebrations. As one Catholic author writes, "A solemnity is a liturgical celebration that is different from feast days and memorials. All three honor the Saints or special aspects of Jesus and Mary, but solemnities are the highest degree of celebration and are reserved for the most important mysteries of the Faith."[23] In Catholic circles, the celebration of Mary on this day as a solemnity takes precedence over The Feast of the Circumcision of the Lord, which also occurs on January 1.

The honor attributed to Mary among Roman Catholics has been unsettling to Protestants since the time of the Reformation. While Martin Luther, Zwingli, and others certainly held her in much higher regard than many Protestants today, John Calvin, for example, struggled with the wording "Mother of God." However, Calvin did affirm the Greek term *theotokos* given its theological import (*theotokos* is often translated "God-bearer"). Mary is *theotokos*, not *christotokos* ("Christ-bearer" or "bearer of Christ"), the latter being the title which Nestorius preferred. Nestorianism denied the intrinsic and integral unity of Jesus' divinity and humanity and was

---

22. Refer to the Cross and Livingstone, eds., "Mary the Blessed Virgin," in *The Oxford Dictionary of the Christian Church*.

23. Fenelon, "5 Things You Might Not Know."

II—Christmastide: Jesus Is Born!

condemned at the ecumenical Council of Ephesus in 431 AD. The council chose the term *theotokos* in order to convey the fundamental unity of Christ's person involving his divine and human natures (without thereby seeking to suggest a confusion of the two natures). The one who was born of Mary was God in the flesh. It is important to honor Mary as the God-bearer for this reason, if for no other. It should be noted that the teaching of the virgin birth (see the Apostles' Creed), which preceded the affirmation of *theotokos*, also challenges Docetism, which is the heretical notion that Jesus only appears to be human. Jesus is fully divine and fully human. Mary stands at the crossroads of the all-important discussion of the divine and human Jesus.[24] For all the differences between the Catholic and Protestant traditions in consideration of Mary, her significance doctrinally in terms of *theotokos* and the virgin birth should serve as important points of connection at the crossroads of the debate.

Protestants often raise concerns over what they take to be an elevation of Mary as co-mediator of salvation. While it is certainly important to challenge any such associations, which would minimize Jesus' singular mediatory role, it is also important to cherish Mary for her place in the history of salvation. As with her import for connections in the midst of theological debates involving her, Mary stands at the crossroads as a connection between the Old and New Testaments, and between Jesus' incarnate life up to his death and his resurrection and ascension. She stands with men and women of old who were of the ancestral line of Jesus, as well as people of faith (see Matthew's genealogy at 1:1–17). Mary remains standing at the cross along with a few other women and John, while Peter, the supposed rock, is nowhere to be found at Jesus' crucifixion and death (John 19:25). Mary is also standing or seated in the upper room with other followers of the resurrected and ascended Jesus as they prayerfully await the Holy Spirit's descent (Acts 1:13–14; cf. Acts 1:4–5).

Moreover, Mary stands at the crossroads of faith and obedience in the midst of doubts and human frailties. Mary is a person of elevated faith and obedience. Consider how she is troubled and bewildered by the angel's greeting and declaration that she would give birth to the Son of God (see Luke 1:29, 34, and 35). And yet, she responds in obedient faith: "Behold, I am the servant of the Lord; let it be to me according to your word" (Luke 1:38; note also the exuberant note of praise and thanksgiving in her song of praise, the *Magnificat*, in Luke 1:46–55). Moreover, I can think of no saint of old who

---

24. For an excellent treatment from a Protestant evangelical perspective on the significance of Mary, which includes historical theological considerations, see Timothy George's article titled "Blessed Evangelical Mary." See also his book *Blessed Evangelical Mary*.

Mother Mary Stands at the Crossroads of the New Year

experienced more pain and loss in obedience. Jesus' lonely life and the extreme opposition he faced would pierce her own soul as his loving mother, as Simeon declared (Luke 2:35). For all Mary's elevated faith and obedience, she was also flawed. Thus, we can identify with her in many ways, as we stand at the crossroads of faith and doubt, obedience and disobedience, in the new year. Mary's flaws of presuming on Jesus and intruding from time to time should not cause us to minimize her importance but endear her to us. Like her, do we not try to get Jesus to reveal his glory prematurely in our life situations? (See John 2:1–4.) Do we not try to get him back in line and save him from looking bad and losing total control? (See Mark 3:20–21, 31–35; see also Luke 2:41–52.) In each instance referenced here, Mary (and Joseph in Luke 2) experience Jesus' loving rebuke. Mary's God-endowed faith and obedience in the midst of her frail humanity should inspire us to follow in her footsteps, just as she follows in the footsteps of her son and Lord.

As we cross over from the old year into the new, may we learn from Mary and cherish her as one who stands at the crossroads as a point of connection in various spheres: ecumenical discussions on Jesus' identity, the Old and New Testaments with the formation of Jesus' community of disciples, and last but not least, faith and obedience to the Lord. May we learn from the *theotokos*—who is far more than *christotokos* in her elevated obedience. May Mary and her *Magnificat* inspire us to cherish the faith and bear our crosses magnificently as we follow Jesus at every juncture on the journey in this new year.

III

Epiphanytide: God Is with Us!

Many put away the Christmas lights as soon as Christmas is over. Life returns to a mundane and dim normal. But how can that be if the one whose birth we awaited and longed for finally arrived and is now present in our midst? Surely the light does not grow dim again, not even as we approach the Lenten season. After all, God is "with us"—Emmanuel. Jesus manifests the divine presence in his entire incarnate state.

"Epiphany" means manifestation and refers to Jesus' manifestation to the Gentiles in the form of the Magi, as recorded in Matthew chapter 2. While often neglected today, the season that features Epiphany on January 6 is known as "Epiphanytide." Still, many churches celebrate Epiphany season from January 6 with the visit of the Magi to the Transfiguration just before the beginning of Lent. Epiphanytide highlights the manifestation or disclosure of Jesus and his glory. We will highlight this theme of manifestation in the following essays. Here it is important to note that Epiphanytide overlaps with the first phase of Ordinary Time in the liturgical calendar. There are two phases of Ordinary Time. The first transpires between Christmastide and Lent, along with Epiphanytide. We will hold off treating "Ordinary Time" until the second phase, which occurs between Pentecost and Christ the King Sunday at the end of the church year.

Clement of Alexandria's reflection on Jesus as the Sun of Righteousness bears on all seasons of the Christian calendar, including Epiphanytide. Just when people are experiencing the post-Christmas and New Year blues, we should find Clement's meditation uplifting. Clement defined happiness and satisfaction quite differently than many of us do today. For him, Jesus truly is the reason for the season, indeed all seasons, as the Sun of Righteousness who illumines our path, opens hearts and imaginations, and shapes

III—Epiphanytide: God Is with Us!

our lives. Here's Clement's take on Christian salvation in the *Exhortation to the Heathen*, chapter 11: "How Great Are the Benefits Conferred on Man through the Advent of Christ":

> For "the Sun of Righteousness," who drives His chariot over all, pervades equally all humanity, like "His Father, who makes His sun to rise on all men," and distils on them the dew of the truth. He has changed sunset into sunrise, and through the cross brought death to life; and having wrenched man from destruction, He has raised him to the skies, transplanting mortality into immortality, and translating earth to heaven . . . having bestowed on us the truly great, divine, and inalienable inheritance of the Father, deifying man by heavenly teaching, putting His laws into our minds, and writing them on our hearts.[1]

As the Sun of Righteousness—the Son of God—races across the heavens, breaking through the secular eclipse, will we receive him again and again so that his light breaks in through the windows of our hearts to illumine our minds? Or will other stories eclipse him in our imaginations and shape our lives in the coming days and year ahead?

Permit Jesus to illumine your path as he reveals or manifests his glory in the midst of the mundane. Follow him on the path of discipleship as he reveals his glory in the miracles and transfigured presence. As we follow his lead, dying to ourselves and taking up our crosses and obeying him, we will see him more clearly and love him more dearly, longing for the day when faith becomes sight.

---

1. Clement, "How Great," 203–4.

EPIPHANY: WHAT WE WORSHIP IS QUITE REVEALING

Epiphany is often taken to signify the first manifestation of Jesus to the Gentiles with the visit of the Magi (See Matt 2).[2] As the story in Matthew's Gospel discloses, the Magi from the East pursued a star that led them to where the young child Jesus and his parents lived. When they found him, the Magi presented gifts of frankincense, gold, and myrrh.

Why did the Magi present the child with gifts? Was it based on what he had accomplished as "King of the Jews"? Was it because King Herod, and the peoples in the region celebrated him as "King of the Jews"? (see Matt 2:2). No, if anything, when Herod and the people of Jerusalem heard their announcement, they were "troubled." In other words, Jesus was not welcome (read Matt 2:1–3).

It does not appear that Herod expressed even the slightest sense to the Magi of his emotional disturbance over the news that the king of the Jews had been born. It was only after the Magi had been warned in a dream not to return to Herod that they realized Herod was not pleased with their report.

As the rest of Matthew 2 reveals, Herod intended to have the child killed (Matt 2:13–18). Herod was given to fits of jealousy and deception and would do anything to secure and strengthen his hold on power. The massacre of the children two years of age and younger in Bethlehem and its vicinity was consistent with his character and intrigues in his later years.[3]

Why, you ask, would Herod care about some small child? What threat could a boy from Bethlehem pose to a mighty king in Jerusalem? It is because Herod now had competition as king. Perhaps Herod's own lack of rightful claim to the throne made things worse for him. After all, his appointment came from Rome, unlike Jesus, whose recognition came from

---

2. Refer to Cross and Livingstone, eds., *The Oxford Dictionary of the Christian Church*, "Epiphany," 557.

3. Perowne, "Herod."

III—Epiphanytide: God Is with Us!

the God of Israel. Further to this point, Jesus was no mere child. Herod feared that this child was the Messiah based on the Magi's report. And so, he inquired of his own religious authorities where the Messiah was to be born. Their response only confirmed his suspicions: the Messiah would be born in Bethlehem. The religious leaders informed Herod of Micah's prophecy (see Matt 2:6).

If they had known about it, I doubt Herod's hostility would have kept the Magi from coming to worship Jesus. They had probably endured many obstacles and challenges along the way in their spiritual pilgrimage. What drove them forward was the star and their awareness that the child who was born King of the Jews was worthy of worship.

How can a child be worthy of worship? It was not based on Jesus' performance, given how young he was at the time. Nor was his worthiness based on star power and fame. His parents, the shepherds, and a few others like Mary's cousin Elizabeth may have been Jesus' only real admirers up to this time. Moreover, his worthiness was not based on being born into nobility or affluence. In contrast to all these motivations, the Magi found Jesus worthy of worship because of the claims associated with him. Jesus was born a king, the Messiah, a being worthy of worship independent of performance, fame, and social status and wealth.

We learn a lot about the Magi's character based on who they worshiped and why. Just like Epiphany, which means manifestation, their supreme regard for Jesus manifests not only Jesus but also reveals a lot about themselves. They worshiped Jesus based on their understanding of his identity and inherent worth. They listened to God rather than people, just as they obeyed the warning in the vision not to return to Herod rather than follow Herod's instruction to come back and tell him where the child was (Matt 2:8, 12).

In our day, we often worship someone based on performance, celebrity status, or riches. Such priorities or "e-valu(e)-ations" manifest or reveal as much about us as they do about the objects of our worship. Like King Herod, or much later in Matthew's Gospel, the rich young ruler (see Matt 19), we miss out on the manifestation of Jesus in our midst. At best, we settle for moralistic therapeutic deities[4] whose daily performance are subject to our review: "What have you done for me lately, God?"

When such motives shape and drive our worship, we often sell our souls to the highest bidder. This value system fails to account for the Bible's teaching on what is valuable and falls far short of the judgment of the Magi—Gentile outsiders from the East who came to worship the one born

---

4. For a discussion of this theme, see Smith, "'Moralistic Therapeutic Deism.'"

Epiphany: What We Worship Is Quite Revealing

King of the Jews. If these Gentile outsiders from afar got the point, shouldn't we who know the Bible better be even more discerning?

It is important that we value the Creator and creation based on inherent value rather than external considerations and what we attribute to them. Otherwise, we cheapen the Creator and creation. In addition, we also cheapen and shortchange ourselves.

With this point in mind, I draw attention to a striking statement by Rabbi Jonathan Sacks. Sacks reminds us that the Jewish faith places high value on the Creator and creation. They are never subject to market preference and supply and demand:

> The concept of the holy is precisely the domain in which the worth of things is not judged by their market price or economic value. And this fundamental insight of Judaism is all the more striking given its respect for the market within the marketplace. The fatal conceit for Judaism is to believe that the market governs the totality of our lives, when it in fact governs only a limited part of it, that which concerns the goods we think of as being subject to production and exchange. There are things fundamental to being human that we do not produce; instead we receive from those who came before us and from God Himself. And there are things that we may not exchange, however high the price.[5]

To build on Sacks's concern, it is not only Judaism's "fatal conceit," but Christianity's, too. Thank God that the Magi and Jesus' parents did not offer up Jesus in exchange for their own safety or status in Herod's court. What or who they honored and worshiped said a lot about them. What about us?

---

5. Sacks, "Markets and Morals."

EPIPHANY, BAPTISMAL THEOPHANY, AND JESUS' LIFE AS A RICH TAPESTRY

Many Christians celebrate the Epiphany or manifestation of the Lord in early January and remember Jesus' baptism a week later, though originally, they were celebrated together. Each event and celebration in their own way highlights the profound realization that God is with us—Emmanuel (Matt 1:23).[6]

To build on previous entries on Epiphany, Epiphany marks the occasion of God's Son revealing himself as human, namely Jesus. Meaning "manifestation" or "divine manifestation," it derives its name from "the Greek 'epiphania,' which denotes the visit of a god to earth."[7] For centuries, Christians have associated the Epiphany celebration with the encounter of the three kings from the East and Jesus, recorded in Matthew 2:1–12.

Further to what was stated above, the Western church often celebrates the Baptism of the Lord on the Sunday following Epiphany, though the Eastern church still celebrates it on Epiphany Sunday.[8] There are similarities between the two celebrations.[9] Before discussing a few of these similarities, we need to reference the biblical account of Jesus' baptism.

Matthew 3:13–17 recounts Jesus' baptism. Jesus appears to John the Baptist to receive his baptism of repentance. Jesus' desire to be baptized by him troubles John since, as he asserts, he needs Jesus to baptize him (Matt

---

6. Epiphany originated in the Eastern church in the third century in honor of Christ's baptism and was introduced in the Western church in the fourth century. The Western church eventually replaced the connection to Christ's baptism with his manifestation to the Magi representing the Gentiles. However, the Eastern church still associates Epiphany with Christ's baptism. See Cross and Livingstone, eds., *The Oxford Dictionary of the Christian Church*, "Epiphany," 557.

7. Catholic Online, "Feast of the Epiphany."

8. Cross and Livingstone, eds., *The Oxford Dictionary of the Christian Church*, "Epiphany," 557.

9. Refer here for similarities: Kozlowski, "Epiphany and Baptism."

3:14). Still, John consents when Jesus insists that it must be done to fulfill all righteousness: "But Jesus answered him, 'Let it be so now, for thus it is fitting for us to fulfill all righteousness.' Then he consented" (Matt 3:15).

Now for a few similarities. We find certain parallels between Jesus' manifestation as a small child to the wise men from the East and his determination to be baptized as an adult in the Jordan River. The wise men honor him as a divine king, as they come to worship him and present him with their gifts (Matt 2:2, 11). Later, as Jesus is baptized, the Spirit descends upon him and God declares him to be his beloved Son with whom he is well-pleased (Matt 3:16–17). The Eastern church, which still celebrates this baptismal event on January 6, refers to the celebration as the "Feast of the Theophany."[10] The Feast of Theophany highlights the truth that the baptism not only reveals Jesus, but the entire Trinity as well. Just as the wise men honor Jesus as divine royalty, God acknowledges him as his beloved Son in his baptism and anoints him by the Spirit. Jesus' baptism signifies his anointing as king or firstborn of all creation, the most exalted among the kings of the earth (see Ps 89:27; Col 1:15). Moreover, the wise men's third gift, myrrh, and John's baptism of repentance signify Jesus' connection with us in our human frailty.[11] As the writer of Hebrews claims, "For we do not have a high priest who is unable to sympathize with our weaknesses, but one who in every respect has been tempted as we are, yet without sin" (Heb 4:15).

For Jesus to complete our salvation as the God-Man, he had to identify with us in every way, which his baptism by John signified. The one who identifies with us in baptism is not a half human, but a full human made up of body and mind or soul. Gregory of Nazianzus puts it this way in his famous critique of Apollinarianism, with its denial of Jesus possessing a human mind or soul:

> If anyone has put his trust in Him as a Man without a human mind, he is really bereft of mind, and quite unworthy of salvation. For that which He has not assumed He has not healed; but that which is united to His Godhead is also saved. If only half Adam fell, then that which Christ assumes and saves may be half also; but if the whole of his nature fell, it must be united to the whole nature of Him that was begotten, and so be saved as a whole. Let them not, then, begrudge us our complete salvation,

---

10. Orthodox Church in America, "Feast of the Theophany."

11. Regarding myrrh and humility: R. T. France notes that myrrh, as an aromatic substance, was associated with death and burial. Undergoing death and burial, Jesus takes on our human frailty to the full. See France, *The Gospel of Matthew*, 75–76.

III—Epiphanytide: God Is with Us!

or clothe the Saviour only with bones and nerves and the portraiture of humanity.[12]

Epiphany and Jesus' baptism manifest the mystery of our complete salvation through Jesus, who is fully God and fully human. Only as he assumes our full humanity "united to His Godhead" in the incarnation does he heal it, as Gregory argued.

Both celebrations—Epiphany and Jesus' baptism—declare the profound mystery of the incarnation, which John's Gospel refers to as "the Word became flesh" (John 1:14) and which involves body and soul. Jesus is: the eternal Word made flesh (John 1:14), the most exalted of the kings of the earth (Ps 89:27), the firstborn over all creation (Col 1:15), God's beloved Son in whom he is well-pleased and on whom the Spirit descends (Matt 3:16–17), who fulfills all righteousness (Matt 3:15), who is our high priest who identifies with us fully in our total humanity, yet without sin (Heb 4:15), to bring us to God through his sacrifice unto death and resurrected life (1 Pet 3:18). May we who have seen his star from nations far and wide come to worship him who was born king of the Jews, bowing low and laying our gifts before him in joyful homage (Matt 2:2, 10–11). May we receive his baptism of the Holy Spirit and fire and pray that we are wheat, not chaff (Matt 3:11–12).

No one or two days can mark the significance of this divine and human manifestation. As has been said of the celebration of Epiphany, so it should be said of Jesus' baptism and incarnation as a whole:

> Epiphany is a complex feast. Originating in the Eastern Church and formed by the mentality of a people whose thought processes differ sharply from our own, the Epiphany is like a rich Oriental tapestry in which the various themes are woven and interwoven—now to be seen in their historical setting, again to be viewed from a different vantage point in their deep mystical significance.[13]

Like Epiphany, Jesus' baptism and entire incarnate life reflect the profound truth that what we find as a small child and as a man being baptized in the Jordan is none other than God with us—Emmanuel (Matt 1:23).

Jesus' entire life is like a rich tapestry that is an integrated whole. This complex weave makes it possible for church traditions to present Epiphany/Epiphanytide as a liturgical season from January 6 to Ash Wednesday at the

---

12. Nazianzus, *On God and Christ*, 158.
13. Catholic Online, "Feast of the Epiphany."

Epiphany, Baptismal Theophany, and Jesus' Life as a Rich Tapestry

beginning of Lent. The last Sunday associated with Epiphany is Transfiguration Sunday, which we will engage in a later entry.

The celebration of Epiphany as well as the Lord's Baptism should not end today. Keep them in mind as we move forward toward his Transfiguration (Matt 17:1–13). Until Transfiguration Sunday, and long after, may we continue to marvel at Jesus, who is "Emmanuel"—God with us (Matt 1:23).

EPIPHANYTIDE: SEEING JESUS IS BELIEVING AND FOLLOWING

Many churches celebrate Epiphany Season from January 6 with the visit of the Magi to the Transfiguration just before the beginning of Lent. Epiphanytide focuses on the manifestation of Jesus and his glory. In the Western church tradition, Epiphany Sunday focuses on the visit of the Magi whereas the Sunday following Epiphany reflects on the manifestation of the triune God at Jesus' baptism (see Matt 2 and 3 respectively for treatment of these two accounts). To truly see Jesus is believing and following, as the Magi followed the star in the east to worship him and obey God rather than Herod in returning home another way to protect the infant Jesus (Matt 2:1–12). Similarly, John the Baptist submits to Jesus' determination to be baptized by John in fulfillment of all righteousness. John prepares the way for him and relinquishes the spotlight joyfully so that Jesus' star shines brighter and brighter, and John's less (Matt 3; John 1:19–42; 3:22–30). As passages in John 1 and John 3 indicate, John the Baptist delights in pointing others—including his own disciples—to Jesus so that they turn to him. As Jesus' ultimate identity is disclosed to them, they believe and follow him. Here we find a theme often developed on the second Sunday following Epiphany, namely, the calling of Jesus' disciples.

John's Gospel develops what becomes an Epiphanytide theme in accounting for John the Baptist's rationale for his ministry of baptism—that Jesus may be *manifested* or revealed. John 1:31 reads: "I myself did not know him, but for this purpose I came baptizing with water, that he might be revealed to Israel." May our entire existence as believers reflect John's singular passion: that Jesus may be revealed—to Israel and to the world! May those who hear of Jesus truly see, which involves believing and following him.

The canonical Gospel writers share John the Baptist's singular passion to see Jesus revealed not simply to the Magi or to John the Baptist, but to a

Epiphanytide: Seeing Jesus Is Believing and Following

multitude of others. To this end, they draw attention to Jesus' calling of his first disciples who will take the good news of Jesus to Israel and the world.

John's testimony about Jesus certainly draws attention to the Lord to such an extent that two of his disciples depart to follow Jesus. Jesus tells them to come and see where he lives. One of them is Andrew, who tells his brother Peter about Jesus. Peter also turns to follow him. Later Philip tells Nathaniel about Jesus. In each of these episodes, we find manifestations of Jesus to the people and how he calls his disciples to him. Notice the emphasis on revealing, seeing, and beholding in this entire section. Here are several examples:

John the Baptist: "that he might be revealed to Israel." (1:31)

John the Baptist: "Behold, the Lamb of God!" (1:36)

Jesus to Andrew and a fellow disciple of John: "Come and you will see." (1:39)

Philip to Nathaniel: "Come and see." (1:46)

Jesus about Nathaniel: "Behold, an Israelite indeed, in whom there is no deceit!" (1:47)

We will come to one last example shortly. Before doing so, it is worth noting that John the Baptist indicates he did not know who Jesus was as the Lamb of God who baptized with the Holy Spirit apart from God revealing it to him (read John 1:32–34).

At the close of John chapter 1, we find Jesus knowing who Nathaniel is in the depths of his being and from a distance. Jesus does not need anyone to reveal it to him. After all, as we are informed in John 2, Jesus knows what is in people's hearts (John 2:23–25). However, Nathaniel is skeptical when Philip declares he has met the one prophesied by the Law and Prophets, since Philip added that Jesus is from the seemingly God-forsaken town of Nazareth (1:45–46). Nathaniel only realizes Jesus to be the Messiah based on Jesus' assertion that he knew who Nathaniel was from afar.

Jesus then makes a staggering claim, namely that Nathaniel will see God's angels ascending and descending on Jesus—the Son of Man (read John 1:49–51). Jesus is alluding to Jacob's encounter with God when he fled from his brother Esau to his uncle Laban's house (Gen 27:41—28:22). God gave Jacob a dream in which angels were ascending and descending at the very spot where Jacob slept. Jacob named the spot Bethel, the place or house where God dwells. Jesus is the ultimate dwelling place of God. That is why he performs all manner of miraculous signs that reveal his glory, as John's Gospel portrays.

III—Epiphanytide: God Is with Us!

Jesus reveals his glory to people through miraculous signs so that they might recognize who he truly is and believe. However, he does not need anyone to reveal to him what's inside people. He already knows (read John 2:23–25).

In the next essay, we will reflect on the first miraculous sign that John's Gospel highlights—the turning of water into wine at the wedding of Cana. Jesus reveals his glory to his disciples there and they believe in him (John 2:1–11). As with his first disciples, those who really see Jesus believe. Those who truly believe follow. There is no such thing as detached observation. Jesus calls those who want to know more about him to "Come and see." Real faith is not simply head knowledge. Nor does it end with heart knowledge only. It also entails hands and feet knowledge, whereby we get up, follow, and obey him.

Are we content with observing Jesus, critically redacting him ideally or historically, studying what he is as fully divine and fully human without coming to terms with who he is in his person and who he is who calls us to respond? There can be no abstract consideration of Jesus or discipleship, or focused consideration on the disciple. They are nothing more than dead ends. "Come and see" refers to *him*—to Jesus, not to his divinity or humanity in the abstract, nor to ourselves apart from him. Come and see him, as revealed in his active signs that manifest the glory of his person.[14] Seeing Jesus is believing and following. If we would see him, we must follow him. As Dietrich Bonhoeffer writes in *Discipleship*, "*only the believers obey, and only the obedient believe.*"[15] We close with another quotation from Bonhoeffer's *Discipleship*:

> Discipleship is commitment to Christ. Because Christ exists, he must be followed. An idea about Christ, a doctrinal system, a general religious recognition of grace or forgiveness of sins does not require discipleship. In truth, it even excludes discipleship; it is inimical to it. One enters into a relationship with an idea by way of knowledge, enthusiasm, perhaps even by carrying it out, but never by personal obedient discipleship. Christianity without the living Jesus Christ remains necessarily a Christianity without discipleship; and a Christianity without discipleship is always a Christianity without Jesus Christ. It is an idea, a myth.[16]

---

14. As I reflect on the canonical Gospels' manifestation of Jesus to those who follow him, I call to mind two passages in Bonhoeffer: *Christ the Center*, 44–45; *Discipleship*, 58–59, 63.

15. Bonhoeffer, *Discipleship*, 63.

16. Bonhoeffer, *Discipleship*, 59.

Epiphanytide: Seeing Jesus Is Believing and Following

Let us move from the myth to the reality of Jesus' manifestation during and beyond Epiphanytide, which inevitably leads us to believe in and follow him.

EPIPHANYTIDE: JESUS' SIGNS AIM AT FAITH, NOT FANFARE

One of the main events in Jesus' life that the church celebrates during Epiphanytide is the miraculous sign of water being turned into wine at the wedding at Cana in Galilee. The event is recorded in John 2:1–11. It is the first of the recorded signs in this Gospel. The story goes that a major mishap occurs at a wedding that Jesus, his family, and disciples attend. They have run out of wine! For some of us, that may be like forgetting to bring the wedding cake. For others of us, it's even worse. So, Jesus' mother gets involved in problem-solving by offering Jesus' services. Maybe she had witnessed him in similar situations at home, where he was asked to create a full menu of food out of nothing and in short order for unsuspecting guests that had just arrived at their house. But Jesus does not appear to be so inclined at the wedding to lend a hand to get the master of ceremonies and newly married couple out of their bind. When his mother tells Jesus that they have run out of wine, he responds: "Woman, what does this have to do with me? My hour has not yet come" (John 2:4). Undeterred by his apparent lack of enthusiasm (likely intended to create space for his ultimate mission in life), Mary tells the servants, "Do whatever he tells you" (John 2:5).

Regardless of his apparently initial reluctance, Jesus springs into action and tells the servants what to do: fill five very large jars to the brim with water. These jars could hold twenty to thirty gallons of water, and were the kind used for ceremonial cleansing. The servants follow his command. Jesus then tells the servants to have the master of the feast sample the contents of the jars. When he does, he is amazed. Jesus has turned the water into wine, and the last wine is far better than the first. The usual plan at weddings was to serve the best wine first until people had "drunk freely," then serve the "poor wine." Not so in the case of this wedding. The best is unintentionally, though miraculously, saved for last (John 2:6–10).

Epiphanytide: Jesus' Signs Aim at Faith, Not Fanfare

Besides demonstrating that Jesus can be the life of the party, and that he cherishes marriage, what is most important for the purposes of John's Gospel as well as Epiphanytide is that this miracle serves as a sign aimed at creating faith. As with all of Jesus' miraculous signs recorded in John's Gospel, the point as far as John is concerned is that people believe. Let's look at the bookend treatments of "signs." They are recorded in John 2:11 and 20:30–31.[17]

In John 2:11, we find that the turning of the water into wine creates faith in the hearts of the disciples. They have an epiphany. In other words, they see Jesus' glory and believe in him: "This, the first of his signs, Jesus did at Cana in Galilee, and manifested his glory. And his disciples believed in him" (John 2:11). In John 20:30–31, we find an explicit indication of the Gospel writer's aim in composing this book: "Now Jesus did many other signs in the presence of the disciples, which are not written in this book; but these are written so that you may believe that Jesus is the Christ, the Son of God, and that by believing you may have life in his name" (John 20:30–31). Throughout this Gospel, we find Jesus performing other miracles, including the healing of the lame man in John 5, the feeding of the five thousand in John 6, the healing of the blind man in John 9, and the raising of Lazarus from the dead in John 11. The raising of Lazarus points to the ultimate sign to follow: the hour of glory coming to fruition with Jesus' death by crucifixion and resurrection from the dead. Jesus says as much when he declares, "The hour has come for the Son of Man to be glorified" (John 12:23). He is referring to his victory over death that ensues.

As we are informed in John 20:30–31, the purpose of the miraculous signs, like John's Gospel as a whole, is to create faith. They are not intended to produce fanfare.[18] Of course, many follow Jesus for a time because of the miraculous signs he performs, only to abandon him when they realize he

---

17. "Signs" function prominently in John's Gospel, so much so that different commentators have conceived the fourth canonical Gospel according to "signs" and "glory" or "passion." For others, the entire Gospel is one of signs. Raymond E. Brown outlines the "Book of Signs" and "Book of Glory" structure and C. H. Dodd conceives the "Book of Signs" and "Book of the Passion" framework. See Brown, *The Gospel According to John (I–XII)*, cxxxviii–cxxxix; Dodd, *Interpretation of the Fourth Gospel*, 289. See D. A. Carson's critique of this overarching approach in Carson, *Gospel According to John*, 103–4.

18. As I write in my commentary on John's Gospel on the nature of the canonical Gospels: "John's words recorded as John 20:30–31 specify the nature of 'Gospel' literature. What is a Gospel? A biography? A history? A theology or catechism? A Gospel includes elements of each, but cannot be identified with any one of them. A Gospel is a category unto itself; it is God's good news written to help people come to faith and grow in their faith in Jesus, their Messiah." Metzger, *The Gospel of John*, 21. See also the discussion of this theme in Carson, "Matthew," 38–39.

III—Epiphanytide: God Is with Us!

is not their father's Oldsmobile (remember that car model?!), a run-of-the-mill Messiah.

One of the clearest illustrations of this problem is recorded in John 6. The exceptionally large crowd that Jesus feeds with only a few loaves and fish is utterly amazed. But while they declare with fanfare that he is the great prophet Moses spoke about (John 6:14), they do not truly believe in him. They wish to make him an imperial king by force, so Jesus departs (John 6:15). Still, they catch up with him and urge him to perform another miraculous sign, such as making more bread to feed the hungry masses again (John 6:25–40).

The crowd loves fanfare and full bellies. They want the bread that Jesus provides, but not Jesus as the bread of life. When the conversation takes a turn for the harder words, the crowd and many of his disciples abandon him. His claim to be the bread that comes down from heaven and that they must eat his body and drink his blood signifies that he is not merely Joseph's son, nor an imperial messianic figure. Jesus comes to take away the sins of the world. Only those whom he has chosen remain (John 6:41–69). When Jesus asks the twelve if they, too, will abandon him, Peter remarks in his typical, genuine fashion: "Lord, to whom shall we go? You have the words of eternal life, and we have believed, and have come to know, that you are the Holy One of God" (John 6:68–69).

Unlike the lame man who does not believe (John 5) and the religious leaders who seek a way to destroy Jesus after he raises Lazarus from the dead (John 11), it is only blind men who receive their sight and who do not fear the establishment that can shun and kick them out of polite society (John 9), and fishermen like Peter who—unlike the crowd—hang their lives like fishing nets on his words (John 6), that truly see his miraculous signs and believe.

How about us? Are we like the crowd or those followers who follow Jesus at first because of full bellies and fanfare, but who abandon Jesus when he does not operate like a deity on demand or when his words become difficult to swallow (John 6:52–66)? Are we like the lame man who comes up lame in his response to Jesus making him whole by turning Jesus over to the authorities who persecute Jesus for healing the man on the Sabbath (John 5:1–17)? Are we like the religious establishment, who fears that if Jesus continues to gain steam, the Romans will take away their established positions and their nation (John 11:45–53)? Or are we like Peter and John who see Jesus' miraculous signs and truly believe? As we engage Jesus today during Epiphanytide, may we realize that Jesus' miraculous signs great and small in our midst are not ends in themselves, nor aimed at creating a buzz or fanfare. Their intent is to reveal Jesus in his glory so that we might find eternal life through abiding faith in him (John 20:30–31).

JESUS' BABY DEDICATION REVEALS THE NEW WORLD ORDER

Usually, a baby dedication is sweet, uneventful, and yet memorable for the family and close friends. The worst thing that can happen at a baby dedication or baptism is that the infant may start to cry. Based on what occurs at Jesus' dedication in the Temple recorded in Luke 2, memorable is correct, but certainly not uneventful or sweet. This event recorded in Luke 2 stands at a crossroad in the church calendar, as it marks the first recorded instance of Jesus and his mission being revealed/manifested to the public. Celebrated on February 2, the Presentation of the Lord or dedication closes out the longer version of Christmastide as well as the birth narrative (forty days after Jesus' birth), is a key date during Epiphanytide, and foreshadows Lent as well as Good Friday and Easter. Jesus' baby dedication in the Temple in Jerusalem reveals the new world order that Jesus' life inaugurates. So much for the possibility of Jesus' baby dedication being uneventful.

Jesus' parents' determination to have Jesus' dedication or purification in the Temple marks them as an observant Jewish couple. They are pious and devout, as are Simeon and Anna who approach and give glory to God for the baby Jesus. We will focus on the encounter with Simeon. One of the most striking features of the narrative is the emphasis on the Holy Spirit. Three times, the text mentions Simeon's vital connection to the Spirit: "the Holy Spirit was upon him" (Luke 2:25); "it had been revealed to him by the Holy Spirit that he would not see death before he had seen the Lord's Christ" (Luke 2:26); "and he came in the Spirit into the temple" (Luke 2:27).

Given that the location is the Temple in Jerusalem, which was viewed as the place where God dwelt, and given the emphasis on the Holy Spirit's guiding presence in the story, we should be expecting something eventful to transpire. Indeed, it does. Simeon's prophetic pronouncement about Jesus leads Jesus' parents to marvel. He is Israel's glory and the Gentiles' light of

III—Epiphanytide: God Is with Us!

revelation. Many will rise and fall because of him and Mary will also endure a pierced heart (Luke 2:29–35).

The scene was certainly eventful, indeed momentous, and memorable, but by no means sweet. Why not sweet? As Simeon says to Mary, many in Israel will fall and rise on account of Jesus' divinely appointed call. And given that many will fall and rise because of him, many will oppose Jesus (Luke 2:34). Simeon adds in his words directed to Mary: "a sword will pierce through your own soul also," even while the "thoughts from many hearts may be revealed" (Luke 2:3).

While the meaning surrounding the sword piercing is not entirely clear, it is likely the case that Mary will encounter untold grief in witnessing her son's appointed call. As much as he loves his mother and family and nation, Jesus will make very clear that he is about his heavenly Father's mission. As Luke's Gospel recounts in what immediately follows, Jesus later tells his parents in the very Temple in Jerusalem when he is twelve: "Why were you looking for me? Did you not know that I must be in my Father's house?" (Luke 2:49). Just as his parents marveled at Simeon's words, no doubt grasping for their meaning, here we find Joseph and Mary at a loss for comprehension. Even so, Mary held tight to Jesus' words and took them to heart: "And they did not understand the saying that he spoke to them. And he went down with them and came to Nazareth and was submissive to them. And his mother treasured up all these things in her heart" (Luke 2:50–51).

Later we find Jesus distancing his mission from filial piety and familial ties in even more striking terms: "Then his mother and his brothers came to him, but they could not reach him because of the crowd. And he was told, 'Your mother and your brothers are standing outside, desiring to see you.' But he answered them, 'My mother and my brothers are those who hear the word of God and do it'" (Luke 8:19–21; see also Luke 11:27–28).

Imagine how such words would hit his hearers given the honor due to parents in traditional Jewish society! Consider, too, how they would strike Mary's heart! It is important to point out that Jesus means no offense or harm to Mary, but to make clear to his mother and brothers and everyone else that his ultimate loyalty is to his heavenly Father's call and divine vocation and the family of faith that holds firmly to Jesus' word. Ponder, too, Jesus' distancing himself from Mary at the wedding in Cana in telling her "Woman, what does this have to do with me? My hour has not yet come" (John 2:4; even so, Mary is not deterred and instructs the attendants at the wedding to do what Jesus tells them based on her request to him to help in view of the wine running out). There's no question that Jesus loved and honored Mary. Even on the cross, in his hour of untold agony, he accounts for her own travail and vulnerability and ensures that she will be cared for after his death and departure (John 19:25–27).

To return to Luke's Gospel, we find that it is not simply Jesus' family that Jesus distances himself from in fulfilling his divine appointment. Jesus also challenges established orders of national allegiance, power and hierarchy, and religious purity codes of conduct. Regarding national allegiance, while Jesus provides salvation for his own people, he is salvation for "all peoples" (Luke 2:31). "He is a light for revelation to the Gentiles," not only "for glory to your people Israel" (Luke 2:32).

Moreover, as already noted, within Israel itself, not all will respond well to him. Many of his own people will fall, though many will rise, on account of him (Luke 2:34). Mary's own song at the news that she will bear the Messiah makes a similar claim (read Luke 1:51–53).

Luke's Gospel makes very clear how Jesus breaks through social barriers involving Jews and Gentiles, rich/powerful and poor, and clean and unclean to bring the fullness of salvation to all people.[19] Jesus' rejection in Nazareth (which involves Jesus' claim that he will work wonders among the Gentiles, as in the days of Elijah and Elisha, and not among his own people due to their hardness of heart; Luke 4:16–30), his cleansing of the leper with his own hand (Luke 5:12–14), eating with tax collectors and sinners (Luke 5:27–32), and blessing of the poor with the kingdom and cursing of the rich (Luke 6:20, 24) certainly did not win him friends in established circles. Here we find that Jesus is salvation for all people, as God does away with the old rule and establishes the new world order in Jesus through the Spirit.

As we remember Jesus' dedication or purification in the Temple this day, may we seriously ponder the state of our hearts and presumed allegiance to him. Do filial piety, national pride, and established hierarchies and structures overshadow him and the family of faith that holds firmly to his word? May we ask God to purify our hearts and may we dedicate ourselves anew to treasuring Jesus' word and finding the fullness of salvation in him.

---

19. For a keen discussion of this theme, see Green, *The Gospel of Luke*, 394–95. Green's treatment includes mention of Mary's *Magnificat* and Simeon's pronouncement.

TRANSFIGURATION: TRANSITIONING TO LENT AND LATER

The Feast of the Transfiguration occurs later, on August 6. Still, today we join with others across the globe in highlighting the Transfiguration as the culmination and close of Epiphanytide and transition to Lent.

All three Synoptic Gospels highlight the Transfiguration. We will focus on its appearance in Matthew 17. As a precursor, Matthew 16 includes Jesus' confession of Jesus as the Christ, Jesus' rebuke of Peter for resisting Jesus' claim that the Lord must suffer and be killed by the authorities before rising from the dead, and Jesus' call for his disciples to carry their crosses and follow him (Matt 16:13–28). The chapter closes with these words: "For the Son of Man is going to come with his angels in the glory of his Father, and then he will repay each person according to what he has done. Truly, I say to you, there are some standing here who will not taste death until they see the Son of Man coming in his kingdom" (Matt 16:27–28).

Chapter 17 begins by ushering in the Transfiguration scene, according to which Jesus takes Peter, James, and John with him onto a mountain. There Jesus reveals his glory to his disciples. Moses and Elijah appear and talk with him, no doubt highlighting that Jesus is the fulfillment of the Law of Moses and the prophets who wear Elijah's mantle (Matt 17:1–3).

Before we proceed further with the text, it is important to highlight the title of this essay: this account transitions the church from Epiphanytide, which accounts for numerous manifestations of Jesus' glory, to Lent, which is the season preparing Jesus' people for the Lord's passion and inviting us to participate with him in his suffering. This being the case, the Transfiguration serves as a sign of encouragement, as it follows on the heels of Jesus' prediction of suffering and death, as well as his call to his disciples to take up their crosses and follow him. Jesus promises that some of those with him will see his future kingdom glory before they experience death.[20] Again,

---

20. See Smith, "Jesus' Transfiguration."

the Transfiguration serves as a sign of encouragement as it foreshadows Jesus—the Son of Man—coming in his kingdom glory at the end of the age (Matt 16:28). We must keep this account before us, as we come down the mountain with Jesus and the three disciples, and as we join them on the path to Golgotha.

Of course, as is well known, not everyone accepts the traditional account of Jesus coming in his glory at the end of the age. The great liberal biblical scholar/historian, philosopher, and missionary medical doctor, Albert Schweitzer, conceived Jesus' greatness differently than orthodox theology. Jesus' greatness is not bound up with bringing about "the eschatological conditions," but in "destroying them." Here's the full context for his statement:

> There is silence all around. The Baptist appears, and cries: "Repent, for the Kingdom of Heaven is at hand." Soon after that comes Jesus, and in the knowledge that He is the coming Son of Man lays hold of the wheel of the world to set it moving on that last revolution which to bring all ordinary history to a close. It refuses to turn, and He throws Himself upon it. Then it does turn; and crushes Him. Instead of bringing in the eschatological conditions, He has destroyed them. The wheel rolls onward, and the mangled body of the one immeasurably great Man, who was strong enough to think of Himself as the spiritual ruler of mankind and to bend history to His purpose, is hanging upon it still. That is His victory and His reign.[21]

Contemporary New Testament scholar and biblical historian N. T. Wright provides a different assessment, and one with which I resonate. It is worth quoting his summation at length:

> Suppose that, after all, the ancient Jewish story of a God making the world, calling a people, meeting with them on a mountain—suppose this story were true. And suppose this God had a purpose for his world and his people that had now reached the moment of fulfillment. Suppose, moreover, that this purpose had taken human form and that the person concerned was going about doing the things that spoke of God's kingdom coming on earth as in heaven, of God's space and human space coming together at last, of God's time and human time meeting and merging for a short, intense period, and of God's new creation and the present creation somehow knocking unexpected sparks off one another. The earth shall be filled, said the prophet, with the knowledge of the glory of YHWH as the waters cover the

---

21. Schweitzer, *Quest of the Historical Jesus*, 370–71.

III—Epiphanytide: God Is with Us!

> sea. It is within some such set of suppositions that we might make sense of the strangest moment of all, at the heart of the narrative, when the glory of God comes down not to the Temple in Jerusalem, not to the top of Mount Sinai, but onto and into Jesus himself, shining in splendor, talking with Moses and Elijah, drawing the Law and the Prophets together into the time of fulfillment. The transfiguration, as we call it, is the central moment. This is when what happens to space in the Temple and to time on the sabbath happens, within the life of Jesus, to the material world itself or rather, more specifically, to Jesus's physical body itself.[22]

Apart from the resurrection, the Transfiguration does appear as the "strangest moment of all." Indeed, it "is the central moment" in "the heart of the narrative." It highlights the fact that biblical history—and so, the church calendar that reflects it—comes to a culmination in Jesus standing on the mountain in his unveiled glory.

At some point, though, we have to come down from this climax of Jesus' glorious manifestation on the mountain. We must take note of the reality that it is not simply biblical scholars and historians who debate Jesus' identity and mission. The New Testament accounts reveal that the original disciples struggled, too, just as we all do. Not only does Peter wrongly rebuke Jesus for prophesying his own death (Matt 16:22), but also this same Peter wanted to erect booths in honor of Jesus, Moses, and Elijah. In effect, Peter mistakenly put them on the same level. Whereas Jesus rebuked Peter for standing in the way of his cross (Matt 16:23), there on the mountain God silenced Peter (read Matt 17:4–5).

How were Peter, James, and John to process what they had experienced? For a time, they would have to keep it to themselves. As they descended the mountain, Jesus commanded them to tell no one of the vision they had seen on the mountain until after he rose from the dead (Matt 17:9). Not only do they appear to have kept it quiet for a time, but they may even have forgotten that the Transfiguration occurred or concluded that it was nothing more than a daydream. How could those who had witnessed the revelation of Jesus' unveiled glory be hiding in fear and despair after Jesus' death unless they had forgotten or had written it off as illusory? They are a lot like the rest of us, as we move from Sunday worship to the daily grind in the valley below every week.

Jesus and the three disciples get a more immediate reality check when they come down the mountain and witness firsthand the other disciples'

---

22. Wright, *Simply Jesus*, 142–43.

Transfiguration: Transitioning to Lent and Later

lack of faith. The disciples who remained behind in the valley below could not cast out a demon from a boy because of their "little faith." Jesus appears exasperated with them before stepping in, rebuking the demon, casting it out, and miraculously healing the boy (Matt 17:14–21).

How often do we fail to trust in the Lord, even after he has manifested his glory to us again and again? How often do we bring Jesus down to the level of great prophets like Moses and Elijah, or award greater significance to Jesus because of famous people sharing the limelight with him? How often do we fail to account for the fact that whether Jesus veils or unveils his glory, he is the same Lord? How often does the manifestation of Jesus reveal not only Jesus, but also the state of our own hearts? How often does the suffering that awaits Jesus and those who follow him take our minds off the glory of his kingdom to come?

In the light of such questions involving our struggles with faith, may we pray that the Spirit of God transfigure—that is, transform and revolutionize—our hearts and imaginations. In view of the Transfiguration, may we not lose sight of our hope in the coming of Jesus' kingdom in its fullness when we come down the mountain this week and move forward to Lent.

IV

Lent: Die to Self to Gain Jesus!

The Christian liturgical season of Lent begins on Ash Wednesday and leads up to Easter Sunday. Lent focuses on purification from sin involving selfish desire, while also highlighting the need for death to self in pursuit of vital, life-giving union with Jesus. Lent is counterintuitive to two contrasting types in contemporary culture: first, the prosperity gospel devotee who only values celebration; and second, the nihilist who perceives all life as suffering and all suffering as meaningless.

Regarding the prosperity gospel mind-set, Lent instructs us that there can be no uniquely Christian abundant life that does a detour around fellowship in Christ's sufferings. As the Apostle Paul exemplifies for us, the godly Christian wants to know Christ, which entails not only knowing experientially the power of Jesus' resurrection but also knowing the fellowship of sharing in his sufferings and becoming like him in his death in order to attain to the resurrection from the dead (see Phil 3:10).

Regarding the nihilistic framework, Lent also instructs us that suffering authentically as a Christian never entails suffering for suffering's sake, but suffering for Jesus' sake. Again, as Paul articulated in Philippians 3, Lent leads us down the path of union with Christ whereby dying to ourselves entails gaining more and more of him who will lead us into the fullness of resurrected life.

I appreciate how the Reformed Church understands Lent:

> Lent invites us to make our hearts ready for remembering Jesus' passion and celebrating Jesus' resurrection . . . As a period of preparation, Lent has historically included the instruction of persons for baptism and profession of faith on Easter Sunday; the calling back of those who have become estranged from the

IV—Lent: Die to Self to Gain Jesus!

church; and efforts by all Christians to deepen their piety, devotion, and readiness to mark the death and resurrection of their Savior. As such, the primary focus of the season is to explore and deepen a "baptismal spirituality" that centers on our union with Christ rather than to function only as an extended meditation on Christ's suffering and death...[1]

Lent directs us to deepen our experiential understanding of Jesus' suffering and death and to enhance our union and communion with him.

---

1. Steenwyk and Witvliet, *Worship Sourcebook*, 557–58. Here are some works related to Lent that the reader may find helpful: Brueggemann, *Way Other Than Our Own*; Orbis, *Bread and Wine*; Rohr, *Wondrous Encounters*; Tickle, *Eastertide*.

ASH WEDNESDAY: LAMENT INDIFFERENT FAITH

It is easy to become indifferent to others' sorrows and sufferings when we live in relative comfort surrounded by modern-day conveniences. It is also easy to discount and become indifferent to our own sorrows when a prosperity gospel culture of celebration and happiness surrounds us. On Ash Wednesday and throughout Lent, we should lament the loss of lament in the American church today. Soong-Chan Rah writes,

> The American church avoids lament. The power of lament is minimized and the underlying narrative of suffering that requires lament is lost. But absence doesn't make the heart grow fonder. Absence makes the heart forget. The absence of lament in the liturgy of the American church results in the loss of memory. We forget the necessity of lamenting over suffering and pain. We forget the reality of suffering and pain.[2]

Fortunately, or better, providentially, the Jewish and Christian liturgical seasons include holy days and seasonal markers to help us account for sorrow and suffering rather than discount them. The Jewish holiday of Purim occurs in February or March every year and involves what Rabbi Jonathan Sacks calls *"therapeutic joy"* at God's deliverance of the Jewish people from ethnic cleansing while enduring foreign rule in exile, as presented in the book of Esther.[3] The Fast of Esther occurs the day before Purim and has a decidedly different tone, as Jews remember Queen Esther's great courage in risking her life to go before the Persian emperor without permission in order to intercede on behalf of her own people.[4] Esther called on her fellow Jews to fast in solidarity before she approached the throne room. In addition

---

2. Rah, *Prophetic Lament*, 13.
3. Sacks, "Therapeutic Joy of Purim."
4. Chabad.org, "Fast of Esther."

IV—Lent: Die to Self to Gain Jesus!

to Purim and the Fast of Esther, the Jewish Scriptures include a book called Lamentations, which tradition tells us was written by the weeping prophet, Jeremiah. Jeremiah wept over Jerusalem's destruction and his people's exile due to sin and rebellion. Lament also makes up 40 percent of the Psalms. And yet, unfortunately, as Rah and others note, the theme of lament and psalms of lament are often missing in the church's worship today.[5] What we often find is an imbalanced theology of celebration and with it triumphalism that serves what Walter Brueggemann calls the "haves" rather than a theology marked by suffering which features the "have-nots."[6]

In addition to Esther's Fast, Purim, Lamentations, and the Psalms, the Christian calendar accounts for lament during the season of Lent. Lent is a season where many Christians choose to give up certain comforts to identify with Christ's sufferings. Lent entails fasting and prayer. Ash Wednesday marks the first day of the season of Lent. It officially takes place forty-six days before Easter. According to one Methodist site,

> Ash Wednesday emphasizes two themes: our sinfulness before God and our human mortality. The service focuses on both themes, helping us to realize that both have been triumphed through the death and resurrection of Jesus Christ.
>
> During some Ash Wednesday services, the minister will lightly rub the sign of the cross with ashes onto the foreheads of worshipers. The use of ashes as a sign of mortality and repentance has a long history in Jewish and Christian worship. Historically, ashes signified purification and sorrow for sins.[7]

Further to what was stated above, Lent is a time when many Christians give up consumer comforts like chocolate, ice cream, or coffee. Lent is not a time to give up sorrow, but to embrace it as well as Christ's sufferings and those of his people. What happens, though, to our identification with Christ and his people in their sufferings if we only make room in our corporate worship each Sunday for celebration and triumph? Perhaps indifference toward those who suffer grows and overtakes us.

In a letter ". . . For Lent 2015," Pope Francis encouraged Christians to go beyond renouncing comforts to fast from indifference toward others. The pope spoke of indifference as a global problem:

> As long as I am relatively healthy and comfortable, I don't think about those less well off. Today, this selfish attitude of

---

5. In *Prophetic Lament* (13), Rah points to the following works: Hopkins, *Journey*, 5–6; Meyer, "A Lack of Laments," 67–78; and Pemberton, *Hurting with God*, 441–45.

6. Brueggemann, *Peace*, 26–28.

7. Aledo United Methodist Church, "Ash Wednesday."

Ash Wednesday: Lament Indifferent Faith

indifference has taken on global proportions, to the extent that we can speak of a globalization of indifference. It is a problem which we, as Christians, need to confront.[8]

The pope encouraged the faithful to care for the global church as it endures suffering and persecution. He quoted 1 Corinthians 12:26. Here Paul writes, "If one member suffers, all suffer together; if one member is honored, all rejoice together." In addition to identifying with the sufferings of fellow Christians, we should sensitize ourselves to the sufferings of those from other faith traditions, including Jews and Muslims. Honoring the Fast of Esther and Purim helps us to connect to Jewish people as they remain vigilant in the face of threats to destroy them and celebrate God's deliverance with "therapeutic joy." Respecting Muslims' practice of Ramadan, which takes place around this time of year, and which involves soul-searching, prayer, and fasting, is also important to confront globalized indifference.[9]

Moreover, we need to guard against indifference to our own sorrow and suffering. How can we account for others' suffering if we won't even make space for lament in our lives? With this question in mind, it is important to mention that my beloved mother Audrey passed away just before Ash Wednesday and the beginning of Lent. The loss of my mom will be with me throughout the rest of my life. I do not intend to get over it, as we are often encouraged to do with suffering. While I cherish the relational gain of my cherished parents' William and Audrey's enduring impact on my life, I also cherish the fact that I miss them greatly. Where there is no great loss, there is no great love.

My parents expressed deep empathy for others in their loss in view of the heavenly Father's deep and abiding love that would lead him to give up his Son—such "searing loss"—to take away our sin, to pay our ransom, and bring us home. It was fitting that Francis Ortega's rendition of "How Deep the Father's Love for Us" played in the background when my mother passed away in the presence of family to go to her eternal rest with Jesus.

On Ash Wednesday, during Lent, and throughout the church calendar year, I pray that God will sensitize my heart to Christ's sufferings, the sufferings of the global church, and people of all walks of life as they struggle and endure hardship. May we who are followers of Jesus not give into the "globalization of indifference." Let us not ignore or speed through Lent. May

---

8. Francis, "Pope Francis For Lent 2015," prologue.

9. One article goes so far as to employ Purim and the preceding Fast of Esther as pivotal means to cultivate Shalom and unify Jews, Muslims, and Christians. Waskow, "Renewal of Purim."

IV—Lent: Die to Self to Gain Jesus!

we participate in Jesus' suffering and never inoculate ourselves from others' grief or suppress our own.

LENT AND BLACK HISTORY MONTH: LITURGIES OF LAMENT AND CELEBRATION

In the prior entry on Ash Wednesday, I argued that a liturgy that makes no space for lament caters to the "haves." A liturgy of suffering features the "have-nots."[10] A truly Christian liturgy rightly conceived accounts for both lament and celebration, and in view of Jesus' cruciform glory, must move *through* lament to celebration. Thus, we must keep Lent if we wish to honor Easter.

Black History Month, which runs throughout February, often overlaps with Lent, which begins in February or March. Black History Month accounts for lament and celebration. It laments the oppression committed against African Americans and celebrates their achievements in the face of overwhelming obstacles. Like the Lenten and Easter seasons, Black History Month moves through lament to celebration.

James Cone, the father of Black Theology, rightly highlighted the need for Christian theologians to prioritize themes of oppression and liberation. He went so far as to call Jesus black, as Jesus identifies with the oppressed or have-nots against oppression.[11] Indeed, Jesus liberates the poor, the downtrodden, the marginalized in an all-encompassing manner of soul and body. As we find in Matthew 5, Jesus blesses the poor in spirit, just as he blesses the poor in Luke 6, while cursing the rich oppressors (similar themes appear in James 1 and 2). We must account for both passages in distinct though inseparable relation. Gordon Fee and Douglas Stuart put the matter well:

> In Matthew the poor are "the poor in spirit"; in Luke they are simply "you poor" in contrast to "you that are rich" (6:24). On such points most people tend to have only half a canon. Traditional evangelicals tend to read only "the poor in spirit"; social

---

10. Brueggemann, *Peace*, 26–28.
11. See Cone, *Black Theology*, 119–24.

IV—Lent: Die to Self to Gain Jesus!

activists tend to read only "you poor." We insist that both are canonical. In a truly profound sense the real poor are those who recognize themselves as impoverished before God. But the God of the Bible, who became incarnate in Jesus of Nazareth, is a God who pleads the cause of the oppressed and the disenfranchised. One can scarcely read Luke's Gospel without recognizing his interest in this aspect of the divine revelation (see 14:12–14; cf. 12:33–34 with the Matthean parallel, 6:19–21).[12]

Many white evangelical Christians may argue that all this about the black Jesus, oppression, and liberation is nothing more than identity politics and a form of the social gospel. They easily forget that every theology has an identity that is culturally and politically embedded. What passes for authentic theology and liturgy is often no more than a contextualized Eurocentric ethnic form of theology that caters to dominant culture ways of life that have become homogenized due to familiarity. They also appear to replace a social gospel with an otherworldly gospel. In contrast, the whole gospel features salvation of the whole person in the whole community where the kingdom of heaven flourishes on earth. In place of a materialistic social gospel or a pie-in-the-sky asocial gospel, the gospel is relational and social and addresses our total human condition.

What is needed, then, is a liturgy that accounts for blackness, namely themes of oppression and liberation, and not simply personal salvation. Just as the church historically accounted for red martyrdom (persecution where Christians shed their blood for their faith) and white martyrdom (asceticism/monasticism where Christians deny themselves for their faith),[13] we need to account for black martyrdom. Black martyrdom involves living in solidarity with the oppressed in view of Jesus who comes to set the captive free.

The US calendar formally features black history only one month of each year. The rest of the year generally features white history. Lent only occurs over forty days during the church calendar cycle. But we must not allow it to recede into distant memory as we proceed toward Easter and

---

12. Fee and Stuart, *How to Read the Bible*, 125.

13. There are at least four forms of martyrdom discussed in various sources: red, white, blue, and green. Thomas Cahill discusses "green martyrdom" and associates it with the distinctive witness of Irish monasticism. See Cahill, *How the Irish Saved Civilization*. Red stands for the shedding of blood and death. White stands for asceticism. Blue stands for penitence. Here's a brief summary of the latter three forms: "White martyrdom was the daily living of the ascetic life for Christ's sake; red, of course, meant the shedding of blood and death itself for Christ's sake. Blue martyrdom, which seems to have been a particularly Irish development, stood for the way of the penitent in penance, in bewailing of sins and in labour." Jones et al., eds., *The Study of Spirituality*, 221.

Lent and Black History Month: Liturgies of Lament and Celebration

Ascension. After all, "the black Jesus" became poor so that we could become the riches of God (2 Cor 8:9). When he ascended, he led captives in his train and gave gifts to humankind (Eph 4:8). Here I am not promoting a form of prosperity gospel teaching, but simply that God cares for the whole person and brings about liberation from oppression for the captive and seeks to make us spiritually, physically, and socially whole through the realization of God's eschatological kingdom in which we participate presently and which will be realized in full one day.[14] The vital connection between Lent, Easter, and Ascension signifies that Jesus' glory ever remains cruciform.

As noted in the last entry, 40 percent of the psalms feature lament,[15] and all four Gospels give significant attention to the way of the cross and Jesus' passion. Given these factors, maybe we should feature lament in our liturgy 40 percent of the year. In that case, forty-plus days of Lent are not enough. Nor are thirty days for black history. We must account for lament as well as celebration, along with black martyrdom, throughout the year, if we are to cherish the have-nots with whom Jesus identifies as the Suffering Servant and man of sorrows, familiar with suffering (Isa 53:3).[16]

---

14. Note that while many white evangelicals look down on the prosperity gospel movement, we have a tendency to promote it in more subtle terms with our implicit or explicit adherence to a riff off of Max Weber's thesis of the Protestant work ethic. Prosperity reflects assurance of God's favor and blessing as a result of our hard work. See Weber, *The Protestant Ethic*.

15. Pemberton, *Hurting with God*, 441–45.

16. Here it is worth accounting for Cone's connection between the Suffering Servant and the black Jesus: "If Jesus is the Suffering Servant of God, he is an oppressed being who has taken on that very form of human existence that is responsible for human misery. What we need to ask is this: 'What is the form of humanity that accounts for human suffering in our society? What is it, except blackness?' If Christ is truly the Suffering Servant of God who takes upon himself the suffering of his people, thereby establishing the covenant of God, then he must be black." Cone, *Black Theology*, 129.

FORTY DAYS OF LENTEN PURPOSE

Lent commemorates Jesus' forty days of temptation by Satan in the wilderness prior to the start of his public ministry. Apart from the Sundays during the Lenten season, Lent is in effect forty days. Lent begins on Ash Wednesday and ends with Easter Sunday.[17] Many of us are familiar with the "Forty Days of Purpose" study by Rick Warren that addresses what he takes to be God's five purposes for human life. The Lord Jesus didn't have Pastor Warren's study to hand when enduring temptation, though we would no doubt find it very helpful in our day. What Jesus did have to hand were the Scriptures on which he had meditated his whole life and a vital relationship with God his Father. Contrary to those who think all suffering and tribulation are without meaning and purpose, Jesus' wilderness trials convey deep meaning and purpose for his public ministry and entire life. The same goes for Lent: Lent's purpose does not begin and end with forty days but bears significance for our entire lives. "By the solemn forty days of *Lent* the Church unites herself each year to the mystery of Jesus in the desert."[18]

In what follows, we will engage these three questions: Where do Jesus and we find our ultimate security in life? In what do Jesus and we find ultimate satisfaction and sustenance for life? How do Jesus and we endure temptation involving scarcity, especially as it gnaws at our sense of ultimate security and satisfaction? (At this point, pause to read Matthew 4:1–11, which provides one of the biblical accounts of Jesus' temptation in the wilderness).

In Matthew's temptation account, Satan attacks Jesus' identity, sense of worth, and values when Jesus is very tired, painfully hungry, and extremely

---

17. Refer to Cross and Livingstone, eds., *The Oxford Dictionary of the Christian Church*, "Lent," 971–72.

18. Catholic Church, *English Translation Catechism*, #540. It is important to note that Lent is ultimately about our union with Christ and not simply reflection on his suffering and death, as noted in the introduction to the Lenten season.

vulnerable. Take note. The same may very well happen to us during Lent, and in seasons where we experience loss and deprivation.

Notice how Satan questions Jesus and challenges him to prove he is the Son of God. In the first two temptations, the devil tries to trip Jesus up with "If you are the Son of God, . . ." He challenges Jesus to prove to him that he is God's Son by taking matters into his own hands and looking to himself rather than his Father for his daily sustenance, by turning stones into bread to ease his hunger. The devil also tries to push him to throw himself over a cliff to see if God's angels will come to his aid and catch him as he falls. Lastly, the devil tries to bargain with Jesus. Jesus will receive all the kingdoms of the world in their glory in exchange for worshiping Satan. In each case, Jesus thwarts Satan with Scripture. He depends on the very Word of God.

No doubt, in addition to the written Word of God, the Father's declaration at Jesus' baptism immediately prior to the wilderness temptations left an indelible impression on Jesus and helped to sustain him: "And when Jesus was baptized, immediately he went up from the water, and behold, the heavens were opened to him, and he saw the Spirit of God descending like a dove and coming to rest on him; and behold, a voice from heaven said, 'This is my beloved Son, with whom I am well pleased'" (Matt 3:16–17).

We don't know much about Jesus' earthly father Joseph, other than that he was a righteous man who cared for his family. After the age of Jesus at twelve, though, we find no mention of him being involved in Jesus' life. Perhaps he had passed away before Jesus' baptism. What we do know is that as early as his twelfth year of life, Jesus experienced a vital relationship with God as his heavenly Father and that his ultimate purpose and allegiance was with God, not his earthly parents: "Why were you looking for me? Did you not know that I must be in my Father's house?" (Luke 2:49).

Many of us struggle with father wounds that eat at our souls and sense of identity. We look for all kinds of things to fill the void in life, whether other relationships, belongings, performance and prowess, and various kinds of status. We can take comfort from Jesus' life that one's ultimate worth and satisfaction should be with God who longs to parent us and care for us during good times and bad.

If Jesus had not been grounded in his relationship with his heavenly Father, he would have gone off the rails, perhaps not during the temptation in the wilderness, but later. Perhaps he would have taken matters into his own hands and not gone to the cross in humble and free obedience to the Father's will (Matt 26:39).

Jesus' temptation in the wilderness over forty days helped him assess his spiritual state and locate where he found his ultimate value, worth, and satisfaction. How about us? Where do we find our ultimate security in life? In what do we find ultimate satisfaction and sustenance for life? How do we endure temptation involving scarcity, especially as it gnaws at our sense of ultimate security and satisfaction?

Of course, we are to work for our daily bread. Of course, we are to trust God for deliverance from evil. Of course, we are not to have any other gods before us. But what will make us immune to taking matters into our own hands and testing rather than trusting God to meet our needs and give us a vital sense of ultimate security and satisfaction?

Whether or not we struggle with father wounds involving our earthly fathers, we need to come to terms with finding our ultimate significance and purpose in life in relation to our heavenly Father, just as Jesus did. Jesus was secure in his heavenly Father's embrace and found his ultimate satisfaction and sustenance in life in relation to God's declaration of love and good pleasure and in God's written Word. Jesus knew that the heavenly Father's embrace is all-important, and that in due course, he would faithfully deliver him from temptation and have his angels minister to Jesus' various needs. Jesus also clearly knew that Satan could not be trusted and that he only wanted to trip Jesus up. Jesus discerned all too well that people are fickle, and as we see following Palm Sunday, the cheers of the crowds easily turn to jeers.

How about us? As we deal with various insecurities and scarcity in life during Lent and beyond, where do we fix our gaze? How do we seek to fill the hole not simply in our stomachs, but in our souls? May the forty days of Lenten purpose help us answer these questions as we make our way forward with Jesus to Good Friday and onward to Easter Sunday.

ESTHER'S FAST, PURIM, LENT, AND INTERNATIONAL WOMEN'S DAY

The book of Esther does not mention God anywhere, but it is obvious that divine providence permeates the book. God preserves the Jewish people while under hostile Gentile rule in a foreign land. The Fast of Esther and Purim, which the book of Esther documents, highlight God's people's suffering and deliverance from their enemies in the Persian Empire.

Whether it is providential or coincidental, the Fast of Esther and Purim overlapped with the Christian season of Lent and International Women's Day in 2020. The connection goes deeper than sharing dates on a calendar from time to time. Like Esther's Fast and Purim, Lent also entails fasting in keeping with Jesus' suffering for the deliverance of God's people. International Women's Day, with its emphasis on gender equality, women's achievements, and confrontation of inequality, immediately preceded the Fast of Esther and Purim in 2020, as it fell on March 8. Esther's Fast occurred on March 9 and Purim began on the night of March 9 and ran through March 10. Purim occurs every fourteenth day of the Hebrew month of Adar, which is at the end of winter or early spring.

Much has been made of Esther's import for women's rights. The book focuses primarily on the providential protection of the Jewish people under oppressive foreign rule, as noted above. Even so, it bears import for Jewish and Christian feminist concerns and advocacy for women and recognition of their accomplishments while enduring and confronting patriarchy over the centuries up to the present day. This entry will highlight certain features of Esther as a Jewish and Christian canonical book, including Esther's Fast and Purim, that features God's people's liberation and bears upon women's dignity and equality.

Any fair engagement of a particular text must account for its argument and context rather than run roughshod over them with an alternative agenda and in an anachronistic manner. Esther is not first and foremost about

IV—Lent: Die to Self to Gain Jesus!

contending against patriarchy. Nor does it present our heroine as an ancient identical twin of a self-avowed modern Western feminist. The same would be true for the canonical Gospels' purpose(s) about Jesus' aim and how the women express their agency in an ancient middle Near Eastern patriarchal world. Scripture is not made of one seamless cloth regarding women either. One finds in Jewish Scripture and tradition an evolution of thought enhancing greater respect and affirmation of women's status as equals.[19] We find this dynamic at work in Esther.

The book of Esther offers various portrayals of women. Take for example Vashti's strong resistance to the king's command to entertain his guests. Her refusal leads to her dethronement. Compare her with the young maiden Esther as she makes her appearance in chapter 1. Whereas Vashti is defiant (Esth 1:10–12), Esther is compliant (Esth 2:1–18), as she is prepared to visit the king's chamber in view of his selection of a queen to replace the deposed Vashti. Still, Esther evolves as a person. At first, she takes orders from the royal court (Esth 2:8–18) and her relative and patron Mordecai (Esth 2:10, 20; 4:8). But later she engages Mordecai dialogically as an equal (Esth 4:10–14), and then goes so far as to give him orders as the heroine of her people (Esth 4:15–17). Esther also goes before the king without an invitation, which could get her killed (Esth 4:8–17). She risks all in order to denounce the evil royal official Haman and advocate for her people's liberation (Esth 7–8).

No matter how one views the subject, women's status was precarious in the Persian empire, as illustrated in the treatment of Vashti and Esther. The consequence of Queen Vashti's refusal to be put on display as the equivalent of a concubine and sex object for the king's drunken guests to gawk at lustfully was severe. She was deposed and made an object of derision. The empire's patriarchal leaders feared that if she were not made an object lesson, other women would follow her example and refuse to submit to male rule (Esth 1:13–22). No doubt, Esther was viewed as a model replacement—beautiful and submissive (Esth 2:5–18). Like other women, including the queen herself, Esther's likely fear and deep reservation about being an object of sexual pleasure for the king would not matter in the slightest to the reigning forces. Such was the tragic and heinous state of affairs in which they found themselves.

Some critiques of Esther portray her as "passive and devious," according to Michael V. Fox. Fox finds such judgments "misguided." In contrast, Fox points out how Esther underwent a metamorphosis: "Esther has a great

---

19. On this subject, see Hauptman, *Rereading the Rabbis*.

challenge thrust upon her. In facing it, she gains three powers that could not have been foreseen from her early behavior: agency, strategy, and authority."

As the narrative unfolds, Esther models courage in going before the mercurial king (Esth 4:11; 5:1–4), cunning in how she entraps Haman in his hubris and hatred of the Jews (Esth 5:9–14), and compassion in how she advocates for her people (Esth 4:15–17). Esther becomes a model for Jewish leadership while in bondage in exile. Regarding this matter, Fox writes,

> In Esther, the author has created a model for Jews in the diaspora, who in the absence of a national state and army, must rely on their own courage and ingenuity to deal with dangers . . . This picture should not, however, be understood as a reassessment of woman's stature. Rather, it is an attempt to reconceive the status of Jews in a new context.[20]

Even if the book of Esther does not argue for a reassessment of women's place in the ancient world, it certainly goes a long way toward opening the door to new possibilities. We should honor Esther's accomplishments as a courageous, cunning, and compassionate leader on behalf of God's suffering people. Esther leads us forward in demonstrating human agency in contending against the objectification and oppression of people wherever it is found.

Like Jesus after her, Esther puts people's interests above her own. As a result, she faces the very real threat of losing not only her position as queen but also her life. We find this theme of self-sacrifice in play in the Fast of Esther. The text in Esther 4 reads:

> Then Esther told them to reply to Mordecai, "Go, gather all the Jews to be found in Susa, and hold a fast on my behalf, and do not eat or drink for three days, night or day. I and my young women will also fast as you do. Then I will go to the king, though it is against the law, and if I perish, I perish." Mordecai then went away and did everything as Esther had ordered him. (Esth 4:15–17)

Like Moses before her, God raises up Esther as a savior for her people Israel. Together they foreshadow Jesus who delivers his people from their bondage to sin and liberation from oppression. During Lent, Christians

---

20. Fox, "The Women in Esther." In addition to Fox's online article from which the quotes are taken, see his earlier work on which the article builds: Fox, *Character and Ideology*. In his online treatment, Fox affirms the feminist perspective of Sidnie Ann White (also known as Sidnie White Crawford), as set forth in White, "Esther: A Feminist Model." See also her encyclopedia article on Esther: Crawford, "Esther: Bible."

IV—Lent: Die to Self to Gain Jesus!

would do well to remember the Fast of Esther and Purim, which their Jewish brothers and sisters honor (as instituted in Esther 9:20–22).

May we take to heart God's providential care for Israel and the church. May we also honor great leaders like Esther and follow their example. You don't need to be Jewish to honor Esther's Fast and Purim. But you do need to believe God providentially cares for Abraham's people. You don't need to be a man to be a great leader of all the people or a woman to honor International Women's Day. But you do need to stand with women in cherishing their accomplishments and confronting inequity and abuse committed against them wherever it exists.

WHAT DID GOD GIVE UP FOR LENT?

Many Christians celebrate Lent, which is a forty-day season of prayer and fasting that ends the day before Easter. Christians who observe Lent give up creaturely comforts and habits of various kinds, such as chocolate, coffee, and cigarettes. As noted in the Ash Wednesday essay, Pope Francis has called on Christians to give up the global problem of indifference during Lent.[21]

Lent is a season leading up to Easter, when we reflect on God's own self-denial. By no means indifferent, God in Christ provides us with the surest sign of love that makes a fundamental difference in our lives. What did God give up for Lent? It wasn't chocolate, coffee, cigarettes—or even broccoli! God gave up his Son. Paul tells us in Romans 8: "He who did not spare his own Son but gave him up for us all, how will he not also with him graciously give us all things?" (Rom 8:32) From a biblical perspective, it is impossible to establish and cultivate strong relationships apart from self-denial. God goes to the greatest lengths possible during the season of Lent—indeed during his Son's entire incarnate life[22]—to break through our indifference and build lasting relationships of trust and intimacy with us. He does so by giving up his most prized "possession"—Jesus.

Paul tells us that this God who gives up his Son for us will graciously give us all things in relation to him (Rom 8:32). From the immediate context of Romans 8, such gifts do not include the removal of suffering and self-denial in this life. The Apostle writes of our need to suffer with the Lord (Rom 8:17) and that nothing can separate us from God's love in Christ, including persecution (Rom 8:35). We are children and heirs of God and fellow-heirs of Christ (Rom 8:16–17). We will share in his glory in his coming kingdom,

21. Francis, "Pope Francis for Lent 2015," prologue.

22. Many refer to the forty days of fasting in the wilderness that Jesus endured prior to his public ministry as providing the biblical basis for Lent. The belief that Jesus was in the tomb for forty hours before rising from the dead also serves as a reason for many observers.

IV—Lent: Die to Self to Gain Jesus!

which far exceeds our present state of suffering (Rom 8:18). Our eternal inheritance is sure—nothing can separate us from the everlasting love of God in Christ (Rom 8:37–39).

God gave up his Son in order to gain him back along with us at Easter. Jesus is the firstborn of many brothers and sisters who are conformed to his image—the new humanity that God creates in Jesus' resurrection from the dead (Rom 8:29).

All of us who claim Christ must give up indifference and the refusal to identify with him in his sufferings so as to gain the glory that awaits us in relation to him (Rom 8:17). I imagine that the twenty-one Egyptian martyrs who experienced martyrdom at the hands of ISIS just prior to Lent several years ago envisioned this hope of sharing in Jesus' glory, as "Jesus" was the last word on their lips.

What words are on our lips this day? Are they words that testify to indifference toward others or solidarity with them and identification with Jesus, God's Son? Are they words like Paul's, who exalts in God's tenacious and glorious love that sustains him in the midst of suffering?

> Who shall separate us from the love of Christ? Shall tribulation, or distress, or persecution, or famine, or nakedness, or danger, or sword? As it is written,
>
> "For your sake we are being killed all the day long;
> we are regarded as sheep to be slaughtered."
>
> No, in all these things we are more than conquerors through him who loved us. For I am sure that neither death nor life, nor angels nor rulers, nor things present nor things to come, nor powers, nor height nor depth, nor anything else in all creation, will be able to separate us from the love of God in Christ Jesus our Lord. (Rom 8:35–39)

In view of nothing being able to separate us from God's love in Christ Jesus, may we not remain separate from others in a state of indifference during Lent and beyond.

Paul suffered greatly for the faith for the sake of Christ and his people (see 2 Cor 11:23–29). By no means was he indifferent to their concerns. He was willing to suffer greatly because of gaining a glowing glimpse of what awaits those who will share in Jesus' glory: "For I consider that the sufferings of this present time are not worth comparing with the glory that is to be revealed to us" (Rom 8:18). It is not that he suffered for drudgery's sake, missing out by not eating chocolates. Paul's situation was not what we find in the movie *Chocolat*, which chronicles the opening of a chocolate shop in an old-fashioned, prudish French town just before Lent, which fostered in

What Did God Give Up for Lent?

the town a revolutionary spirit of self-abandon. No, Paul was revolutionized by Jesus' love and joy to give up creaturely comforts for him and others to gain far more.

In the end, it is not ultimately about what we give up at Lent, but about what God gave up in surrendering his Son to death in order to gain Jesus back along with us for the glory of his everlasting love. Now, I'll eat and drink to that!

LENT: GIVING UP VICE TO GAIN THE SAVIOR

People often associate Lent with giving up some vice for God. It might be cigars or alcohol or sweets, or something a bit more devious. Now if spinach or prunes counted, I think you would find a lot more people claiming to keep the fast.

But Lent is not only about giving up vice. It is also about gaining. What do we gain? The virtuous Savior. Just as Jesus went into the wilderness and suffered hunger and thirst for forty days to encounter and experience God in a more intense manner while being tempted by the devil (see Matt 4:1–11), so we give up something during Lent to gain more of Jesus. We give up vice to gain and savor the Savior.

The Apostle Paul wrote during his first Roman imprisonment (he was imprisoned on account of his bold Christian witness) that for him "to live is Christ, and to die is gain" (Phil 1:21). While he did not likely pen those words during the Lenten season, nonetheless, his words bear on the subject of Lent.

Paul was pondering what stood before him—possible death, or release from imprisonment. Regardless of the possibility of death, he did not fear. Why? Death simply entailed his departure to be with Christ, which is "better by far" (Phil 1:23, NIV). After all, Paul's whole existence was Christ. Even so, Paul determined for the sake of his brothers and sisters in Christ here on earth that it was best for him to remain on earth for a time to support and build up the Christian community (Phil 1:24–26).

Later, in Philippians 3, Paul returned to the Christocentric thrust of his life, and how suffering loss was central to his spiritual participation in Jesus' life (read Phil 3:7–16). The fellowship of sharing in Jesus' sufferings was not an ellipsis for Paul. It was essential (see Phil 3:10). Part of suffering loss involved dying to the egoistic drive of pursuing perfection by way of self-righteousness (Phil 3:7–8), something in which Paul had excelled (Phil 3:1–6). Paul's rejection of self-righteousness and challenge to others who still embraced it did not go over well in many circles. Much of the suffering Paul experienced was at the hands of those who did not give up their egos "during Lent" and throughout the year to embrace a righteousness by faith in Christ Jesus for a lifetime.

It is important to note here that there is nothing inherently good or virtuous about giving up something like a vice as a Christian if it is not ultimately tied to gaining Jesus by faith. They belong together. For Paul, you could not have one without the other: suffering and savoring intimacy with the Savior went together.

Like any intimate relationship, it is not only the good times that cultivate intimacy. Suffering together also builds the relationship. So it is for the believer with Jesus.[23] Here I call to mind my mother and father. My parents were married for more than sixty years. When they took their wedding vows, they did not only take seriously the parts about "better" and "richer" and "health." There was no ellipsis, that is, no omission of words that involved suffering, pain, and difficulty. They embraced their entire wedding vows throughout their marriage, which lasted until my father died of cancer several years ago: "to have and to hold, from this day forward, for better, for worse, for richer, for poorer, in sickness and in health, to love and to cherish, till death do us part."

In her last years of life, my mother cherished my father as much as she ever did and longed to see him. So it was for Paul in his walk with Christ. He longed to see Jesus, and he viewed participation in the bad times as well as the good times—that is, participation in Jesus' sufferings as well as his resurrection glory—to be essential to his faith. One of the fundamental differences between a healthy marriage in the here and now and what Scripture refers to as the church's marriage to Christ Jesus is that the latter lasts forever. Thus, what we give up now to gain greater intimacy with Jesus has far greater significance. After all, the bond is eternal.

Paul's passion in his Christian life was to connect with the whole Christ, and nothing but the whole Christ. For him, loss and suffering were not the end goal. They were simply the vehicle on the path for gaining Christ Jesus. How about us during Lent and beyond? Do we look at suffering and loss as an obstacle, or as an opportunity to gain Christ Jesus? What are you giving up during Lent? And what—or better whom—do you hope to gain by faith through it?

---

23. N. T. Wright refers to this identification with Jesus in his suffering as "mutual belonging." The word for Paul's "partnership" with Christ in his suffering is *koinonia* (see Phil 3:10). For Paul, suffering with Christ "expressed a mutual belonging for which modern English does not provide exact words." Wright, *Paul*, 278.

LENTEN EXTRAVAGANCE

John 12:1–8 is a fitting text to consider for this Sunday in Lent. The text narrates Mary's anointing of Jesus for burial with an extremely expensive perfume made of pure nard. Only a few verses separate Jesus' anointing in Bethany at Mary's, Martha's, and Lazarus's home and Jesus' triumphant entry into Jerusalem. We honor Jesus' triumphant entry next week on Palm Sunday. What we find here in Jesus' anointing is the equivalent of Lenten excess or extravagance (pause to read John 12:1–8). Mary's anointing of Jesus with such expensive perfume may lead one to think the text does not fit Lent. After all, rarely if ever does one find Lent and excess or extravagance in the same sentence, except by contrast. Why is that? Lent is a season in the Christian liturgical calendar that is intended to prepare Jesus' followers for Easter through reflection, prayer, and fasting, just as Jesus prayed, meditated, and fasted in the wilderness prior to beginning his public ministry.

Here is a helpful explanation of Lent, which also serves to highlight the tension in making a connection between Lent and excess or extravagance:

> Lent is a time of repentance, fasting and preparation for the coming of Easter. It is a time of self-examination and reflection. In the early church, Lent was a time to prepare new converts for baptism. Today, Christians focus on their relationship with God, often choosing to give up something or to volunteer and give of themselves for others.[24]

If Judas were around today, he would most likely take issue with equating excess and Lent, since in this biblical account, he takes issue with Mary anointing Jesus with nard. His stated reason is that the perfume could be sold so that the money could be spent on the poor, which on the surface appeared reasonable. D. A. Carson provides fitting context for this reaction:

---

24. The People of the United Methodist Church, "What is Lent?"

Lenten Extravagance

The objection Judas raises has a superficial plausibility to it. The sum of "three hundred denarii" (RSV), the value of the perfume, must not be estimated according to the modern value of an equivalent amount of silver, but according to wages of purchasing power. One denarius was the daily wage given to a common day-laborer; three hundred denarii was therefore the equivalent of *a year's wages* for a fully employed labourer (no money would be earned on Sabbaths and other holy days). The sum was enormous. Either Mary and her family were very wealthy, or perhaps this was a family heirloom that had been passed down to her. Either way, Judas displays a certain utilitarianism that pits pragmatic compassion, concern for the poor, against extravagant, unqualified devotion.[25]

As Carson notes, Judas's objection has a certain "superficial plausibility to it." However, the text informs us that he does not care for the poor. Nor does he care for Jesus, as he will soon betray him for silver (see Matt 26:14–16). What Judas does care about is confiscating the money and pocketing it. As Carson asserts, "his personal greed for material things masquerades as altruism."[26] He was responsible for the moneybag and would often help himself to what was in it (John 12:6). Jesus rebukes Judas, making clear that while they can always give to the poor, they will not always be able to prepare him for burial, which Judas will help to expedite in betraying Jesus to his enemies (John 18:1–3).

As an aside, I wonder if Martha also took issue with Mary here. Luke's Gospel narrates another time when Jesus is in their home and Mary is at his feet listening to him teach along with his disciples. Martha rebukes Mary for not helping her with serving. Jesus gently rebukes Martha, stating that Mary has chosen well whereas Martha is "distracted with much serving" (Luke 10:40; see Luke 10:38–42). Certainly, Martha loves Jesus, as did Lazarus their brother. But Mary is found in both Luke's and John's accounts given to pure, undistracted devotion. Such pure devotion is a rare find, like the perfume made of pure nard.

Certainly, Lent is a season marked by self-examination, restraint, and self-sacrifice. Such sacrifice is on display here, as Mary does not keep the perfume for herself, or sell it and spend it on herself. Rather, she pours it out on Jesus. For his part, the Lord is not gloating over this act of extravagance, or caught up in self-adulation. This anointing is to prepare him for his ultimate act of self-sacrifice, as the text informs us—his burial following death on the cross (John 12:7).

25. Carson, *Gospel According to John*, 429.
26. Carson, *Gospel According to John*, 429.

IV—Lent: Die to Self to Gain Jesus!

A footnote in the text informs us that a denarius was the equivalent of a laborer's day's wage. So, as Carson notes, 300 denarii are approximately a year's wages. Perhaps Mary has saved up for years to buy this perfume. Or perhaps someone had given it to the family in view of the death of Lazarus, whom Jesus had raised back to life (John 12:1). Lazarus's death and resurrection serves as a sign of Jesus' death and resurrection to follow. Lazarus's resurrection was the last straw for Jesus' enemies, since many people came to believe in Jesus through it. They now sought to kill Lazarus as well, to do away with the evidence of Jesus' miraculous power and true identity (See John 12:9–11).

This is not the first time Mary had poured perfume on Jesus. John 11:2 tells us that she had earlier done the same thing—poured perfume on Jesus and wiped his feet with her hair (compare with John 12:3). Some claim that Mary is the sinful woman who poured perfume on Jesus' feet and wiped them with her hair in a Pharisee's house out of deep gratitude for Jesus having forgiven her of her sins (see Luke 7:36–50). Whatever the case, we can take from this account and the one in John 11 that Mary loves Jesus purely, as signified by the perfume made of pure nard. This act of extravagant devotion and personal sacrifice of resources prepares Jesus for his ultimate sacrifice. So, it is fitting that we recount this story at Lent prior to Jesus' week of passion that follows the triumphant entry into Jerusalem.

Today, this week, God's Spirit may prompt us in pure devotion from a grateful heart to give extravagantly to the Lord Jesus in personal self-sacrifice, like Mary. Perhaps we have experienced the equivalent of the Lord raising our brother from the dead, like Lazarus (see John 11), or the Lord forgiving us our many sins like the woman often associated with Mary (see Luke 7). Since Jesus was anointed for burial so long ago by Mary, and given that he was raised from the dead to die no more, we can give to Jesus by giving to the poor this Lenten season, since they are still with us, as Jesus said (John 12:8).

Perhaps if we are miserly in our presumed devotion to Jesus, we will be miserly in our care for the poor. If we are extravagant in responding to Jesus' superlatively extravagant and unsurpassed grace, we will respond in kind toward those in need around us during Lent and beyond. In reflecting on Jesus' statement about his impending departure from his disciples and the ongoing presence of the poor, one commentator on this passage argues, "This does not mean that the poor are not important. On the contrary, Jesus establishes a parallel between himself and the poor. Now he is present, and Mary rightly feels the need to be extravagant. When he is no

Lenten Extravagance

longer present in the flesh, the poor will still be there—to be served with the same extravagance."[27]

Those who are forgiven much love much. Those who are given much renounce much in gratitude, not from guilt or grudging obligation, but for the sake of others in Lenten excess and extravagance.

---

27. González, "April 7."

V

Holy Week: Jesus Dies to Bring New Life!

In a consumer culture that views religion in privatized terms of individualized, specialized care, we may have a hard time conceiving Holy Week as the beginning of a holy war. We're not talking about a holy war of Christendom defending the Holy Land or preserving some semblance of Christian America. Rather, we have in mind Jesus presenting himself as the royal priest who confronts the religious and political establishment fixated on temple worship, nationhood, and empire, so as to free and lead his people out of Egypt and into the Promised Land.

We need to ask ourselves based on Holy Week, what kind of life does Jesus die to give us? The American Dream and the life of health and wealth to which we feel accustomed and entitled? If so, Holy Week becomes a very hollow week. Rather than build stockpiles of ammunition to protect his self-interests or build our stock portfolios, Jesus' aim is to share life with us—forever—in the miraculous freedom of divine love. From Palm Sunday to Jesus cleansing the Temple, weeping over Jerusalem, Maundy Thursday, Good Friday, and Holy Saturday, Jesus reveals just how far he is willing to go. He takes away our false hopes and faulty aspirations for making nation states and our individual lives great again by dying to such drives and the vicious circle of eye-for-an-eye retribution that secures the gains of greedy empires and persons. The Holy Week cycle destroys this circle and leads us forward to Easter and newness of life.

Will we follow Jesus or become enslaved to other powers, perhaps even the religious establishment that aligns itself with Caesar at the people's expense? Dostoyevsky gets at this in "The Grand Inquisitor" in *The Brothers*

V—Holy Week: Jesus Dies to Bring New Life!

Karamazov. Jesus returns to earth at the time of the Spanish Inquisition. Eventually he stands trial before the Grand Inquisitor. His crime? Instead of offering bread and enslaving their consciences, Jesus sought to free people for love, only to experience their rejection of him. Sound familiar? The punishment for Jesus' "misdeed"? The Inquisitor condemns him once again to death.

> Thou didst desire man's free love, that he should follow Thee freely, enticed and taken captive by Thee. . . .
> . . . Hadst Thou taken the world and Caesar's purple, Thou wouldst have founded the universal state and have given universal peace. For who can rule men if not he who holds their conscience and their bread in his hands? We have taken the sword of Caesar, and in taking it, of course, have rejected Thee and followed him.[1]

How will we respond in our own day? Like the crowds at Jesus' trial before Pilate, like the masses that follows the Cardinal's lead? Or like Peter, Mary and the rest of his disciples whose lives Jesus' love has freed as he leads them to the Promised Land?

---

1. Dostoevsky, *The Brothers Karamazov*, 283, 286.

PALM SUNDAY, HOLY WEEK, AND HOLY WAR

Palm Sunday marks the beginning of Holy Week with Jesus' triumphal entry into Jerusalem (Matt 21:1–11). On this day, we celebrate Jesus in his humble glory riding a donkey into the city of David, as the crowds and children cry out, "Hosanna to the Son of David! Blessed is he who comes in the name of the Lord! Hosanna in the highest!" (Matt 21:9). The crowds throw palm branches on the path before Jesus to celebrate him as their approaching king (Matt 21:8), who came to bring lasting peace and gracious justice.

Many expected Jesus to deliver them from their Roman oppressors in keeping with their Messianic expectations. Like his disciples, they had no idea that Jesus would bring peace and justice paradoxically through the Roman symbol of oppression—the cross. In less than a week from Palm Sunday, Jesus would bear nail marks in his hands. How did they respond to his strategy for bringing about victory, when they saw it all play out? How about us?

Like the crowds, we may respond well during Palm Sunday celebrations. For instance, you will find many churches marking the occasion by distributing palm branches to those gathered for worship. This is a helpful, symbolic act. Palm Sunday helps us look back and forward at the same time: we look back to Jesus' first coming leading up to his sacrificial death for the sins of the world followed by his resurrection to new life. We also look forward to his second coming, when he returns to rule the world with a just peace. At that time, multitudes from among the nations will worship him (see Rev 7:9–10).

Not everyone marks Palm Sunday joyfully, though. In Matthew's Gospel account, for example, many do not cast palm branches before Jesus' path. They do not approach Jesus with an open hand of praise, but a closed fist, as revealed behind the scenes and within a few days (see these accounts of how some of the rulers, people, and Romans reacted to Jesus: Matt 21:15,

V—Holy Week: Jesus Dies to Bring New Life!

45–46; 26:1–5; 27:15–31). How do you and I approach Jesus today—with an open hand revealing our palms, or a closed fist?

As with the rulers noted in Matthew 21, we might not be able to see Jesus working wonders if we are consumed with power and control, whereas the blind, lame, and little children can truly see him (Matt 21:14–15). These vulnerable ones have everything to gain and nothing to lose as a result of Jesus, whereas leaders may fear losing their grip on power, to which they hold tightly with a closed fist. They cannot reach out and touch Jesus, like those longing for him, though they long to seize him and do him in (Matt 21:45–46). What about us? Did we journey with Jesus through the season of Lent with his disciples simply to take matters into our own hands, like Judas did in his conspiracy with the establishment?

In our individualized, privatized religious culture, we may find it difficult to grasp the political overtones of all that transpired during Holy Week, which really initiated God's holy war against idolatry, pride, and injustice. In Jesus' day, there was no separation of church and state, or more accurately, temple and state. Going back to the time of God's deliverance of Israel from Egypt through Moses and Aaron, God tabernacled with his people. Later, King Solomon built a temple for God's glory to dwell in Jerusalem, the city of his father, King David. Now here's David's greater Son, Jesus, riding into Jerusalem as a humble prince of peace. The crowds cheer because they recognize Jesus as David's greater Son (Matt 21:9). Immediately following this event according to Matthew's Gospel, Jesus cleanses the temple (the second temple, which was reconstructed in remembrance of Solomon's). Kings and priests as well as prophets all shared the same public space in Jewish history. Jesus intertwines and integrates all three functions of king, priest, and prophet in his own person.

It is worth noting that the Roman Emperor also operated as a priest in addition to king. Here's what N. T. Wright has to say about Tiberius, who like Caesar Augustus before him was hailed as divine:

> After Augustus's death, he too was divinized, and his successor, Tiberius, took the same titles. I have on my desk a coin from the reign of Tiberius (there are plenty of them, readily available). On the front, around Tiberius's portrait, it says, "Tiberius Caesar, son of the Divine Augustus." On the back is Tiberius portrayed, and described, as "chief priest." It was a coin like this that they showed to Jesus of Nazareth, not long after he had ridden into Jerusalem, when they asked him whether or not they should pay tribute to Caesar. "Son of God"? "High priest"?[2]

---

2. Wright, "On Palm Sunday."

Palm Sunday, Holy Week, and Holy War

While many of the Jewish authorities wished for their Roman oppressors to be overthrown, they sought to trap Jesus at points by trying to get him to challenge Caesar's authority as divine king and chief priest (Matt 22:15–22). Politics and religion were not separate, but one.

The Jewish religious establishment also questioned Jesus' authority to cleanse the temple. Matthew's Gospel transitions immediately from Jesus' triumphal royal entry on Palm Sunday to his priestly temple cleansing scene (Matt 21:12–17). A few chapters later Jesus weeps over Jerusalem during Holy Week. Why? Rather than turn to him for his kingly and priestly rule of peace—which would have brought about their deliverance, the Jewish nationalists determined at an opportune time to pursue direct confrontation with Rome in pursuit of liberty from its tyrannical power. In Luke's Gospel, the lament over Jerusalem immediately follows the triumphal entry and immediately precedes the temple cleansing (read Luke 19:41–44).

Wright observes that Jesus

> continues with the warning of what was going to happen to Jerusalem, because, as he says, "You didn't recognise the time of your visitation by God." This is the moment, and you were looking the other way. Your dreams of national liberation, leading you into head-on confrontation with Rome, were not God's dreams. God called Israel so that through Israel he might redeem the world; but Israel itself needs redeeming as well. Hence God comes to Israel riding on a donkey, in fulfilment of Zechariah's prophecy of the coming peaceful kingdom, announcing judgment on the system and the city that have turned their vocation in upon themselves, and going off to take the weight of the world's evil and hostility onto himself, so that by dying under it he might exhaust its power.[3]

Here we witness Jesus' form of holy war. It does not involve an eye for an eye retributive pursuit of justice, but grace. Wright's own teacher G. B. Caird argued that "Evil is defeated only if the injured person absorbs the evil and refuses to allow it to go any further."[4] This is exactly what Jesus did. He took the evil and hostility upon himself and exhausted it, as Wright notes. As a result, Jesus' embrace and embodiment of grace threatened the logic and foundation stone of the Roman system of retributive justice, otherwise known as the *Pax Romana* or Roman peace.[5] If redemption is stronger than

---

3. Wright, "On Palm Sunday."
4. Caird, *Principalities and Powers*, 98.
5. Along similar lines see Jürgen Moltmann, *The Crucified God*, 136–45, for his distinct treatment of Jesus' confrontation of the Roman rule of retribution by nonviolence

V—Holy Week: Jesus Dies to Bring New Life!

evil, hostility, and retribution, having exhausted them, Rome rules the shadowy old world order, not the new age reality of the Messianic kingdom. Palm Sunday with its exemplification of Jesus' humble lordship, gracious disposition, and redemptive and equitable rule begins Holy Week. It also sweeps us up in Jesus' ride into Jerusalem on a donkey to bring about God's holy war. As the New Testament proclaims, the resurrected Jesus will conquer the world's hostility by reigning in cruciform glory.

---

and grace.

MAUNDY THURSDAY: JESUS' LAST STAND IS EVERLASTING

On Maundy Thursday, we remember Jesus' Last Supper with his disciples where he washed their feet, followed by final instructions to them and his high priestly prayer. Together they serve as the tactical moves for the Lord's last stand against his adversaries.

Now if you were preparing for battle with your enemies, wouldn't you be padding the upper room, lower rooms, and surrounding premises with sandbags while stockpiling ammunition? In contrast, Jesus prepares for his last stand with a family meal, a foot washing, a farewell discourse,[6] and intimate prayer to his heavenly Father (see John 13–17). Given Jesus' Passover sacrifice of himself that the church remembers on Good Friday to bring liberation from bondage in Egypt or the Empire and his resurrection from the dead on Easter Sunday, what transpired in his last stand is everlasting. Thus, we are called to live into this everlasting kingdom reality signified by Maundy Thursday ("Maundy" is derived from the Latin word for "command" and refers to Jesus' command on that Thursday evening to his disciples after the foot washing at the Last Supper to love one another as he has loved them; see John 13:34). What does it entail for us? This entry will provide an answer to the question.

The United States prizes autonomy and is a fast-food society. As a result, it is easy to discount family meals and hospitality. And so, we may easily bypass what occurred on Maundy Thursday as nothing more than quaint and dispensable. To the contrary, it is qualitatively all-important and indispensable for the Christian movement and what transpired on Good Friday. N. T. Wright has this to say:

> When Jesus wanted to explain to his followers what his forthcoming death was all about, he did not give them a theory, a

---

6. For further reflection on this theme, see Metzger, *Gospel of John*, 167–71.

V—Holy Week: Jesus Dies to Bring New Life!

model, a metaphor, or any other such thing; he gave them a *meal*, a Passover meal.[7]

Many people claim that the meal was the equivalent of the Passover Seder.[8] In this view, Jesus is the head of his family made up of his followers. The only difference is that this head of the home and rabbi offers his own body and blood as the sacrificial lamb, which is signified by the bread that he breaks and wine that he pours out at the meal.

John's Gospel is the only canonical Gospel account that does not record the institution of the Lord's Supper on Maundy Thursday. John's Gospel is also the only canonical Gospel that records the foot washing. Most of us have never had someone wash our feet at a meal, and likely never by the head of the home or table. But just as Jesus offers himself as the Passover sacrifice (Luke 22:14–20), so he washes his followers' feet during the supper:

> Now before the Feast of the Passover, when Jesus knew that his hour had come to depart from this world to the Father, having loved his own who were in the world, he loved them to the end. During supper, when the devil had already put it into the heart of Judas Iscariot, Simon's son, to betray him, Jesus, knowing that the Father had given all things into his hands, and that he had come from God and was going back to God, rose from supper. He laid aside his outer garments, and taking a towel, tied it around his waist. Then he poured water into a basin and began to wash the disciples' feet and to wipe them with the towel that was wrapped around him. (John 13:1–5)

Jesus' unassuming act was too much for Peter. At first, he refused to let Jesus wash his feet (John 13:6, 8). But given our culture of familiarity with the passage and our culture in which familiarity easily breeds contempt, we may not find the foot washing so radical and feel we are entitled to Jesus stooping low to tend to us. But it is radical and momentous. Again, here's Wright:

> Within the gospels' recounting of that ultimate Passover, one scene stands out with special poignancy and power. John's Gospel displays deft artistry and fathomless theology throughout, but especially in the footwashing scene in chapter 13. In a few lines we glimpse a tableau both intimate and touching and scary and dangerous. Having begun his gospel with the all-creative

---

7. Wright, *Day the Revolution Began*, 182.

8. For a treatment of parallels between the Last Supper and the Passover Seder, see Jeremias, *Eucharistic Words of Jesus*, 42–61. For an overview as well as critique of the Last Supper as a Passover Seder, see Klawans, "Last Supper a Seder?"

Maundy Thursday: Jesus' Last Stand Is Everlasting

Word becoming flesh and revealing God's glory, John begins the shorter second half with an acted parable of the same thing. Jesus removes his outer garments and kneels down to wash the disciples' feet, summing up all that is to come in this act of divine humility, of loving redemption, of cleansing for service. For John, as indeed throughout the New Testament, Jesus' vocation to rescue the world from its plight, and in so doing to reveal the divine glory in action, is focused, symbolized, encoded in an action simultaneously dramatic, fraught with cosmic significance, and gentle, tender with human emotion. If you want to understand the great mysteries of Christian theology, of Trinity, Incarnation, and atonement itself, you could do worse than spend time with this scene.[9]

Jesus calls on his followers to care for one another in the same manner (John 13:12–17). If we thought Jesus went too far with washing his disciples' feet, we may think he went beyond the breaking point with calling them to care for one another in the same servant-like manner. Even if we like the title of servant-leader or lead servant, we easily take offense if we're not esteemed in ministry. My colleague Albert Baylis put it well when he remarked: we all want to be called servants until someone treats us like one.

The challenge to our sense of entitlement does not end there. Not only does Jesus wash Peter's feet, but he also washes the feet of Judas, whom the Lord knew would betray him that very night. Jesus breaks bread with the very one who would hand him over to be broken and poured out in death. However, rather than protect himself, Jesus offers himself as a willing sacrifice in order to destroy hatred with love and bring new life.

If we had more time and space, we would discuss the farewell discourse recorded in chapters 14–16 and Jesus' high priestly prayer in chapter 17. The church recalls these subjects and the other themes noted here on Maundy Thursday. In each and every one of them—from the family meal and foot washing to the farewell discourse and prayer to his Father as well as the betrayal—Jesus models humility, vulnerability, and the desire for relational intimacy that mark his kingdom glory and vision for our lives as his kingdom community.

May we follow suit. We have every reason to be inspired by Jesus' glorious, all-powerful example of holy and pure love on Maundy Thursday and Good Friday, and his resurrection from the dead on Easter Sunday. As a result of the bodily resurrection, what transpired at Jesus' last stand in his battle to the death with his enemies inaugurated the eternal kingdom reality. Humility, vulnerability, and relational intimacy win out in the end. Will we

---

9. Wright, "The Royal Revolution."

V—Holy Week: Jesus Dies to Bring New Life!

live into this reality or go back to the way things used to be before Jesus' last and everlasting stand?

DON'T PASS OVER THE PASSOVER ON GOOD FRIDAY

The New Testament is a very Jewish book. There is no way around it. One cannot understand what is going on anywhere in the New Testament without a grasp of what goes on everywhere in the Hebrew Scriptures. In fact, the Scriptures that Christians often refer to as the Old Testament are foundational to the New Testament and find fulfillment and perfection in the New. Good Friday—the day the church generally associates with Jesus' death—is no exception given that Jesus' death and resurrection are vitally connected to Passover.[10]

The canonical Gospels record the significance of Jesus choosing Passover (see Exod 12) rather than the Day of Atonement (see Lev 16) or one of the other two pilgrimage feasts (the Feast of Weeks and Festival of Booths; Deut 16:16) for his grand, climactic entrance into Jerusalem. N. T. Wright has this to say about Holy Week and its relation to Passover as the occasion when Jesus confronts the nationalistic piety centered in the Temple establishment:

> All four gospels make clear one vital point: that Jesus chose Passover to go to Jerusalem and confront the Temple establishment with his radical counter-claim, knowing where it would lead. He didn't choose Tabernacles or [Hanukkah]; he didn't choose the Day of Atonement. He chose Passover, because Jesus' understanding of his own vocation was to accomplish, once and for all, the New Exodus for which Israel had longed. Passover-imagery isn't just miscellaneous decoration around the edge

---

10. Religion scholar James Tabor argues that Jesus died on Thursday, not Good Friday, in "Jesus Died on a Thursday." Regardless of the day that Jesus' death occurred during Holy Week, the connection between Passover and Jesus' passion and resurrection is an intimate one for the New Testament community. For another article discussing their historical connection, refer to Fredriksen, "When Jesus Celebrated Passover."

107

V—Holy Week: Jesus Dies to Bring New Life!

of an atonement-theory whose real focus is elsewhere. It is the flesh-and-blood reality.[11]

Jesus presents himself as the embodiment of the Temple where God meets with his people. In fact, he told the Jewish authorities at the time of the first of several Passovers recorded in John's Gospel that he would destroy the temple of his body and raise it up in three days. Thus, he had the authority to cleanse the Temple in Jerusalem (John 2:13–22; see also Matt 21 for Jesus' confrontation with the Temple authorities as the final Passover draws near).

Again, as Wright indicates, the canonical Gospels present Jesus choosing the Passover for his climactic action of salvation for his people. Even so, the New Testament also presents a connection to the Jewish Day of Atonement or Yom Kippur, which occurs in the autumn of the year. According to the Epistle to the Hebrews, Jesus has entered the Holy of Holies as the great and sinless high priest who has offered his own pure blood once and for all as eternal cleansing from our sin (see Heb 9).

It is all too easy for us to privatize Jesus' message and not see him as bringing deliverance for his people from established nationalistic theopolitical structures that enslaved them. Such enslavement involving nationalism brought about their demise as the Jewish people sought vengeance against Rome. Their rebellion led to Rome's destruction of Jerusalem and the Temple in AD 70. Jesus desired to spare his people just as he seeks to spare us from all-consuming nationalistic and individualistic idols as well as vengeance that leads to self-destruction.[12] But all too often, we hide behind our idols, including holy buildings and cities, holy books, and holidays of religious and national prominence, and fail to account for Jesus' presence in our midst as the replacement or fulfillment of these types, as the case may be, at the end of the age. As the book of Revelation reminds us, God and the Lamb are the Temple in the eschaton, not some building no matter how prominent or cherished: "And I saw no temple in the city, for its temple is the Lord God the Almighty and the Lamb" (Rev 21:22).

For the sake of security and autonomy, we are tempted to stay put and not take to heart that the celebration of Good Friday and Easter overlap with Passover, the ultimate pilgrimage feast. But as we come to terms with

---

11. Wright, "The Royal Revolution."

12. Wright argues that while the Jewish authorities believed Jesus' approach and political and eschatological reinterpretation of the Scriptures and sacred symbols would lead to their destruction, it is Jesus' reinterpretation that would lead to their preservation and victory as a people. See Wright, *The Challenge of Jesus*, 54–73.

Don't Pass Over the Passover on Good Friday

Jesus offering himself as the ultimate Passover Lamb[13] and leading his people in pilgrimage out of Egypt to the Promised Land, we realize we cannot stay put. We must press forward and not return to Egypt. As Hebrews 11 makes clear, like Abraham and other saints of old, we still have not found what we are looking for (Heb 11:39–40). The Promised Land—which will appear before us as the new heavens and earth dawn—beckons us. The Spirit and the Bride say come (Rev 22:17).

So, don't pass over the Passover as we celebrate Good Friday. It's time to leave Egypt or Rome or whatever nation or city typifies Empire at a given time. And for those who have already left, don't go back. Too much is at stake. Go forward to enter the promised rest. Remember that Jesus has conquered the grave and has authority and power and glory over all kingdoms of the world. He has won while Caesar has lost, a point that Revelation brings home, declaring: "Worthy is the Lamb who was slain, to receive power and wealth and wisdom and might and honor and glory and blessing!" (Rev 5:12).[14] Good Friday's here. But Easter Sunday's coming.

---

13. John the Baptist refers to Jesus as the Passover Lamb as recorded in John 1:29 and Paul does as well in 1 Corinthians 5:7. Revelation 5:6, 12 refer to Jesus as a lamb that was slain.

14. It has been argued that "You are worthy" and "our Lord and God" greeted Emperor Domitian when he appeared in triumphal procession. The Apocalypse commandeers such language and applies it to the Ancient of Days and to the Lion who is the Lamb slain and raised bodily to new life. In effect, John seeks to convey to his readers that Caesar loses; Christ wins. See the following treatments of this theme: Mounce, *The Book of Revelation*, 126–27. Lilje, *Last Book of the Bible*, 108–9; Stauffer, *Christ and the Caesars*, 150–59; and Coleman, *Singing with the Angels*, 40–41.

HOLY SATURDAY: WHOLLY IN THE DARK?

We often skip over the Saturday that falls between Good Friday and Easter. We simply pass through it and so lose out on its monumental significance. It's almost as if we are wholly in the dark about Holy Saturday's import.[15]

Speaking of being in the dark, that's exactly where Jesus and his disciples were on Holy Saturday. For his part, Jesus was dead in the darkened grave. For their part, his followers were spiritually at a dead end. Who knows what thoughts they had of Jesus and their relation to him? Had they been deceived? Was he a messianic imposter? How could the One who was to lead Israel out of Egypt into the Promised Land die as a sacrificial victim to the victimizing evil empire of Egypt/Babylon/Rome? Imposing doubts darkened the disciples' minds. They did not realize until later that Jesus was not only the New Moses to deliver them from bondage in Egypt but also the Passover Lamb.

If the disciples and we come into the light of the entirety of Holy Scripture that provides 20/20 vision, we will find that Holy Saturday is critically important for our faith. It is a date to mark on our church calendars. Without it Good Friday's not so good, and Easter's not so hopeful. In what follows, we will provide three reasons why Holy Saturday is wholly relevant to our faith and lives.

First, identification. Holy Saturday signifies that Jesus' passion is our passion. He endures what we endure. He does not excuse himself from fully identifying with us. If we die, he dies. He accepts our human limitations and submits himself to bearing the burden of our fallen and sinful state. Here it is worth accounting for Tania M. Geist's reflection on Pope Benedict's 2013 meditation on the theological significance of the Shroud of Turin for Holy

---

15. For a novel and robust analysis of Holy Saturday, see Lewis, *Between Cross and Resurrection*.

Holy Saturday: Wholly in the Dark?

Saturday. Benedict considered the crucified man emblazoned on the burial garment to be Jesus. Geist writes,

> Insofar as the Shroud symbolizes Christ's suffering and death, however, it also conveys a message of hope and life. Benedict mused that the image on the Shroud functions like a photographic negative, its contrast of dark and light being essential. So too with the paschal mystery, wherein "the darkest mystery of faith is at the same time the most luminous symbol of boundless hope. Holy Saturday is the 'no man's land' between death and Resurrection, but One has entered into this 'no man's land.'" And the One who has entered has come to share in our death, in a historic and unrepeatable gesture of "the most radical solidarity."
>
> Benedict sees this to be the true power of the Shroud and what it represents: that in his descent, Christ takes on our suffering, our sins—"*Passio Christi. Passio hominis* [the passion of Christ and his passion for humanity]."[16]

Yes, Holy Saturday conveys "the most radical solidarity" between Jesus, God, and us. Such solidarity highlights God's exceeding goodness that we also find displayed on Good Friday.

There is more, though. Second, annihilation and transformation. Holy Saturday signifies that we are dead to the old-world system and can "walk in newness of life" given our baptismal union with Jesus in his death and burial, as Paul writes in Romans 6 (read Romans 6:1–4). If Jesus were not dead and buried, our sinful state and old humanity would not be dead and buried. But given that Jesus who bore our sins on the cross died and was buried, we are dead to sin as we have been "baptized into his death" (Rom 6: 3). The annihilation of our old humanity makes possible the transformation of our humanity in accordance with Easter's emphasis on new life. As the link between Good Friday and Easter, Holy Saturday underlines and highlights God's goodness in terminating the old order of being and points forward with hope to Easter and the transformation of our existence as the new humanity.

Lastly, attention. Just as the chief priests tried to be attentive, so should we be, albeit for different reasons. The chief priests wanted a guard posted to keep Jesus' disciples from stealing the body (Matt 27:62–66). But it was pointless to try and keep him in the tomb. The guards became like dead men when the angel appeared Easter morn (Matt 28:4). And for those who argue that the disciples were responsible for Jesus' body's disappearance,

---

16. Geist, "Benedict XVI's Theology."

V—Holy Week: Jesus Dies to Bring New Life!

think again. From the likes of the disciples at the time of Jesus' death and his post-crucifixion appearances, this clueless and cowardly band could not have put together a cunning and courageous, risky plan to steal the body of their fallen Lord and claim that he had been raised from the dead.[17]

The disciples were not attentive to Jesus' prophetic hints offered throughout the Gospels. They had no clue of Jesus' imminent resurrection. Would we be more cognizant, though? Hindsight's always 20/20. Not so with peering into the future, especially in view of the traumatic days when Jesus suffered and died. Jesus' followers could not come to terms and fathom all that Jesus had told them would occur, including the bodily resurrection from the grave. Still, as Jesus instructed them on Maundy Thursday, they were to watch and pray. Easier said than done in their case, and no doubt our own: "And he came to the disciples and found them sleeping. And he said to Peter, 'So, could you not watch with me one hour? Watch and pray that you may not enter into temptation. The spirit indeed is willing, but the flesh is weak'" (Matt 26:40–41).

In talking about the need for attentiveness during Passover and beyond, we can learn a thing or two from God's command to Israel at the time of the first Passover celebration and Exodus: "In this manner you shall eat it: with your belt fastened, your sandals on your feet, and your staff in your hand. And you shall eat it in haste. It is the Lord's Passover" (Exod 12:11).

No doubt, Jesus' exhortation to watch and pray during the Passover celebration in Jerusalem during Holy Week bears some similarity to the first Passover whereby the Israelites were to be ready to set out on mission at any moment. When they did depart, it was with the urgent pleading of Pharaoh and the Egyptians (Read Exodus 12:29–42). The Israelites did indeed leave in haste. So, no wonder they were encouraged to keep watch. As Exodus 12:42 indicates, Passover is a night of watching or vigil: "It was a night of watching by the Lord, to bring them out of the land of Egypt; so this same night is a night of watching kept to the Lord by all the people of Israel throughout their generations" (Exod 12:42).

While eating the Passover meal, the Israelites were to be prepared for departure, for missional sojourn—with belts and sandals fastened, staff and food in hand in haste. If that were true of them, what about us? What are we waiting for? The answer: for God to call us to embark. We are to wait on God attentively rather than sit back and relax or take matters into our own hands. Be vigilant and wait, which is not easy for us, especially when we

---

17. Wright comments that the disciples' bewilderment (see John 20:1–18) points to the authenticity of the resurrection account. Wright, "Uncomfortable Truth."

Holy Saturday: Wholly in the Dark?

don't know what to do, as on Holy Saturday when Jesus' first disciples were totally in the dark.[18]

God's goodness, divine comfort, and hope are on display on Holy Saturday. The disciples could not have concocted or comprehended that Jesus was the Suffering Servant and Paschal Lamb. Only he and his Father knew in advance of Good Friday and Easter that it was he who had to suffer vicariously for the deliverance of the world. He had to suffer as a silent lamb led to slaughter (rather than suffer as the leader of a violent rebellion of a loyal remnant like the Maccabean martyrs, as some maintained), whom God would use to free the world from the evil and idolatrous empire and bring about the new creation.[19] Only Jesus knew that the Father would raise him from the darkness of the tomb. Although Jesus' followers could not do anything to keep Jesus from falling into the hands of his enemies, and although they could not have stolen his body from the grave, God was in control and everything was in his hands, including their own lives. No one could snatch them from Jesus' or his Father's hands (John 10:28–30).

In view of what has been shared, watch and pray. Do not be taken by surprise. The Passover Lamb's blood has been spilt and the Angel of Death has passed over our heads and homes while God liberates us from captivity. Watch and pray, for not only does the Passover Lamb identify with us in our suffering, but also as the New Moses and High Priest, he transforms our state of being from slaves to God's firstborn heirs, a royal priesthood and holy nation, God's chosen people (1 Pet 2:9). God will lead us into the light of day and out of Egypt into the Promised Land. Those who are attentive and waiting on God will find in view of Holy Saturday how good and hopeful Good Friday and Easter truly are.

---

18. Wright, "God in Private and Public."

19. See here the following interview between Michael Bird and Wright: "N. T. Wright: The Church Continues." Refer also to this discussion in Wright's work, *Day the Revolution Began.*

VI

Eastertide: Jesus Is Risen!

Eastertide extends from Easter Sunday through Pentecost. As we saw with Holy Week, Jesus presents himself as the ultimate Passover Lamb. He is also the Royal Priest who leads his people from exile in Egypt to the Promised Land. Easter is not an isolated event. It looks backward to the prior seasons of the church calendar, which move toward it. Easter also looks forward as it culminates in Jesus' second coming at the close of the age.

If we account for the entire biblical drama, we must come to terms with the Jewish Passover, Jesus' Passover, and the church's Passover. They are of one cloth, or better, one loaf of unleavened bread. Thus, it should pose no difficulty for understanding that Passover shapes the church's worship experience and liturgy.[1] Similarly, given that Eastertide ends with Pentecost, which is also the occasion for the Jewish Feast of Weeks, we see the relation of God's giving of the Law to Moses on Sinai and the giving of the Spirit to the church through whom God's saints speak the words of the New Covenant promises in Christ. As Chrysostom put it, the apostolic community "did not come down from the mountain carrying, like Moses, tablets of stone in their hands; but they came down carrying the Holy Spirit in their hearts . . . having become by his grace a living Law, a living book."[2]

If we do not account for the biblical backdrop and story line that involves Passover and the Feast of Weeks, we might as well replace Jesus as the Paschal Lamb and the Spirit as the dove who brings tongues of fire with the Easter bunny and chocolate eggs. Such secular imagery makes as much

---

1. Greenacre and Haselock, *The Sacrament of Easter*, 52.
2. John Paul II, *Veritatis Splendor*, section 24.

VI—Eastertide: Jesus Is Risen!

sense of Easter and what ensues for the life of God's ecclesial people as Jesus and the Spirit removed from the biblical drama.

EASTER: NEW CREATION AND VOCATION IN THE PROMISED LAND

Holy Week is like a garment, blanket, or tapestry made of one cloth, and without any holes in it. There is one golden thread that ties together all the events the church celebrates this week. That golden thread is Jesus and his mission. So while we may tend to think that everything culminates at Good Friday with the cancellation and eradication of sin in Jesus' death on the cross, or perhaps that it all comes crashing down and gets swept away on Holy Saturday as Jesus lies buried in the grave, we need to realize that the story's not over. Jesus rises from the grave. But even here we must be careful to guard against thinking of the events as simply one patch on a very spotty quilt. The entire Bible is the story of God's deliverance and healing of the nations and world through his Suffering Servant and chosen people. So how does all this bear on what transpired during Holy Week and up to today—Easter Sunday?

Certainly, the idea of holy war highlighted on Palm Sunday comes into play. Maundy Thursday, Good Friday, Holy Saturday, and Easter Sunday continue this theme. God delivers his people from bondage in Egypt through his Suffering Servant Jesus and takes them to the Promised Land. There they serve as a royal priesthood and holy nation formed by the Messianic seed of promise and who are children of Abraham's faith. They are called to bless all peoples for the glory of God on earth. The first epistle of Peter puts it this way: "But you are a chosen race, a royal priesthood, a holy nation, a people for his own possession, that you may proclaim the excellencies of him who called you out of darkness into his marvelous light" (1 Pet 2:9).

So, what does this entail for our understanding of Easter? And how might making sure we see all the events of Holy Week and the "Old" and "New" Testaments as one piece be important to our life and witness? If Easter is the whole progression of Holy Week, and if the "Old" and "New"

VI—Eastertide: Jesus Is Risen!

Testaments are really "Older" and "Newer," or the beginning and end of one narrative, what will that entail for human existence?

Many view Easter as a form of validation of Jesus' claims and actions prior to going to the cross. In other words, the resurrection serves as apologetic proof. Certainly, this emphasis has its place. For example, in his speech at Pentecost, the Apostle Peter makes clear that God validated Jesus' identity and activity and that the resurrection demonstrates that he is Lord and Christ (Acts 2:22–36). While this is certainly true, there is indeed more to the tapestry.

Many will also emphasize that Easter is the elevation of believers from sin and death to eternal life involving purification from sin and personal salvation. Here one calls to mind Paul's words that if Jesus is not raised from the dead, our faith is meaningless, and we are still dead in our sins (1 Cor 15:17). The point on elevation, then, is certainly part of the fabric. But there is still more to the tapestry of Scripture.

It is also important to conceive of Easter as the beginning of the new creation and vocation to victorious and abundant life in the Promised Land. Again, if as we have argued in the Good Friday entry, Good Friday's relation to Passover is not a coincidence, but an indication that Jesus is leading his people out of bondage and into the Promised Land, then we must come to terms with an all-encompassing and earth-dwelling view of salvation that looks very different than the perspective that God will whisk us away from this evil world to an eternal abode in the sweet by-and-by. On this "whisk away" view, the church is simply a weigh station where we can unload some of our baggage for an easier lift off.

In an interview with *Christianity Today*, N. T. Wright makes the following assessment of the resurrection, which bears on what has been stated so far and on our public worship:

> In the West we have been so seduced by the Platonic vision of "heaven" that the resurrection of Jesus is seen simply as the "happy ending" after the crucifixion, and as the prelude to his "going to heaven" so that we can go and join him there later. This misses the central point that the resurrection of Jesus is *the beginning of the new creation, in which we are to share already in the power of the Spirit.* This affects everything, from prayer and the sacraments to mission and service to the poor. And yes, it ought to be reflected liturgically in whatever tradition we stand. Playing this back to the meaning of the cross, we realise that new creation is now happening because the dark powers that have kept the world enslaved to sin and death have been defeated. Perhaps there are themes there which could be brought

Easter: New Creation and Vocation in the Promised Land

more explicitly into our Good Friday commemorations as well. But the Christian life is meant to be a sustained and focused celebration of that achievement. Present suffering and struggle are held within the narrative of Jesus' victory on the one hand and the final redemption of all creation on the other. That is what climactic passages like Romans 8 are all about. I would love to see churches trying out different ways of embodying all of this in the way we order our public worship.[3]

If we account for the entire biblical tapestry, we will come to see the church as a royal priesthood and holy nation, a people belonging to God (1 Pet 2:9). We will realize that the church is not a building but a community that participates in Jesus' mission as the New Moses, Royal Priest, and Passover Lamb. Our liturgy is not a private ritual, but a public pageant. Our aim is not simply about proving a point that Jesus is Lord or getting people saved. Rather, the proof is in the pudding that Holy Week and Easter Sunday are ultimately about God making all creaturely life whole in and through Jesus in the Spirit of Pentecost who raises Jesus from the dead. We can find no better liturgical explanation for seeing Easter in view of the entire biblical tapestry and the entire biblical tapestry in view of Easter than the following reflection from the Orthodox Church. Thomas Hopko writes:

> In the Orthodox Church the feast of Easter is officially called Pascha, the word which means the Passover. It is the new Passover of the new and everlasting covenant foretold by the prophets of old. It is the eternal Passover from death to life and from earth to heaven. It is the Day of the Lord proclaimed by God's holy prophets, "the day which the Lord has made" for His judgment over all creation, the day of His final and everlasting victory. It is the Day of the Kingdom of God, the day "which has no night" for "its light is the Lamb" (Rev 21.22–25).[4]

In view of what has been claimed in this entry about Easter, what then is the import for the life and liturgy of the church? How will it affect our way of being in the world as the community of the Royal Priest and Pascal Lamb who conquers Egypt and leads us as his royal priesthood, holy nation, and temple people to the Promised Land? *Pray that* God's heavenly kingdom will come to earth. *Partake of* the sacraments as being baptized into Jesus as he crosses the Red Sea and Jordan River, and as we drink of him for nourishment as we pass through the wilderness into the land flowing with

---

3. For more on Wright's interview with Bird, see "N. T. Wright: The Church Continues." See also Wright, *Surprised by Hope*; *Day the Revolution Began*.

4. Hopko, "Easter Sunday."

VI—Eastertide: Jesus Is Risen!

milk and honey. *Provide for* the well-being of the widow, orphan, and alien in their distress (Deut 10:18; Jas 1:27). *Participate in* the Easter pageantry that does not end on Sunday or with the close of Eastertide. Rather, it carries on throughout the year. The golden thread of Jesus and his mission weaves its way through the tapestry of the church calendar until Christ the King Sunday, which celebrates his reign over all the nations and creation, and which will come to fruition with the dawning of the new heavens and the new earth.

This golden-threaded tapestry weaves all saints together as the church militant, the church expectant, and the church triumphant throughout the ages and across the globe. Together we chant "Jesus is risen! He is risen indeed!" Together we cry "Come, Lord Jesus, come!" Amen.

THANK GOD IT'S DIVINE MERCY SUNDAY

No doubt you've heard the saying "Thank God it's Friday." People can't wait to get off work and enjoy their weekends. But what if their lives are difficult not simply during the week, but also on the weekend? Thus, it's not enough to look forward to having a few days off from work. One must look forward with expectation for signs of divine mercy throughout the week, including today, which is Divine Mercy Sunday.

Today is the second Sunday of Easter, which as stated above, is also Divine Mercy Sunday. It is associated with Faustina Kowalska (d. 1938), later known as St. Faustina, who was a Polish girl of poor education and humble means who lived during the Great Depression in Poland. She claimed to have visions of the risen Jesus that lasted for years.[5] Regardless of what many people then and now think of visions of the risen Jesus, one thing is certain: the risen Jesus does indeed reveal himself uniquely to each one of us, manifesting his divine mercy. Perhaps the question we should ask ourselves is: are we looking or listening carefully and with expectation for revelations of Jesus' divine mercy?

We find such unique revelatory manifestations of mercy in the resurrection accounts in chapters 20 and 21 of John's Gospel. Consider Jesus' appearance to Mary Magdalene, as well as to Thomas—known as the Twin, and to Simon Peter, among others. We will consider each encounter in subsequent essays, beginning here with Jesus' interaction with Mary Magdalene in the garden where the tomb lies open.

Mary Magdalene came early to the tomb on Sunday morning to mourn over her deceased Lord. To her deep chagrin and dismay, she found the stone rolled away and Jesus' body missing. She beckoned Peter and the beloved disciple (John) to come and see for themselves that Jesus' body was missing. Though Peter and this other disciple came and observed that what

---

5. Rabenstein, "Kowalska, Faustina," in *New Catholic Encyclopedia*, 243–45.

VI—Eastertide: Jesus Is Risen!

Mary had said was true, they soon departed. However, Mary remained (see John 20:1–10).

Just as Mary was not prepared for the empty tomb, so she was not prepared for what happened next. First, Mary saw two angelic beings inside the tomb after Peter and John had departed. Then, to her utter amazement, the risen Jesus appeared to her. It is quite striking that instead of appearing first to Peter and John, Jesus appeared first to Mary, who initially mistook him for a gardener. But when Jesus called Mary by name, her eyes were opened, and she recognized the Lord (read John 20:11–18)

Perhaps it was the intonation, or just perhaps that he knew Mary by name. No anonymous gardener would have known her name, but Jesus knew Mary by name, just as he knows each of us by name. Jesus knows exactly how to engage each person who seeks after him, whether it be Mary, Thomas, Peter, or any of the other disciples, as well as you and me.

Like Faustina, Mary Magdalene no doubt experienced her own form of great depression, as her crucified Lord's dead body had been taken from her. Perhaps like Faustina, she is not someone to whom we would naturally expect the resurrected Lord to appear. Surely, in our natural way of thinking, we would expect the Lord to appear to his enemies to confound and overwhelm them, or to leading citizens who would instantly become distinguished followers, unlike the band of misfits Jesus led for three years in his public ministry. But instead of his adversaries or the brightest and best, Jesus appeared to Thomas and Peter, Mary and Faustina.

Here in these revelatory encounters we find evidence of divine mercy. No one deserves God's revelatory mercies, neither Mary nor Faustina, neither Thomas nor Peter, neither the rich and powerful nor Jesus' enemies, neither you nor me. So it always comes as a bit of a shock when Jesus mercifully reveals himself to us at the empty tombs of our own lives. And given that Jesus reveals himself mercifully to us, we should not be surprised when he reveals himself to those we would never expect to be recipients of his mercy and grace.

Moreover, we should be signs of God's revelatory mercy to all those around us, including those the world would ignore or slight, like Mary and Faustina. In honor of those often bypassed as seemingly unworthy of God's mercy (as if anyone is worthy of God's mercy!), I close with words that Faustina recorded in her diary to mark the Feast of Mercy that Roman Catholics and many Anglicans celebrate this day:

> On one occasion, I heard these words: My daughter, tell the whole world about My Inconceivable mercy. I desire that the Feast of Mercy be a refuge and shelter for all souls, and especially for

Thank God It's Divine Mercy Sunday

poor sinners. On that day the very depths of My tender mercy are open... Let no soul fear to draw near to Me, even though its sins be as scarlet. My mercy is so great that no mind, be it of man or of angel, will be able to fathom it throughout all eternity.[6]

You don't have to be Catholic or Anglican to appreciate these unfathomable words. You can be Catholic or Anglican, Baptist or Reformed, Independent or institutionally indifferent. But don't be indifferent to God's inconceivable mercy poured out on your behalf. In a world marked by indifference and intolerance, thank God for Divine Mercy Sunday.

---

6. Kowalska, *Diary*, 699.

WE SEE JESUS WHEN BREAKING BREAD TOGETHER

Have you ever pondered the significance in Luke 24 of the disciples recognizing the resurrected Jesus when he broke bread with them? (Read Luke 24:30–31.) Then and now, the resurrected Jesus breaks through and reveals himself to us when we break bread together.

You may recall the context for this text. Two of Jesus' disciples were walking along on the road to Emmaus and discussing Jesus' crucifixion as well as the flash news report that Jesus had been raised from the dead. Little did they know, but the stranger who walked up alongside them and joined in their conversation was none other than Jesus. The text simply tells us: "While they were talking and discussing together, Jesus himself drew near and went with them. But their eyes were kept from recognizing him" (Luke 24:15–16). What was it about the breaking of bread that led the disciples to recognize Jesus? And what difference does this text make for us today in view of the resurrection?

To answer these questions, we will first account for what David Lertis Matson and others have pointed out about the centrality of bread in Jesus' day as well as in the church. As Matson notes, bread, like salt, was critically important to people's sustenance. Matson also makes clear the thematic significance of breaking bread in Luke's two canonical books—the Gospel of Luke and the Acts of the Apostles. Matson goes so far as to claim that

> it is Luke among the writers of the New Testament for whom "breaking bread" becomes a "classic" way of referring to the Lord's Supper (Luke 9:16; 22:19; 24:30, 35; Acts 2:42, 46; 20:7, 11; 27:35). Of the many references listed here, the meal scene embedded in the story of Emmaus (24:13–35) is the most theologically charged: only after Jesus instructs the two disciples on the road to Emmaus and breaks bread in their house are they able to recognize the risen Lord in their midst (24:30). At story's

> end, Luke summarizes the entire sequence of events thusly: "Then they told what had happened on the road, and how he had been made known to them in the breaking of the bread" (24:35) ... As the climax to the first of Luke's two volumes (Luke 1:1–4; Acts 1:1), the Emmaus narrative occupies a strategic "pivot" position, allowing the reader to look "backward" to the table fellowship practice of Jesus in the Gospel of Luke and "forward" to the depiction in Acts of believers breaking bread in their homes.[7]

We find in this explanation the answer to the first of our questions above, namely, "What was it about the breaking of bread that led the disciples to recognize Jesus?" Jesus had made quite clear, as did Luke, that table fellowship was constitutive of Jesus' way of being and mission in the world. We truly see Jesus in this humble act of fellowship.

Two other claims stand out to me in Matson's article. They will help us address the second question above, namely, "What difference does this text in Luke 24 (and related biblical texts) make for us today in view of the resurrection?" One is Matson's claim that "The New Testament bears ample witness to the fact that the earliest struggles of the church involved matters of table fellowship."[8] The other is Matson's reflection that "When we gather together to celebrate the Lord's Supper, we must do so with the firm conviction that the risen Lord is present with us, revealing himself to us. Like the disciples at Emmaus, our prayer must always be: 'Stay with us, because it is almost evening and the day is now nearly over.' For when we do, we continue to encounter the ever present one in the breaking of the bread."[9]

Now it should hardly come as a surprise that the early church's struggles involved problems with table fellowship given the essentially and radically inclusive nature of their meals. Old barriers were removed, including between Jews and Gentiles. Refer here to Paul's rebuke of Cephas for separating himself from table fellowship with Gentile believers in Antioch in the presence of the visiting Jewish circumcision party from Jerusalem (Gal 2:11–14). The same is true for divisions between Hellenistic Jews and Hebraic Jews. Refer here to the apostles' determination to overcome the blatant disregard of Hellenistic widows in the daily distribution of food in Jerusalem (Acts 6:1–7). We find the same dynamic at work in overcoming divisions involving haves and have-nots, that is, people of different classes. Refer to Paul's challenge to the Corinthian church for the well-to-do

---

7. Matson, "Breaking the Bread," 8.
8. Matson, "Breaking the Bread," 10.
9. Matson, "Breaking the Bread," 12.

VI—Eastertide: Jesus Is Risen!

separating themselves from those of lesser means during the Agape feast in Corinth (1 Cor 11:17–34).[10] Matson's quotation from Philip Francis Esler on Luke's eucharistic theology has a bearing on all such divisions, not just Jew and Gentile, namely Esler's attentiveness to "Luke's persistent emphasis on the fact that the old barriers between Jew and Gentile have been decisively shattered in the eucharistic fellowship of the Christian community and that an era of salvation for all humanity has now been inaugurated, even if there are some who do not yet realize it."[11]

Should we be surprised that we have a hard time seeing and experiencing the risen Jesus if and when we do not have table fellowship with fellow believers, or if we live as if the old barriers between us have not been removed? Yes, Jesus is revealed in the breaking of the bread (Luke 24:30–31, 35). And yes, the old barriers "have been decisively shattered" between us through Jesus' eucharistic meal that remembers and celebrates his death, burial, and resurrection. But still, we must live into this new reality if we are to see and experience the resurrected Jesus as he truly is! May we no longer live as if we are blind to this realization. May we who are from all walks of life come together as Jesus' people at his feast. May we live in expectation that Jesus' resurrected glory breaks through to us as we break down these barriers wherever we find them in the church today.[12]

---

10. See Fee, *First Epistle to the Corinthians*, 533–34.
11. Esler, *Community and Gospel*, 104; quoted in Matson, "Breaking the Bread," 12.
12. I address this theme at length in my volume *Consuming Jesus*.

JESUS' RESURRECTION DOESN'T DEPEND ON FAITH, BUT DEEPENS IT

Jesus' resurrection does not depend on his disciples' faith. However, it should deepen our faith and our engagement in this world whereby we descend into greatness by caring for those often despised and marginalized.

Again, Jesus' resurrection does not depend on his followers' faith, but it should deepen it. Now if Jesus' resurrection depended on his first followers' faith, he wouldn't have risen. They were bewildered and unbelieving. It is worth noting that his first disciples, whose reports serve as the basis for the canonical Gospels, had no idea that he was going to rise bodily, even though he had told them on several occasions that he would rise from the dead. The teaching of the resurrection wasn't on their radar.

Those first disciples and their contemporaries were not gullible people who believed everything they saw and heard. In fact, the vast majority of disciples simply did not believe the reports and sightings at first or were too afraid to share the news with anyone. Take for example the following accounts in Mark 16 (italics added):

> But go, tell his disciples and Peter that he is going before you to Galilee. There you will see him, just as he told you." And they went out and fled from the tomb, for trembling and astonishment had seized them, and they said nothing to anyone, *for they were afraid.* (Mark 16:7–8)

> She went and told those who had been with him, as they mourned and wept. But when they heard that he was alive and had been seen by her, *they would not believe it.* (Mark 16:10–11)

> After these things he appeared in another form to two of them, as they were walking into the country. And they went back and told the rest, *but they did not believe them.* (Mark 16:12–13)

VI—Eastertide: Jesus Is Risen!

There is no reason to wonder why these first disciples doubted. Reports of bodily resurrections were hardly daily occurrences. It wasn't like, "Did you hear about Bob down the street? He died a week ago and rose again yesterday." "Really?! So, too, did my cousin Ernie. It was just this morning. There have been a lot more resurrections of late." Not even close. In fact, the bodily resurrection of an individual from the dead ahead of the general resurrection, never to die again, and whose resurrection has a bearing on all resurrections that follow, wasn't on their Jewish map. Even so, that first report on a Sunday morning over two thousand years ago that Jesus rose from the dead has certainly changed history and the world map.

Even Nietzsche—no friend to Christianity—believed the movement Jesus started brought about the Roman Empire's demise, not when it was in decline, but when it was at its height. In Nietzsche's estimation, a nobler outlook on humanity perished with Christianity's rise, and had only just been reborn with Nietzsche's teaching of the wise, strong, and solitary *Übermensch*, who elevates only himself.

Nietzsche would have us side with him rather than Paul's cruciform Christ. He believed that the church uses the cross to manipulate others to submit to its teaching. Nietzsche's works prize the Greco-Roman elevation of the wise and powerful and mocks Paul's crucified God notion that celebrates the weakness and foolishness of the cross as God's power and wisdom (read 1 Cor 1:18–31). Here's a representative statement from Nietzsche's arsenal:

> *God on the cross*—are the horrible secret thoughts behind this symbol not understood yet? All that suffers, all that is nailed to the cross, is *divine*. All of us are nailed to the cross, consequently *we* are divine. We alone are divine. Christianity was a victory, a nobler outlook perished of it—Christianity has been the greatest misfortune of mankind so far.[13]

But where is that world-changing movement today? Have we been lured or shamed into submission by Nietzsche's rhetorical brilliance and bravado? Remember how the crucified and risen Lord turned the Roman world upside down. If we are to witness that occurrence again, we must reset our spiritual clocks and circle Jesus in his cruciform glory rather than boast in the brightest and best.

Let's not forget what happened to those first disciples to see how Jesus' resurrection should deepen our faith. Those earliest disciples went from being self-concerned cowards after Jesus' death to people of great courage and compassion after Jesus' resurrection. Take for example the healing of the nameless beggar in Jesus' name, as recorded in Acts 3. When called to

13. See Nietzsche, *The Antichrist*, 633–34.

Jesus' Resurrection Doesn't Depend on Faith, But Deepens It

account for the disturbance of the peace, and told to quit speaking in Jesus' name, consider how the two disciples responded, as recorded in Acts 4. Consider also how their inquisitors reacted, taking note that the disciples were simple folk, unschooled and ordinary. They were not the "brightest and best" Christian leaders, or the "significant churches," as we hear celebrated today. Their adversaries came to the realization that what differentiated the disciples, namely Peter and John, was not their superstar skill-sets and upwardly mobile networks, but that they had been with Jesus (read Acts 4:8–22).

The New Testament encourages and exhorts us to descend into greatness by celebrating and proclaiming Jesus whose crucified weakness and foolishness is God's power and wisdom (see 1 Corinthians 1:21–25). As Paul and the New Testament exhort us, may we give ourselves to the weak and unwise, just as Jesus and his first disciples did, and just as many of us were, when Jesus found us. Jesus' resurrection does not depend on our faith. However, Jesus' bodily resurrection should deepen our faith and move us beyond self-centered cowardice to courageous compassion, where we descend to the depths and care for nameless beggars in body and soul, and the weak and unwise, like ourselves. Then people will take note that we have been with the resurrected Jesus, not Nietzsche's *Übermensch*.

SOMETIMES DOUBT IS DEVOTION

You've heard of the doubting Thomas? He's the disciple who would not believe the testimony of his fellow apostles that Jesus had been raised bodily from the dead. He replied that he would only believe if he could place his finger and hand in the risen Jesus' cruciform wounds (read John 20:24–25). I really think his doubt was a form of devotion, as will be argued.

Several days later, Jesus appeared to Thomas in the presence of the other apostles and encouraged Thomas to do exactly what Thomas had told the other disciples he must do if he were to believe that Jesus was indeed alive:

> Eight days later, his disciples were inside again, and Thomas was with them. Although the doors were locked, Jesus came and stood among them and said, "Peace be with you." Then he said to Thomas, "Put your finger here, and see my hands; and put out your hand, and place it in my side. Do not disbelieve, but believe." Thomas answered him, "My Lord and my God!" Jesus said to him, "Have you believed because you have seen me? Blessed are those who have not seen and yet have believed." (John 20:26–29)

Jesus did not rebuff Thomas on account of his doubt by telling him to believe only with the heart or with his naked eyes. Jesus engaged Thomas where he was at, so to speak. In Caravaggio's painting of the encounter, Jesus went so far as to take Thomas by the hand and place the hand in his side. While it is certainly true that the text records Jesus as saying that those who believe without seeing him are blessed, Jesus' statement does not come across to me as a rebuke of Thomas. Rather, it is at this point that John's Gospel turns to those readers, who have never had visible access to Jesus (which includes us) and calls them blessed for simply believing the testimony of faithful witnesses concerning his bodily resurrection.[14] Again, if Caravaggio's painting

---

14. For an important work arguing that the canonical Gospels are based on

Sometimes Doubt Is Devotion

provides any indication of Jesus' intended remarks, it would be that the Lord welcomed Thomas' genuine, honest, and open inquiry.

Remember, too, how devoted Thomas was to Jesus in his discipleship: when he realized Jesus had determined to go up to the vicinity of Jerusalem at a time when his life was at risk there, Thomas urged his fellow disciples to go up with him and die with the Lord (John 11:16). Going further, it is not certain how Thomas died. One report indicates that he traveled as far as India and founded the church there. The report indicates that he died when pierced with the spears of four soldiers. While it is not certain how Thomas died, it does appear certain how he lived, according to John's Gospel—as devoted to Jesus. He would rather have been the doubting Thomas than the gullible Thomas. He did not want to believe in an apparition or a figment of the imagination. Too much was at stake—the real Jesus and faithful witness to the Lord that would lead to his death.

Like C. S. Lewis many centuries later, Thomas was not after convenient or comfortable faith, but honest and true faith. Regarding costly faith, Lewis wrote in *God in the Dock*: "I didn't go to religion to make me happy. I always knew a bottle of Port would do that. If you want a religion to make you feel really comfortable, I certainly don't recommend Christianity."[15]

It is far better to doubt than to engage in easy believism, where ignorance is bliss. Thomas was no cynic. But he was not a silly, drunken fool either. He desired sufficient reason to believe, and Jesus welcomed his search. He will welcome our genuine quest as well. As former atheist now Christian Dr. Sarah Irving-Stonebraker of Western Sydney University wrote in an article for *The Veritas Forum*,

> Christianity, it turned out, looked nothing like the caricature I once held. I found the story of Jacob wrestling with God especially compelling: God wants anything but the unthinking faith I had once assumed characterized Christianity. God wants us to wrestle with Him; to struggle through doubt and faith, sorrow and hope.[16]

While the Lord may not appear in person to take away any doubt you and I may have about him, I do believe he will reveal himself uniquely to those who really seek after him with genuine questions on their minds and in their hearts, like the devoted Thomas. As in the case of Thomas, those who want to remove all doubt from their faith are truly devoted.

---

eyewitness testimony and that the Gospels' original readership would have understood them in this way, see Bauckham, *Jesus and the Eyewitnesses*.

15. Lewis, *God in the Dock*, 58.
16. Irving-Stonebraker, "How Oxford and Peter Singer."

POST-RESURRECTION APPEARANCES
—FAITH RESUSCITATION

If Jesus had not risen from the dead, we could expect that his disciples would have chosen one of two options. According to N. T. Wright, the "normal options open" to the disciples following Jesus' demise were: they could have chosen to go back to fishing and other former occupations, or they could have chosen a replacement as messiah from among Jesus' blood relatives, like James.[17] As the story goes, they did not choose either option. Instead, according to the New Testament witness, following the resurrection, their faith in Jesus underwent resuscitation.

Take Peter, for example. It looks as if he was already leaning toward the first of the two options Wright presents—Peter went fishing, just like he used to do. He's not alone. Some of the other disciples joined him. They fished all night long and caught nothing (John 21:1–3).

The account sounds strikingly familiar. Earlier in the Gospels, Peter and his companions were out fishing all night long but caught nothing (see Luke 5:1–11). Moreover, in both instances (Luke's and John's accounts), Jesus tells them to throw out their nets again. They did not recognize Jesus at first in the account recorded in John 21, not until they cast their nets and haul in an unbelievably large load, just like in the earlier incident.

In John 21:9–13, we find that Jesus prepared a campfire meal of fish and bread for them. This account ends with the narrator stating: "This was now the third time that Jesus was revealed to the disciples after he was raised from the dead" (John 21:14).

As with the earlier accounts, we find a bit of faith resuscitation going on. In John 20, we find that Jesus appeared to the apostles on two separate occasions (after having first appeared to Mary Magdalene). In each instance, the disciples had locked themselves up in a room (John 20:19, 26). Here in John 21, they seem to have had enough courage to venture out to go fishing.

17. Wright, "Christian Origins."

Post-Resurrection Appearances—Faith Resuscitation

Based on the prior two resurrection appearances, the disciples were now fully cognizant of Jesus' resurrection. Yet, it did not keep them from going fishing. In fact, in Peter's case, it was likely that he would return to fishing as an occupation, even though he knew Jesus had been raised.

Why do I think Peter would return to fishing as an occupation? Because he had denied Jesus three times. Peter probably thought that his days of fishing for people as a witness to Jesus (Luke 5:10) were over because of his colossal failure of faith in denying Jesus three times. But Jesus has a way of meeting people where they are and leading them to where he wants them to be. In Luke 5 and John 21 respectively, Peter appeared to acknowledge that he is not worthy of Jesus. In Luke 5:8, we find Peter crying out, "Depart from me, for I am a sinful man, O Lord." In John 21, Peter was cut to the heart with grief when Jesus asked him a *third* time (the same number as his denials) if Peter loved Jesus. While in Luke 5, Peter was told once that he would fish for people, here in John 21, Peter was exhorted three times to feed Jesus' sheep. Peter had denied Jesus three times, but Jesus in turn asked Peter three times if he loves Jesus, and then reaffirmed Peter three times by telling him to get back to following Jesus, not comparing himself with others, and to care for God's flock (read John 21:15–19).

Perhaps you can relate to Peter. You may firmly believe in the resurrection of Jesus, but you have no confidence that you can go through a resuscitation of your faith as an active follower of Jesus because of failures in your life and ministry. Each of us should realize that we are not worthy of Jesus—not even when we are at our best. But we should also realize that if Jesus who alone is worthy tells us to get back up and follow him, who are we to resist?

I asked my wife why she thought Jesus delayed his ascent to his Father's throne for forty days. Her response: "so he could teach the baby birds to fly." Indeed, Jesus wanted these little birds—or "children," as he refers to them in John 21:5—to get back up and follow him and lead his people.

Jesus was not resuscitated, but rather resurrected. However, in the case of his followers, Jesus appeared to his disciples over a forty-day period after his resurrection to bring about the resuscitation of their faith and reignite their witness. So, too, he makes himself known to us today, not just until his ascension (which we celebrate forty days after Easter), but throughout the church year. We should encourage one another—just as Jesus exhorted Peter—in the midst of our doubts about ourselves not to give up, but to undergo a resuscitation of faith. Get back up with rejuvenated faith in view of Jesus' call and get to work. Feed his sheep.

A MOTHER'S DAY TRIBUTE: THE PIERCED HEART

I don't envy mothers, but I sure do respect them. They carry their children for months as they cope with nausea and kicks and then give birth to them, often in searing pain. The pain does not end there for mothers, though, as they bear with the kicks and punches life brings their way through their children's decisions, sorrows, and losses. Of course, there are also the joys of holding their children close and watching them succeed in small and great ways as they grow up and develop. As with most other relationships but in an exceptional way, child-rearing is a mixture of joys and sorrows.

Here I call to mind Mary, the mother of the Lord. I can only imagine what it must have been like for Mary in raising Jesus. I don't envy Mary, but I sure do respect her—unbelievably so. Mary's situation was unique among women and mothers. For one, not many women receive news from an angel that they will bear a child. Moreover, as the angel announced to her, Mary would conceive and give birth differently than the rest of women—as a virgin.[18] Furthermore, the child she would bear was God who came to save the world from sin. I don't know of any other mother who fits that bill. As a result, Mary is blessed among women, just as the son whom she bore is blessed (Luke 1:42). Every generation will call her blessed (Luke 1:48). This news and the future realization of this promise filled Mary's heart with joy.

Still, as with many incredible blessings, there are huge burdens to bear. This was certainly the case for Mary. As Simeon prophesied at Jesus' dedication, a sword would pierce her heart (Luke 2:35). Throughout Jesus' life, Mary's heart experienced the pricking of a sword. As Jesus grew up and eventually went about his mission, Mary felt the pain of his growing independence. As much as Jesus loved her, his love for his heavenly Father

---

18. Here I call to mind the "Annunciation" celebrated earlier in the year highlighting the announcement that Mary would be the virgin mother of Israel's Messiah. See Stuhlmueller and Rouillard, "Annunciation," 473–77, in *New Catholic Encyclopedia*.

A Mother's Day Tribute: The Pierced Heart

was supreme. It is likely that her son's words and actions pierced her heart, as Jesus told his mother and earthly father Joseph that he needed to be about his heavenly Father's business (Luke 2:49), even if it entailed difficulties for them. Jesus' words to those around him in her presence that those who obeyed his teaching were his true mother and brothers must have stabbed her soul (Luke 8:21; cf. Matt 12:49). As with their encounter in John 2 at the wedding at Cana in Galilee, Jesus wanted to make sure his mother realized that he was not there simply to do her bidding: "Woman, what does this have to do with me? My hour has not yet come" (John 2:4).

Above and beyond these events, I can only imagine what it must have been like for Mary when the soldiers cast lots for the seamless tunic (chiton) that she likely had made and had given to Jesus as her parting gift for him when he transitioned from childhood and attained manhood. Surely, a sword pierced her heart at her son's crucifixion (John 19:23–27), just as a spear pierced his side (John 19:34).[19]

Many of Jesus' encounters with his mother sting. It is hard to imagine one using any of these accounts as the basis for a Mother's Day sermon. Perhaps the best model text for Mother's Day in showing Jesus' care for his mother is the painful account of his crucifixion, where in the midst of his overwhelming affliction, the Lord commits Mary to his disciple John for him to take care of her from that point forward: "When Jesus saw his mother and the disciple whom he loved standing nearby, he said to his mother, 'Woman, behold, your son!' Then he said to the disciple, 'Behold, your mother!' And from that hour the disciple took her to his own home" (John 19:26–27). It is a very moving scene. Still, would many mothers want this text to be the basis for a sermon dedicated to them on Mother's Day?

In a Christian culture that often venerates the family to a position of near worship, it is very difficult to take to heart Jesus' relationship with his mother. What Jesus and Mary make so clear to us in these accounts is that our ultimate focus must not be on our nuclear family or some other love, but on God. As the close of Mary's Magnificat emphasizes, Mary understood to some degree that Jesus' birth and life would bring about the climax of salvation history that would benefit Israel and peoples everywhere, especially the lowly (Luke 1:50–55).[20]

---

19. For a contemplative study on Mary's life of great sorrow and resilience, see Giallanza, *Seven Sorrows of Mary*.

20. For a discussion of "traditional" family notions and how they often reflect modern concepts of family rather than Scripture, see the following: Clapp, *Families at the Crossroads*. For a prophetic challenge to the supremacy of family in our society, see Clapp, "Our First Family."

VI—Eastertide: Jesus Is Risen!

Still, handing her son over to God was not easy. Mothers can no doubt relate to Mary's pain to varying degrees, perhaps even in learning how to give one's child to God rather than hold him or her back. I am thankful for my own mother who did not hold me back but gave me up to the Lord. And while my wife's mother in Japan does not know the Lord, she has blessed her daughter and me by not holding her back from our faith journey together. I am grateful for my wife's mother, too.

The preceding discussion reminds me of Jim Elliot's correspondence with his mother and father prior to his departure to Ecuador as a missionary. They were saddened by the news of his eventual departure. In response to their sorrow, he encouraged his parents to consider Psalm 127's discussion of children as a heritage from God and that the person whose quiver is full of children should be glad. A parent whose quiver is full of children will not be dismayed when contending with one's enemies in the gate. Elliot encouraged his parents metaphorically speaking to draw back their bowstring with the mighty arm of prayer and let loose the arrows (that is, their children) against Satan and his host.[21]

Elliot and some of his fellow missionaries were killed by the Huaorani or Auca Indians in Ecuador. Elliot's and his comrades' determination, as well as the commitment of some of their family members to return and minister there, not only led to the conversion of many of the Huaorani to Christ but also to a mass movement in their generation of people committing themselves to global missions. Easily forgotten, but no less important, their mothers and families played strategic roles in raising and releasing them to God. They let loose the bowstring of prayer and fraternal faith rather than nuclear warheads of harbored hate and hurt.

May God fill his quiver with our lives as spiritual arrows in view of Jesus as the hope of salvation who will set the world ablaze with God's fiery love. Like Elliot's mother and father, may we not forget Mary's strategic role in all this. May her story of sacrificial love in raising and releasing Jesus inspire all who nurture and mentor others to take the sting of parenting and offer it up to God in faith along with their children and pray they would become a mighty force of healing in Jesus' name in our world today.

---

21. See Elliot, *Shadow of the Almighty*, 132.

ON MEMORIAL DAYS, HONOR THE DEAD, NOT RELIGIOUS PROPAGANDA

Nations have liturgies, just like religions. National and religious liturgies often blend together, including during times of war and on their memorial days.

Just think of Israel's history. The people of Israel went out to battle in the name of God, proclaiming that God fought for them (Exod 14:14; Deut 3:22; Josh 10:12–14). Other nations made similar claims that their gods fought for them against their enemies. Nation states and empires in the modern period may appear more subdued or subtle in their employment of religion or competing secular worldviews and ideologies during times of war or memorial days, and at memorial sites. Nonetheless, the sentiment is often there in various quarters, sometimes overtly so.[22]

It is important to pause and make clear that this essay is not arguing that religion tends toward promoting violence. In my estimation, "religion" is a construct that can be used by political powers to engage in violent activity. Similarly, a secular national power can also construct "religion" or all-encompassing ideology or slight a particular religion as inherently violent in order to engage in violent activity against it. While religion can be used to promote violence, so, too, can secular and atheistic systems of government.[23]

Now to return to the argument at hand, England's St. Paul's Cathedral, Japan's Yasukuni Shrine, and America's Gettysburg and Vietnam Veterans Memorials all bear tribute to the war dead. Some might balk at the mention of Yasukuni Shrine in this brief list given the intense scrutiny and

---

22. Cooper, "General Casts War."

23. William Cavanaugh challenges the Western liberal democratic "myth" that religion has a fundamental predisposition to promote violence. See Cavanaugh, *Myth of Religious Violence*.

VI—Eastertide: Jesus Is Risen!

controversy surrounding it.[24] Others might puzzle over the mention of Gettysburg and the Vietnam Veterans Memorial since they are not technically religious shrines. Yet the Japanese Shinto shrine in Tokyo pays homage to the nation's war dead, as do many nations' churches and temples; for their part, the American sites noted here have a mystical and spiritual dimension, according to many experts on religion and culture.[25]

I have visited St. Paul's Cathedral, Yasukuni, and Gettysburg, and have been struck by the religious air or mystical aura at each center which hallows the extreme tribute many souls paid to their respective nations. I still recall the deep and long bows of veneration by some Japanese pilgrims at Yasukuni last summer when I was there. However, the spiritual sentiment at Gettysburg did not stand out to me at the outset of my first visit to the site. It was not until a German traveling companion took issue with the narrative of an audio recording that struck him as reverently recounting providential forces that preserved my nation. No doubt, his own nation's history and tragedies associated with the use of religion for Germany's war campaigns made him exceptionally alert and wary of national religious piety in whatever quarter of the globe, especially when it was tied to war.

In the Civil War, both sides of the terrible conflict believed in the same God, used the same Bible and prayed for the Almighty's aid in destroying the other, a point that President Abraham Lincoln made in his Second Inaugural Address.[26] While President Lincoln's remarks in his second inaugural were rather subdued, Mark Twain's "War Prayer" was a literary blitzkrieg against the blinding abuse of religion to carry out war against one's foes.[27] In the case of Lincoln, religion played a role in his Gettysburg Address and his Second Inaugural, not to beat the drums of war, but to beat into submission human pride and presumption that God is on our side, no matter the side, to destroy the enemy. As we honor Memorial Day, we remember the extreme sacrifice of those who have given their lives in battle for freedom. Many of us also lament the horrors of war that brought their lives to an end. May we also remember Lincoln's liturgy at Gettysburg that does not call on the Almighty to win the war for his side, but for everyone to dedicate themselves anew under God to the cause of freedom and peaceful, equitable unity: "we here highly resolve that these dead shall not have died in vain—that this nation, under God, shall have a new birth of freedom—and

---

24. Woolf, "Yasukuni Shrine."
25. Niebuhr, "More Than a Monument."
26. See Lincoln, "Second Inaugural Address," 157.
27. Twain, *The War Prayer*.

On Memorial Days, Honor the Dead, Not Religious Propaganda

that government of the people, by the people, for the people, shall not perish from the earth."[28]

While Lincoln's military means to bring about reunion of the North and South has been severely criticized in various quarters, Lincoln's ultimate hope was that those who fought on both sides of the conflict might ultimately deter the living from further destruction, and that together they might pursue a new birth as a commonwealth. I pray with the same hope in mind for this land and our world today as a community of nations. May we not offer up soldiers' lives as bloody, atoning sacrifices or penal substitutes for ours and others' sins. Rather, may we look to Christ Jesus' atoning death as the substitute for every government's and people's payment by blood for their trespasses, and pursue a just, equitable, global peace that unites nations apart from war.

May we beat our religious propaganda and spiritual pride that often elevates us above God into submission under God as a people, and our swords into plowshares.

---

28. See Lincoln, "Address Delivered at the Dedication," 150.

THE ASCENSION: JESUS HAS SOME SERIOUS HANG TIME

I used to sit and watch with amazement as basketball superstar Michael Jordan ascended to the rim with the basketball in his outstretched hand. His hang time was unbelievable. It was almost as if he defied gravity, as he made his way to the rim for one of his jaw-dropping dunks or reverse lay-ups as a basketball god. Jesus also has some serious hang time. Jesus defies gravity in his ascension. Sorry Air Jordan and Sir Isaac Newton. And yet, when the right time comes, Jesus will return to earth, just like he ascended to heaven. According to Jesus, what goes up must come down. Like and unlike Jordan and the Terminator in their return to the court and screen, Jesus will someday say, "I'm back."

One of the most neglected aspects of Jesus' public ministry is his ascension. The church calendar marks the ascension as having occurred forty days after Easter. Many Christians around the world celebrate the Feast of the Ascension.[29]

Luke gives special attention to the ascension: see Luke 21:26–28; 22:66–71 (cf. Matt 24:50–53, 26:57–68; Acts 1:6–11, and 7:54–60). The apostolic community took great comfort from knowing that the crucified and risen Lord ascended to the right hand of the Father, and that he will return in glory.

Paul (Saul) was present at Stephen's stoning and heard Stephen speak of seeing the ascended Christ (Acts 7:54–60). No doubt, at the time, he scoffed at Stephen's vision. Later, Paul highlights the significance of the ascension for the Christian life: Ephesians 4:1–16 (spiritual unity and gifting) and Colossians 3:1–4 (identity in Christ and spiritual growth).

Luke and Paul are not alone in the New Testament's accounting of Jesus' ascension. Here are a few examples. Hebrews 1:1–3 reveals that Jesus is

---

29. On the ascension, see Quinn and Murray, "Ascension of Jesus Christ," 768–72, in *New Catholic Encyclopedia*.

The Ascension: Jesus Has Some Serious Hang Time

the great prophet, priest, and king. He is the true Word of God who declared that he would reign regally in heaven with the Father, as the heavenly high priest who offered himself as the once-and-for-all sacrifice for sins. In John's farewell discourse (John 14–16), the Lord speaks of the need for him to return to the Father so that the Spirit would come and abide with his people to comfort and counsel them. In Acts, we find that the disciples are to wait for the Spirit upon Jesus' ascent, just as they are to await Jesus' return (Acts 1:4–11). Following almost immediately after the ascension, Christians celebrate the Spirit's outpouring, gifting, and empowerment (Acts 2:1–4) on Pentecost Sunday a week from now.

How seriously do we take the ascension?[30] The ascension did not lead the early church to escape the world, but to live with their feet firmly hitting the ground running forward in mission. The ascension mobilized Christians to live victorious, holy lives in the midst of severe difficulties and persecution, as in the case of Stephen. Take for example this central statement on the ascension in the opening chapter of Acts, which details the missional movement of the apostolic community:

> So when they had come together, they asked him, "Lord, will you at this time restore the kingdom to Israel?" He said to them, "It is not for you to know times or seasons that the Father has fixed by his own authority. But you will receive power when the Holy Spirit has come upon you, and you will be my witnesses in Jerusalem and in all Judea and Samaria, and to the end of the earth." And when he had said these things, as they were looking on, he was lifted up, and a cloud took him out of their sight. And while they were gazing into heaven as he went, behold, two men stood by them in white robes, and said, "Men of Galilee, why do you stand looking into heaven? This Jesus, who was taken up from you into heaven, will come in the same way as you saw him go into heaven." (Acts 1:6–11)

The apostolic community took the ascension very seriously. The ascension of Jesus coupled with the descent of the Spirit at Pentecost made it possible for them to stop staring at the heavens and move forward here on earth by becoming Jesus' witnesses—which involved suffering unto death in many cases—in Jerusalem, Judea, Samaria, and to the ends of the earth (the English word "martyr" is taken from the Greek word for witness—*martus*[31]).

---

30. For books highlighting the significance of the ascension, see the following: Farrow, *Ascension and Ecclesia*; Farrow, *Ascension Theology*; Orr, *Exalted Above the Heavens*.

31. Refer to this article on the subject: "Martyr," 1052–53, Cross and Livingstone, eds., *The Oxford Dictionary of the Christian Church*.

VI—Eastertide: Jesus Is Risen!

Just as Jesus' ascent was no ordinary hang time, so the apostolic community's witness was no ordinary observation.

How about us today? How seriously do we take Jesus' ascension? Are we gazing up at the heavens to the point of being of such heavenly good that we are of no earthly value? Or does Jesus' ascension lead us to be his witnesses here below in a manner that we proclaim and demonstrate Jesus in word and deed in a self-sacrificial loving manner, thereby advancing his kingdom shalom? Ours is a hope that does not avoid the world and its struggles. Rather, the ascended Jesus continues to operate here on earth through his Spirit-filled people.

I don't have Jordan's hang time—not even close. But what other Christians and I do have is the confident assurance that the Jesus who hung on the cross is not dead and buried but raised and seated at God's right hand. He has conquered sin and death. Our salvation is complete. As the Creed declares, he will come again to judge the living and the dead and make all things new. I am hanging my hopes on him.

ASCENSION AND PENTECOST: ABOVE THE FRAY YET ON THE GROUND

Have you heard the saying, "They are of such heavenly value that they're of no earthly good"? Sometimes this statement is taken to refer to Christians whose heads and hearts are above the clouds, lost in thought about spiritual ideals that have no bearing on life here on earth. The dual teaching of the Ascension and Pentecost, which are celebrated on consecutive Sundays, flies in the face of this saying. Those who take to heart this dual teaching and seek to live it out will be of such heavenly value that they will be of great earthly good. They hit the ground running, since the ascended Jesus extends his incarnate ministry through the Spirit in them. They are above the fray, yet their feet are firmly on the ground. We find this dynamic at work in the Acts of the Apostles (read Acts 1:1–11).

Right out of the gate, the author, who is traditionally recognized as Luke, refers Theophilus, the recipient of this book, to his former volume, which is generally understood to be the Gospel of Luke. Luke claims that in his first book (Luke) he recounted "all that Jesus began to do and teach" until his ascension (See Acts 1:1–2). The implication is that Jesus was not finished with working here on earth. Indeed, now he continues to act and teach through his apostolic community. It is worth pointing out at this juncture that according to Acts 1:1–2, we do not extend Jesus' holistic ministry of word and deed. Rather, Jesus extends his ministry through us.

Moreover, just as Jesus is not finished teaching and operating here on earth with his ascension, so the Spirit did not begin his ministry at Pentecost. As Acts 1:2 makes clear, Jesus instructed his followers in his commands through the Spirit prior to Jesus' ascension. We find here biblical support for St. Irenaeus's teaching that Jesus and the Spirit are the two hands of God. God always works through Jesus and the Spirit, who are always operating together.

VI—Eastertide: Jesus Is Risen!

As God's two hands, Jesus and the Spirit reveal that God rolls up his sleeves and gets to work in the dirt and grime of daily life. The ascension shows that Jesus is above the fray, as are his people who have been raised with him in spirit through the Spirit to the heavenly throne. However, while on earth, Jesus entered fully into our struggles and poured out his life's blood, sweat, and tears. Even on earth, while tackling evil head on and identifying with us sinners in our daily struggles, he still stayed above the fray. So, too, through the Spirit, he continues to act in and through his true followers throughout the ages, leading us to place our feet firmly on the ground while staying above the fray and sharing the good news of Jesus in word and deed at great cost to ourselves for the sake of others.

It's easy to lose sight of staying above the fray and needing to get to work. In Acts 1, the angelic messengers appear to challenge the disciples to get to work, "Men of Galilee, why do you stand looking into heaven?" Yes, Jesus will return "in the same way" (Acts 1:11). The implication appears to be *Now, it's time to get to work*, beginning with waiting for the Spirit's descent at Pentecost in a spirit of prayer. The disciples may have been tempted to lose themselves in the cloud that hid Jesus from their sight, becoming of such heavenly value that they were of no earthly good (Acts 1:9). However, the angels snapped them out of their seeming dreamlike state to take action—which is exactly what they did. That is why the book is called "The *Acts* of the Apostles."

The rest of the book is about the apostolic community being Jesus' witnesses in Jerusalem, Judea, Samaria, and the ends of the earth. They preached and taught, they prayed, they performed miraculous signs and healings, they served, they broke bread together, and shared everything in common (see the summary statements in Acts 2:42–47 and 4:32–37). In other words, they were of great earthly good.

The ascension and Pentecost go together, as without the ascension, there is no point of reference for staying above the fray. Persecution ensued as a result of the missional movement of God's Spirit. They could easily have gotten lost as a community in their service and/or in their suffering. They could have easily lost sight of the need to serve others in costly ways, if they had lost sight of Jesus, who poured out his life for the sake of the world. It is important that we ourselves keep in mind Jesus' ascended state and that we reside with him spiritually in our hearts, minds, and imaginations:

> If then you have been raised with Christ, seek the things that are above, where Christ is, seated at the right hand of God. Set your minds on things that are above, not on things that are on earth. For you have died, and your life is hidden with Christ in God.

Ascension and Pentecost: Above the Fray Yet on the Ground

> When Christ who is your life appears, then you also will appear with him in glory. (Col 3:1–4)

It is also important to keep in mind Jesus' return. Colossians 3:4 reminds us that when Jesus appears, we will appear with him in glory.

Lastly, we must also keep in mind that it is vitally important to guard against spiritual insularity and escapism. If we are Spirit-filled people, we will place our feet firmly on the ground and move forward missionally as Jesus' witnesses in word and deed in communal service to the world at large, as the book of Acts models for us. Like the apostolic community that Acts presents to us, may we hold true to the ascended Jesus and descended Spirit and be of such heavenly value that we are of incredible earthly good.

PENTECOST SUNDAY: HAPPY BIRTHDAY TO THE MISSIONAL CHURCH!

Just as we celebrate birthdays of individuals and nations, the church celebrates its birthday. That birthday celebration occurs on Pentecost Sunday.

Pentecost is the fiftieth day after Easter (including Easter). The Old Testament backdrop is the Jewish festival of Shavuot or the Festival of Weeks (Exod 34:22; Num 28:26–31; Lev 23:15–21). This festival occurs fifty days after the Passover celebration. The Passover celebrates God's deliverance of Israel from slavery in Egypt. The Festival of Weeks celebrates God's giving the Ten Commandments to Moses at Sinai for his people. Just as the Law came down from heaven to Israel, so the Spirit of God came down from heaven to the church on Pentecost, fifty days after Jesus' resurrection following Passover. God's Spirit internalizes the Law in God's people, in keeping with the New Covenant (see Heb 8:8–13). One might argue that Israel began as a nation with the giving of the Law at Sinai. So, too, the church began its history with the giving of the Spirit at Pentecost.[32]

Fifty is a number of perfection. In Jewish cosmology, God created the world in seven days (if one includes the day of rest). Seven times seven plus one is fifty, which signifies the perfection of creation in this case. The Festival of Weeks also marks the occasion of the first wheat harvest with the beginning of summer. So, the church is to begin its harvest of Great Commission witness "today," as it participates in Jesus' life and work (Matt 28:18–20). We see evidence of the first fruits of that harvest at Pentecost as three thousand believed and were baptized into the church (Acts 2:41). The Messianic Age, which dawned in the person of Jesus (See Acts 4:16–21), has come in its fullness with the descent of the Spirit (Acts 2).[33]

---

32. For a treatment of the Jewish backdrop to Pentecost, see Longenecker, "Jewish Roots of Pentecost."

33. Consider Kirby, "Pentecost, Its Teachings and Context."

Pentecost Sunday: Happy Birthday to the Missional Church!

Rather than living off the fumes of the past, we need to fan into flame the Spirit's spark in our lives. Just as tongues of fire appeared and rested on the believers and they were filled with the Spirit and proclaimed the good news of Jesus in other tongues (Acts 2:3–4), we must wait on God in prayer, long for the Spirit's movement, and obey Jesus' word by sharing and enacting the good news of the kingdom as the Spirit of God ignites our hearts and lives.

It is very easy for churches to look back nostalgically as the Spirit moved in their midst when they were born. After a few years, church anniversaries can easily move from celebrating the Spirit's ongoing movement to cementing monuments. The classic hymn by C. Michael Hawn "Spirit of the Living God" is an appropriate one to sing today, as we seek to guard against turning Pentecost celebrations and church movements into monuments. May the Spirit fall upon us, free us, fill us, form us.

How can we become more sensitive to the Spirit, seek not to grieve the Spirit (Eph 4:30), not take the Spirit for granted, and be filled with the Spirit, while we seek as churches to be and remain missional movements every year of our lives? The answers we give will either help or hinder us in our efforts to guard against turning the celebration of the church's birth into a memorial monument.

We have come to the end of Eastertide, which begins with Easter Sunday and ends today on Pentecost. This realization that Easter is not simply a day but a season, which culminates in Jesus' ascension and Pentecost, signifies that Easter's import never comes to an end. Thus, the newness of life that Eastertide promises is always there for the taking.

Having reflected on the fact that the Spirit mobilizes the church as a missional movement rather than establishes a monument signifies that Eastertide is not sectarian. How can it be when the Spirit who enlivens the church never closes the divine circle of the Triune life but continues to keep the circle open, flowing outward through the church into the world? Colin Gunton reflects on Basil's point that the Spirit "completes the divine and blessed Trinity." As Gunton argues, the Spirit does so, "not as the one who completes an inward turning circle, but as one who is the agent of the Father's outward turning to the creation in his Son."[34]

On account of Jesus' resurrection and ascension, as well as the Spirit's outward movement in and through the church, the church is the first fruits of God's new creation. The church belongs to the last days and through Jesus in the Spirit orients humanity to the future as God's "pilot project," as

---

34. Gunton, *Act and Being*, 146.

VI—Eastertide: Jesus Is Risen!

Rowan Williams articulates.[35] If, however, Jesus had not been raised and the Spirit had not come, the church would be rotten fruit rather than first fruits. In other words, we would be dead in our sins (1 Cor 15:17).

Jesus was indeed raised never to die again. Thus, Easter is not one day, but a season. Eastertide culminates in the ascension and Pentecost, which entail that Easter's import lasts throughout the remainder of the year or what is called Ordinary Time, indeed until the end of the age.

Step back and ask what difference it makes that the resurrected Jesus ascended to God's right hand on our behalf and sent the Spirit to fill and form us in Ordinary Time until he returns to lead us into the Promised Land. What difference does it make for how we as the church, led by the Spirit, approach the rest of the year as the risen and ascended Jesus' royal priesthood and holy nation, including national holidays like the Fourth of July which lie ahead? What difference does it make for the way we approach time, God's creation, and our fellow humans in all their diversity—such as variation in gender, race, social and economic status, and physical and mental abilities—as we move toward the end of the year with the end of the age in mind?

How often do we connect Easter to the ascension and Pentecost? How often do we connect Eastertide to Ordinary Time through the Ascension and Pentecost? All too often, we approach Easter like Christmas—just as one day and not as a season. We treat it almost as if Jesus were raised and went back to the grave or took off. We need to realize he stayed around forty days or so. He not only stayed but provides staying power in having ascended to the Father from whom the Spirit descended the fiftieth day of Eastertide at Pentecost to fill and form us in Ordinary Time until the end of time. Basil writes,

> The entire season of Pentecost is likewise a reminder of the resurrection we expect in the age to come. If we count that one day, the first of days, and then multiply it seven times seven, we will have completed the seven weeks of holy Pentecost, and the season ends on the same day it began (Sunday) with fifty days having elapsed. Therefore this season is an image of eternity, since it begins and ends at the same point, like a circle.[36]

---

35. "The Church is God's Pilot Project for the human race. The Church of God is what humanity is meant to look like: such a deeply counter-intuitive statement, and yet fundamental for our understanding of the Good News." Williams, "The Church." Williams has also written on the significance of the resurrection: *Resurrection*. See also Peterson, *Practice Resurrection*.

36. Basil, *On the Holy Spirit*, 27.66.

Pentecost Sunday: Happy Birthday to the Missional Church!

Jesus' entire incarnate life culminating in his death, resurrection, and later ascension signifies that lifelong presence is key for his perfection as our redeemer. Similarly, just as he stayed and remained with us before ascending to the Father, it is essential for our perfection that God provides staying power as he forms us in the ascended Jesus through the abiding Spirit during Ordinary Time—the "Season after Pentecost."

VII

Ordinary Time: Follow Jesus in the Spirit to the End!

The church has cycled through the liturgical calendar year in and year out since very early times. But we should not confuse this cycle with a cyclical view of history. Whether we are talking about the "now" and the "not yet" and everywhere in between,[1] or the church through the ages and the church across the globe, the Spirit of Jesus moves us forward as God shapes our imaginations and energies. Such movement does not end with Pentecost but carries on until Christ the King Sunday at the close of the church year. The Lion, who is the Lamb, will reign forever, not the Easter bunny. After all, the Lamb is the Ancient of Days, the Alpha and Omega. To him, a thousand years is like a day. So, no matter how fast the secular hare races, this ancient "tortoise" will arrive first at the finish line.

We have already noted that the church cycle year in and year out does not suggest a cyclical view of history, since the Lord will bring history to a close at the end of the age. There is one other caution that must be issued here. The church calendar views all of history as enchanted so that even what the liturgical calendar calls "Ordinary Time" is by no means ordinary in contrast to Advent, Christmastide, and Eastertide, for example. Nor is it ordinary in the way secular time is, where no moment or day has greater significance than another. Ordinary time in the secular sense suggests that all time is equally mundane, merely sequential or chronological.[2] Ordinary

---

1. For a concise study of the "now" and "not yet" aspects of the kingdom of God, see Ladd, *Gospel of the Kingdom*.

2. See Mircea Eliade's discussion of the Jewish and Christian understanding of time in terms of linear history rather than cyclic time and eternal return: *The Sacred*

VII—Ordinary Time: Follow Jesus in the Spirit to the End!

Time in the Christian sense is also the opposite of disordered time, or time-out-of-sync, time-out-of-whack, which inevitably harms our engagement of God, others, and our world. Ordinary Time involves the quality of *kairos* whereby Jesus' person, teaching, and work break in and shape every aspect of our temporal existence. Time is on his side.

We will account for Ordinary Time in a variety of ways after first presenting in order Trinity Sunday, Corpus Christi Sunday, Father's Day Sunday, and Fourth of July Sunday, which occur one right after the other during Ordinary Time. Given the title "Ordinary Time" and what it entails for order or being "ordered," it is worth mentioning the variety of diverse subjects set forth here. After highlighting Trinity Sunday and the other days stated above, we will devote four essays to the specific theme of Ordinary Time, pause to reflect upon Mary's Assumption and Dormition, and then present two more articles on Ordinary Time. Following these explorations, space will be devoted to the Season of Creation during the month of September, closing it off with treatments of St. Francis of Assisi and St. Kateri Tekakwitha, who were known and honored for their love of creation. Then we will highlight Sukkot, the Jewish Feast of Tabernacles, before focusing on Disability Sunday, which is part and parcel of Disability Month in October. After this analysis, we will engage such topics as Reformation Day and All Saints Sunday, as well as meditate on life's end—for us personally and for the world, which is a featured theme in November. Meditation on life's end is a fitting way to lead up to Christ the King Sunday at the close of the year.

As stated in the introduction, one learns a great deal about someone by looking at their calendars and checkbooks. What a given church or ecclesial tradition puts on their calendar says a lot about their priorities. Do those priorities reflect God's heartbeat revealed in the ascended Christ who through the Spirit of Pentecost seeks to bring order to disordered lives and the creation in our day during Ordinary Time? In the beginning this same Spirit hovered over the waters when the earth was formless and void (Gen 1:2) and was involved in God's creative process, such as breathing life into Adam (Gen 2:7), just as God brought order to all things that he had made through his Logos or Word (see Gen 1:3, 6, 9, 11, 14, 20, 24, 26; cf. John 1:1–3). Check your church and personal calendars to see how well they

---

and Profane. Eliade writes that in Judaism, "Yahweh no longer manifests himself in *cosmic time* (like the gods of other religions) but in a *historical time*, which is irreversible." Eliade, *Sacred and Profane*, 110. He goes on to write that "Christianity goes even further in valorizing *historical time*. Since God was *incarnated*, that is, since he took on *a historically conditioned human existence*, history acquires the possibility of being sanctified" (111).

VII—Ordinary Time: Follow Jesus in the Spirit to the End!

match with God's kingdom mission in the world and where necessary reset your spiritual clock so that sacred time breaks through the secular eclipse.

Mention was made above that Ordinary Time counters disordered time, which is so prominent today. Colin Gunton once remarked that the human attempt to displace eternity has made an eternity out of time. As a result, we are enslaved to it rather than realizing there is a season for everything (Eccl 3:1–8). In a similar vein, Karl Barth spoke of the world spirit that enslaves us to race here and there and everywhere to get someplace fast, but with no apparent benefit in many cases. Here's Barth on time travel through space:

> If only one could say why all these people rushing by so quickly are in such a hurry, why it is that they are so terribly pressed, as may be seen very forcibly today on every street! What do they propose to do with the time and energy saved? . . .
>
> The bondage of the will! People have to do this, we have to do it, even though we do not know why, even though we do not know where the propulsion of the earth-spirit in this form will lead us. Yet we must add to this: No, they do not have to do it, we do not really have to do it, the person who rests in God and is moved by him is sovereign in relation to this very primitive thing, namely, his movement in space, whether in a car or on foot, whether with greater or lesser speed, and he can order it and carry it out meaningfully—and knowing what he is doing. It is, however, one of the strangest symptoms of the basically perverted beginning of our existence, and of the existence of the powers that anonymously control us, that we seem not to be free to do this.[3]

The church calendar orders everything, every moment according to the Eternal Logos who entered time in its fullness, born of a woman, born under Law, in order to redeem those under the Law to become children of God (Gal 4:4–5). In contrast to Barth's "earth-spirit" that propels us forward in disorder, the Spirit of God orders our time in space. God will shape all of history until Christ permeates all things and makes all creation new and beautiful in his time (Eccl 3:11; Rev 21:5). So, slow down rather than get ahead of Jesus. Follow him to the end. Enter your promised rest.[4]

---

3. Barth, *The Christian Life*, 231–32.

4. For a work that draws on the seasons of the year to develop an ecclesiology befitting our situation today as we live in Ordinary Time between Easter and the Lord's return, see Pauw, *Church in Ordinary Time*.

THE TRINITY IS NOT JUST FOR TRINITY SUNDAY, BUT THE WHOLE YEAR

The doctrine of the Trinity is not just for Trinity Sunday, but for every day of the year.[5] Unfortunately, according to Lesslie Newbigin, many Christians from the High Middle Ages up until the latter half of the twentieth century were averse to referencing the Trinity, perhaps even on Trinity Sunday:

> It has been said that the question of the Trinity is the one theological question that has been really settled. It would, I think, be nearer to the truth to say that the Nicene formula has been so devoutly hallowed that it is effectively put out of circulation. It has been treated like the talent that was buried for safekeeping rather than risked in the commerce of discussion. The church continues to repeat the trinitarian formula but—unless I am greatly mistaken—the ordinary Christian in the Western world who hears or reads the word 'God' does not immediately and inevitably think of the Triune Being—Father, Son, and Spirit. He thinks of a supreme monad. Not many preachers, I suspect, look forward eagerly to Trinity Sunday. The working concept of God for most ordinary Christians is—if one may venture a bold guess—shaped more by the combination of Greek philosophy and Islamic theology that was powerfully injected in the thought of Christendom at the beginning of the High Middle Ages than by the thought of the fathers of the first four centuries.[6]

Why the aversion? Perhaps it was due to a growing and pervasive rationalism. Newbigin was not alone in lamenting the lack of Trinitarian thought forms in Western thought. Michael Buckley has also noted the lack

---

5. For a volume addressing how "the triune God of grace" should impact our worship, see Torrance, *Worship*.

6. Newbigin, *The Open Secret*, 27–28.

The Trinity Is Not Just for Trinity Sunday, But the Whole Year

of engagement of Trinitarian theology in Christian apologists' engagement of budding atheists in the modern period.[7] While rationalism is an ongoing problem, other forces that wage war today against robust Trinitarian reflection in many circles are consumerism and pragmatism. We easily settle for quick-fix, base commodity spirituality and short-term solutions to problems. However, quick fix spirituality and pragmatism cannot help us contend against impersonalism and materialism. The increasingly impersonal and materialistic view of the world in the modern age beckons us to give account once again to the Father's interaction with the cosmos—not imposing his will from without—but entering into the world through his Son and Spirit's interpersonal and communal engagement from within the historical process.

While the Trinity is not just for Trinity Sunday, but for every Sunday and every day of the year, it is not the case that just any construal of "the Trinity" suffices. Newbigin took issue with certain social Trinitarian constructs being developed in his day (for example, in Konrad Raiser's ecumenical thought) in such a way that they dominated Christological categories and the gospel message in service to democratic notions of governance. Newbigin challenges this approach: "What gives ground for anxiety here is the positing of a Trinitarian model *against* the model of Christocentric universalism. The doctrine of the Trinity was not developed in response to the human need for participatory democracy! It was developed in order to account for the facts that constitute the substance of the gospel."[8]

While needing to safeguard against excessive or abusive uses of the Trinity for our own ends, we should not throw out the baby with the dirty bathwater. One of the most striking features and implications of Trinitarian reflection for the gospel is that we are not alone. Thus, it would be shortsighted or narrow-minded to limit the Trinity's significance to Trinity Sunday. Jesus goes with us, even as he invites us to go into all the world, as reported in Matthew 28:18–20. The Great Commission is the Great Communion in which we participate in the life of the triune God while bearing witness to the good news of God calling all humanity to respond to his personal love through faith in Jesus every day of the year across the globe. In Matthew 28:18–20, we find that we are called to baptize people into the name of the Father, Son, and Spirit, teaching Jesus' disciples to obey his

---

7. Buckley, *Origins of Modern Atheism*, 33.

8. See the full context of the quotation (7) in Newbigin, "Trinity as Public Truth," 7–8. Never should relationality overshadow God as divine Trinity. Rather, the reverse should always remain the case. Paul Molnar critiques a social-Trinitarian state of affairs in which "Relationality [has become] the subject, and God the predicate." Molnar, *Divine Freedom*, 227.

VII—Ordinary Time: Follow Jesus in the Spirit to the End!

commandments, which are summed up in loving God with all our hearts and our neighbors as ourselves (Matt 22:34–40). As Jesus goes with us, and the Spirit dwells in us and empowers us, we invite people to enter God's community as members of the divine family.

Hierarchal, impersonal, and materialistic constructs of reality that would seek to eclipse the triune God, on the one hand, and democratic notions seemingly imposed on the triune God, on the other hand, will never displace the reality that God in Jesus through the Spirit dwells in our midst as Emmanuel "the whole of every day" until "the very end of the age"[9] (Matt 1:23; 28:20). Only in this relational and mysterious manner can the church truly overcome the impersonal and secular mundane. The Trinity is not just for Trinity Sunday, but for all of us the whole of every day throughout the year and age.

---

9. Carson asserts that Matthew ends with "promise" rather than "commission" (see Matt 28:20). "Our English 'always' masks a Greek expression found only here, meaning 'the whole of every day.' Jesus promises to be with His disciples, as they make disciples of others, not only on the long haul, 'but the whole of every day,' 'to the very end of the age.'" Carson, *God with Us*, 163. Further to this point, I maintain that even and especially in his ascended state, Jesus is present to us through the Spirit in the most intimate way.

CORPUS CHRISTI SUNDAY: DISCERNING CHRIST'S REAL PRESENCE

Today is Corpus Christi Sunday. "Corpus Christi" (the body of Christ) often follows Trinity Sunday in ecclesial celebrations, though not always. Moreover, not all Christians celebrate this day, parallel to how not all Christians share the same view of the Lord's Supper or Eucharist, which this day commemorates. Roman Catholicism, various Orthodox traditions, and some Anglican churches honor this feast to commemorate the institution of the sacrament of Holy Communion.[10] It is most unfortunate that the very institution intended to bring Christians together should be the cause or source of so much division. In what follows, we will seek to discern Christ's real bodily presence that should serve to unite all of us regardless of our important differences on the nature and significance of Holy Communion.

Before we turn to discern what should unite all Christians in discerning Christ's real bodily presence, we must first account for some items pertaining to this feast day of Corpus Christi Sunday. One may ask why the Feast of Corpus Christi is not honored on Maundy Thursday, when the Lord Jesus instituted Holy Communion. The rationale is often articulated that a separate day is required to celebrate the feast, given that Christ's church focuses on the Lord's passion and suffering at that time.

One may also wonder why Corpus Christi appears on the Sunday following Trinity Sunday. In my estimation, it appears quite fitting given that the Eucharist signifies the church's participation in the divine life, namely, what St. Peter refers to as "partakers of the divine nature," which comes about through God's "precious and very great promises" (2 Pet 1:4), and which no doubt includes the New Covenant confirmed with Jesus' broken body and shed blood.

St. Thomas Aquinas speaks to the church's partaking of the divine nature in the words attributed to him for the mass honoring this day:

10. Connell, "Corpus et Sanguis Christi," 272, in *New Catholic Encyclopedia*.

VII—Ordinary Time: Follow Jesus in the Spirit to the End!

> Since it was the will of God's only-begotten Son that men should share in his divinity, he assumed our nature in order that by becoming man he might make men gods. Moreover, when he took our flesh he dedicated the whole of its substance to our salvation. He offered his body to God the Father on the altar of the cross as a sacrifice for our reconciliation. He shed his blood for our ransom and purification, so that we might be redeemed from our wretched state of bondage and cleansed from all sin. But to ensure that the memory of so great a gift would abide with us for ever, he left his body as food and his blood as drink for the faithful to consume in the form of bread and wine.[11]

Indeed, Jesus' followers have been made partakers of the divine nature through the Son of God taking to himself our human nature and becoming human. Here Thomas drinks from the ancient Christian well. As Irenaeus, Athanasius, and others in the historic faith claimed before Thomas, Jesus became what we are so that we might become what he is.[12] Where Thomas and the Roman Catholic tradition since Thomas have often differed from Christendom as a whole concern the statement that Christ has "left us His Body as food and His Blood as drink under appearances of bread and wine." The next statement unpacks further Thomas's perspective:

> O precious and wonderful banquet, that brings us salvation and contains all sweetness! Could anything be of more intrinsic value? Under the old law it was the flesh of calves and goats that was offered, but here Christ himself, the true God, is set before us as our food. What could be more wonderful than this? No other sacrament has greater healing power; through it sins are purged away, virtues are increased, and the soul is enriched with an abundance of every spiritual gift. It is offered in the Church for the living and the dead, so that what was instituted for the salvation of all may be for the benefit of all.[13]

According to Thomas, the sacrament or means of grace entails the substantial changing of the bread and wine into the body and blood of Christ (often referred to as transubstantiation). Many Protestants following Martin Luther took issue with this view of the mass and also the idea often associated with the mass that virtues increase and salvation takes effect by a power of the rite within itself (*ex opere operato*—literally by the work worked). Luther's fear was that this operation "made the sacrament mechanical and

---

11. Aquinas, *Opusculum 57*, 610.
12. See Athanasius, *On the Incarnation*.
13. Aquinas, *Opusculum 57*, 610.

magical" rather than "mystical," as Roland Bainton makes clear in *Here I Stand*.[14] One might counter that it is Christ himself that makes the sacrament efficacious rather than any human agent, including the priest. No doubt, Luther would agree, but as Bainton notes, Luther claimed that faith, which is itself a gracious gift of God to the human agent and not a human work itself, is essential for salvation to be appropriated with or without the sacrament (here I would highlight that in Luther we find "by Christ alone" is accompanied by "by grace alone" and "by faith alone"). Bainton also argues in *Here I Stand* that for Luther, faith is necessary, "since faith is itself a gift of God, but this faith is given by God when, where, and to whom he will and even without the sacrament is efficacious; whereas the reverse is not true, that the sacrament is of efficacy without faith."[15]

More could be said on the nature and significance of the Eucharist, far more than can be discussed in one entry. Christian traditions will debate the relation of Christ's real presence to the sacraments or the necessity of faith for the rite to be efficacious, but we should not debate the importance of the sacrament for vital faith.[16] Nor should we debate the importance of Christ's real presence to us as his people in relation to and beyond the sacrament, nor that we are really his body one to another in the world. In fact, for Aquinas, the real presence of Christ gives rise to a real change in our relationships with God (*theosis*—divinization) and one another. Regardless of what we think of the elements, they convey in an iconic manner the elemental reconfiguration of all life in sacramental terms as the divine love is poured out in our lives and through us to one another.[17] We who are the body of Christ through Christ's own body are not just stuff bound up with what Max Weber calls the modern disenchantment of the world. As those mystically united to Christ and one another through the Spirit, we should not treat one another as mere things, but as iconic persons in communion.

Of course, this is easier said than done. Even more difficult than coming to agreement on the nature and significance of the Lord's Supper or Eucharist is living out what Jesus calls us to be as his people. Not only did

14. Bainton, *Here I Stand*, 131.

15. Bainton, *Here I Stand*, 131.

16. Webber argues that many are entering "evangelically alive liturgical churches," and often because of the weekly Eucharistic meal. Evangelicals are rediscovering the importance of "Table worship" (which Luther and Calvin highlighted). Some are reconsidering the memorialist view of the Lord's Supper "in favor of a view that emphasizes the active saving and healing presence of Christ at the Table." He refers the reader to Justin Martyr's 150 AD account of Christ's Table presence. Webber, *Ancient-Future Faith*, 110–11.

17. For an important discussion of this theme involving Aquinas' view of the Mass and its significance for the church's life, see Hofer, ed., *Divinization*, 66–67.

VII—Ordinary Time: Follow Jesus in the Spirit to the End!

he institute the Lord's Supper on the night of his passion, but also he was passionate at the Last Supper in providing an example for us as his followers to love one another, humble ourselves before one another, and wash one another's feet (read John 13:12–17).

John's account specifies not that we are blessed if we consider Jesus' teachings, know, them or believe in them, but rather if we "do" them. And yet, how unfortunate though equally unsurprising it is that instead of following suit, his disciples immediately following the institution of the Lord's Supper debate who is the greatest among them! (Read Luke 22:24–27.) For his part, Paul instructs believers that we are members or parts of Christ's body following his teaching on the Lord's Supper. He also exhorts believers to love one another as we express our various spiritual gifts through the excellent way of love made available by the same Spirit who gifts us (see 1 Cor 11–14). And yet, Paul rebukes the believers in Corinth that they have partaken of the Agape feast involving the Lord's Supper in an unworthy manner (see 1 Cor 11:17–34) whereby the well-to-do have kept the food to themselves while those without means were on the outside looking in. In other words, the Corinthian church functioned more like a fraternity than a healthy family, in keeping with the social customs of their day.[18]

While it is important to seek to discern the nature and significance of the body and blood in the Lord's Supper or Eucharist theologically, the biblical-theological thrust for Paul in 1 Corinthians 11 is to discern the well-being of the body of Christ as his people (read 1 Cor 11:27–34). Let us examine ourselves to see if we get it right on caring for other members of Christ's body. Based on the Lord Jesus' and the Apostle Paul's exhortation to us, getting it right on caring for one another at the Agape feast and beyond should be what brings all of Christendom together. Let us not fight over our important differences on the nature and significance of the elements and miss out on what is most pressing in importance: loving God's people humbly and sacrificially—so that all are included and so that no one goes without—faithfully declaring that Christ is really present.

---

18. According to Fee, the Lord's Supper was probably part of a common meal. The "haves" and "have-nots" were likely divided during this celebration, as it was "sociologically natural for the host to invite those of his/her own class to eat" in the dining room. Those not of their class (the less fortunate here in Corinth) ate in the courtyard. Fee, *First Epistle to the Corinthians*, 533–34.

WHAT WOULD FATHER'S DAY BE LIKE FOR JESUS?

Father's Day is a national holiday that was first celebrated in Washington state in 1910. Father's Day was later honored nationwide beginning in 1972. As far as I know, the Jewish nation did not celebrate a holiday equivalent to Father's Day in ancient times. So, it is difficult to answer the question set forth in the title of this piece: What would Father's Day be like for Jesus? Yet it is worth exploring as a thought experiment, for we can learn about Jesus' relationship with his earthly father and heavenly Father by trying to answer the question. We may also learn a thing or two about how to relate to our earthly fathers and heavenly Father.

We don't know much about Jesus' relationship with his earthly father, Joseph. We do know that according to the New Testament, Joseph determined not to divorce Mary after the angel announced to him that her pregnancy (Jesus) was conceived by the Holy Spirit, not sexual intercourse with another man (Matt 1:18–25). We also know that Joseph protected Mary and Jesus, as he took them and fled to Egypt after an angel warned him of Herod's plan to kill Jesus, who was a small child (Matt 2:13–15). As Matthew 1 tells us, Joseph was a just man. Lastly, we find that he was devout. Not only did he listen to the angelic witnesses who instructed him about Jesus, but also Joseph and Mary followed Jewish sacred customs and tradition, including Jesus' dedication as a newborn baby in the Temple and later their pilgrimage to Jerusalem for the Passover when Jesus was twelve (Luke 2:22–42).

The last appearance of Joseph in the canonical Gospels takes place in the Temple immediately after the Passover celebration when Jesus was twelve (read Luke 2:41–52). Jesus had disappeared and his parents had no idea where he was. No doubt, Jesus' parents were in a frenzied panic searching everywhere for him. Had he gotten lost? Was he kidnapped? What could have happened to him? Later when they found Jesus, Mary rebuked

VII—Ordinary Time: Follow Jesus in the Spirit to the End!

him, "Son, why have you treated us so? Behold, your father and I have been searching for you in great distress" (Luke 2:48).

I'm not sure how Mary and Joseph responded to Jesus' question, "Why were you looking for me? Did you not know that I must be in my Father's house?" (Luke 2:49). The question might have appeared rather dismissive and disrespectful, though we are told that "they did not understand the saying" (Luke 2:50). We do know from the following statement that Jesus "was submissive to them" in his return to Nazareth during his youth and that Mary "treasured up" all that occurred there in Jerusalem in her heart (Luke 2:51).

Jesus had a way of making sure his parents understood that he was ultimately submissive to his heavenly Father and his Father's divine purpose. A similar example is found in John 2 when Jesus appears frustrated and dismissive of his mother for involving him in dealing with the crisis that there was no more wine at the wedding in Cana in Galilee. Jesus tells Mary that his "hour" has not yet arrived. What he may be doing is reminding her that his ultimate loyalty is to his Father in heaven (read John 2:1–5).

The canonical Gospels make clear that Jesus has a unique, one-of-a-kind relationship with God as an "Abba" (Daddy, Papa) experience.[19] We see this in Jesus' baptism recorded in Matthew 3, where the Father speaks from heaven (read Matt 3:16–17).

Mark's Gospel declares at the very start that Jesus is God's Son: "The beginning of the gospel of Jesus Christ, the Son of God" (Mark 1:1). We also find consideration of Jesus' unique relationship with his heavenly Father in John's Gospel. Take for example the following account. Jesus has just healed a lame man on the Sabbath and is being persecuted for his act of mercy and reference to God as his personal Father. This was a staggering claim, as God was viewed at this time as the Father of the nation, but not of individuals. Jesus' claim puts him on the same level with God, and so, they sought to persecute him all the more: "This was why the Jews were seeking all the more to kill him, because not only was he breaking the Sabbath, but he was even calling God his own Father, making himself equal with God" (John 5:18). In response to their accusations and aim to kill him, Jesus defends his actions and claims by arguing that he simply does what his Father does and acknowledges the Father's honor of him. Like Father, like Son (read John 5:19–24).

---

19. For a classic study of Jesus' use of "abba," see Jeremias, "Abba," 11–65. See also Schillebeeckx, *Jesus*, 256–61. Jeremias argues that "abba" plays a unique and important role in Jesus' life and ministry. It conveys a tender and intimate relationship with his Father that is distinctive of him in contradistinction to Israel and the early church. For a feminist critique of this tradition, see D'Angelo, "Abba and 'Father.'"

What Would Father's Day Be Like for Jesus?

Jesus understood early on (at least from the age of twelve) that his relationship with his heavenly Father was all-important. Jesus' father Joseph was a good and righteous man, but he could never take the place of Jesus' Father in heaven. Jesus would have all of us relate to his Father as "Our Father in heaven," as he instructs his disciples to pray (see the Lord's Prayer recorded in Matt 6:9–13). This Father's name is alone hallowed. His kingdom alone will come in its fullness (see Matt 6:9–10). We are ultimately dependent on the heavenly Father for our daily sustenance, forgiveness of sins, and protection from evil (see Matt 6:11–13).

Mention was made at the outset of this piece that Father's Day was first celebrated in Washington state in 1910. Sonora Smart Dodd and her five siblings had been raised by their dad, who was a widower. No doubt grateful for her father's faithful investment and care for the family, she convinced local establishments to set aside a day to honor male parents. A friend of mine named David also hails from the Pacific Northwest. His father died of cancer when David was a youth. His father told David as his death drew near how much he valued being David's father. He also counseled David on his death bed to see him as his brother from then onward, and to look to God as his ultimate Father to whom he entrusted David's care. David heeded his good father's sound advice. I have admired how David cherishes his heavenly Father's care for him to this day.

Many of us are grateful for our earthly fathers' care for us. Others of us did not experience the blessing of an earthly father's loyal love. Yet all of us can experience what David has encountered—the blessing that comes from knowing God as our heavenly Father. Through faith in Jesus, we can experience the gracious care of God as "Abba" (Daddy Father). Jesus' joy includes making a home for us with his Father who becomes our Father through Jesus. As Jesus told Mary Magdalene, "I am ascending to my Father and your Father, to my God and your God" (John 20:17). Consider also Jesus' high priestly prayer in which he envisions our being with him in his Father's presence—a Father who loves us just as he loves his Son (John 17:20–26). Through faith in Jesus, we receive the Spirit of God who pours God's love into our hearts (Rom 5:5), not fear. As Paul writes, "For you did not receive the spirit of slavery to fall back into fear, but you have received the Spirit of adoption as sons, by whom we cry, 'Abba! Father!'" (Rom 8:15).

No doubt, Jesus would have celebrated the equivalent of Father's Day out of respect for his earthly father, Joseph. However, he would always ensure that his ultimate affection for a father be expressed to God. My friend David to whom I referred above learned early on in life that God alone is our ultimate Father through Jesus and that we can count on him, just as Jesus urged us. Will you and I do the same and trust in Abba?

A FOURTH OF JULY REFLECTION: TAKING EXCEPTION TO AMERICAN EXCEPTIONALISM

On the Fourth of July, Americans celebrate the founding of our great nation, which is a wondrous experiment in the pursuit of democratic ideals. There is much to celebrate for sure: freedom from tyrannical regimes where people have no freedom in the areas of speech and religion, among other human longings and values. Of course, we have had more than our fair or unfair share of overwhelming challenges along the way, such as with the struggles for civil rights for various groups of people, including ethnic minorities and women. Even so, our democracy continues to move forward in pursuit of its values set forth in its founding documents.

Amid the fanfare, I can't help but ask: why must many Americans consider our nation to be the best for it to be great? Certainly, it is a great nation. But who are we Americans to say that it is the best or most exceptional nation on the earth, the exception to the rule? What criterion do we use for our long-standing conviction of our exceptionalism? The largest economy? The greatest military? State of the art health care research? Nations in our time and nations to follow will no doubt debate where such superlatives go on the ladder of greatness.

The origin of American exceptionalism is sometimes attributed to John Winthrop's sermon to his fellow colonists in New England in which he declares, "We shall be as a city upon a hill. The eyes of all people are upon us."[20] However, others claim that it arises in view of the European Enlightenment. Donald E. Pease draws attention to the Enlightenment or secular perspective and then presents an evolution of meaning associated with American exceptionalism. On the variance of meaning, he writes:

---

20. Refer to Winthrop's sermon, "Model of Christian Charity," 304–7. Refer also to this online source where it is found: "John Winthrop Dreams of a City on a Hill, 1630," in *The American Yawp Reader*.

A Fourth of July Reflection

Despite American exceptionalism's standing as an invariant tenet of the national creed, however, accounts of the discourse's content have changed with historical circumstances. American exceptionalism has been taken to mean that America is either "distinctive" (meaning merely different), or "unique" (meaning anomalous), or "exemplary" (meaning a model for other nations to follow), or "exempt" from the laws of historical progress (meaning that it is an "exception" to the laws and rules governing the development of other nations). The particulars attributed to the term have been said to refer to clusters of absent and present elements—the absence of feudal hierarchies, class conflicts, a socialist labor party, trade unionism, and divisive ideological passions, and the presence of a predominant middle class, tolerance for diversity, upward mobility, hospitality toward immigrants, a shared constitutional faith, and liberal individualism—that putatively set America apart from other national cultures. Although historical realities have posed significant challenge, these tenets have proven uncommonly resilient.[21]

Regardless of whether the origin of American exceptionalism is religious or secular in nature, I take exception to America's or any nation's sense of exceptionalism if it is intended to convey a people group or nation's inherent superiority and exemption from laws applying to other people groups or nations.

This problematic sense of exceptionalism is on display in the Bible whenever God's people Israel presume that *God is on their side* because they are Abraham's descendants and because God blessed them and gave them the Promised Land. One instance where such thinking could have gained a foothold or stronghold was when the nation of Israel under Joshua entered the Promised Land to conquer it. But God intervened. As Joshua and the people were about to march on Jericho, Joshua came face to face with an imposing figure with a drawn sword in his hand (read Joshua 5:13–15).

As revealed in this passage, Joshua asks the "man" looming before him whose side he is on, to which the figure responds that he is not on either side. Rather, he has come as the commander of the LORD's most exceptional army of heaven. Joshua falls flat before the heavenly commander in homage and then takes off his sandals in response to the commander's command.

What might this text suggest for the doctrine of national exceptionalism? Do we presume that God is on our side in times of war, just like soldiers of various military forces that have gone into battle throughout history with

---

21. Pease, "American Exceptionalism."

VII—Ordinary Time: Follow Jesus in the Spirit to the End!

"God with us" (in whatever language) etched on their belt buckles, rolling off their tongues, and stirring in their hearts?

I honor the bravery of America's soldiers throughout the generations, who have put themselves in harm's way for our democratic ideals and liberties. Still, the presumption that God is on our side does not pay honor to the commander of the LORD's army—Jesus. Never ask God, "What side are you on?" but "Lord, what side are we on?"

Patriotism is a very good thing—maintaining loyalty to one's nation. However, blind nationalism and exceptionalism that claims that one's country can do no wrong, or that it is synonymous with the kingdom of God, is by no means exceptional from the Bible's vantage point. Even God's chosen people—Israel—had to guard against such presumption or face God's stinging rebuke or worse—destruction and exile. If such is the case with God's chosen people in the Bible, do we think God would excuse us from a similar fate for such presumption?

Concerns over American presumption or exceptionalism have increased due to recent events in US history. September 11, 2001 changed everything for the American imagination. As William Cavanaugh writes, it was a *kairos* or crisis moment of eschatological import for US history. He continues,

> A kind of eschatological sensibility pervades discourse about "9/11," not necessarily in the sense of an end to chronological time, but rather a suspension of ordinary time. We live in a state of exception, a time when exceptional measures such as torture become thinkable . . . *Kairos* is messianic time (see e.g., Acts 3:20), a time for one decisive actor to appear on history's stage. In the language of American exceptionalism, that actor is the United States, the "indispensable nation," as Madeleine Albright called it, the one exceptional nation needed for exceptional times.[22]

It is important that the church in the US does not succumb to such exceptionalism but takes exception to it. But how?

Instead of being eclipsed by the secular calendar and the Fourth of July this week, it would be wise to reflect upon the national liturgy in view of Jesus confronting the religious and political hierarchy during Holy Week (refer back to the essays under the Holy Week section in this book). Remember how Jesus urged Israel's leaders to place their hope in him rather than

---

22. Cavanaugh, *Migrations of the Holy*, 88. The quote from Albright is taken from Andrew Bacevich, *American Empire*, x. For a discussion on church and national calendars, see Watts, *Bowing Toward Babylon*, 68–71.

A Fourth of July Reflection

the Temple or Jerusalem and Israel. They would not listen, which spelled destruction for the people. Their sense of their own indispensability and messianic ambitions as well as the nation's exceptional status clouded their vision, just like it does for those who see this or any country as indispensable.

Given that we are in the Christian season of Ordinary Time (not to be confused with ordinary time as Cavanaugh uses the term in the quote above), let us move further along the path of discipleship toward maturation and place our hope in Jesus as our Messiah. May we the church be exceptional in obedience to the Lord given our calling to be a royal priesthood, holy nation, and people belonging to God (1 Pet 2:9). May we take off our sandals in the Lord's presence, which is holy ground. May we preach against any form of exceptionalism that presents this or that country as an exception to the rule of international law as well as God's Law. May we not beat the drums of war, which only breeds more violence and disorder. Rather, may our hearts beat for the cruciform Christ and take up the cross, not the sword, as we move forward in Ordinary Time awaiting Christ's triumphant return.

MAY JESUS ORDER OUR STEPS DURING ORDINARY TIME

Ordinary Time in the Christian calendar is not about ordinary and ho-hum events, but about the ordering of Christian existence according to Jesus' life and teaching above and beyond the Advent and Christmas, Lenten, and Easter seasons. This essay reflects on what such ordering involves and how important it is for Jesus to order our lives throughout the year, including during Ordinary Time.

Before we go further, let's consider more carefully the meaning of Ordinary Time. Here is what one helpful article explains about Ordinary Time:

> Because the term *ordinary* in English most often means something that's not special or distinctive, many people think that Ordinary Time refers to parts of the calendar of the Catholic Church that are unimportant. Even though the season of Ordinary Time makes up most of the liturgical year in the Catholic Church, the fact that Ordinary Time refers to those periods that fall outside of the major liturgical seasons reinforces this impression. Yet Ordinary Time is far from unimportant or uninteresting.
>
> Ordinary Time is called "ordinary" not because it is common but simply because the weeks of Ordinary Time are numbered. The Latin word *ordinalis*, which refers to numbers in a series, stems from the Latin word *ordo*, from which we get the English word *order*. Thus, the numbered weeks of Ordinary Time, in fact, represent the ordered life of the Church—the period in which we live our lives neither in feasting (as in the Christmas and Easter seasons) or in more severe penance (as in Advent and Lent), but in watchfulness and expectation of the Second Coming of Christ.[23]

---

23. ThoughtCo, "What Ordinary Time Means." While different in meaning and context, it is worth drawing attention to a work that takes up the theme of "ordinary"

May Jesus Order Our Steps During Ordinary Time

There is no better way to live in watchfulness and expectation for Jesus' second coming than to submit to Jesus in ordering our steps according to his life and teaching presented during his first coming. So, as we proceed, let's ask: what's involved in Jesus ordering our steps during Ordinary Time? The answer: total trust and obedience.

Jesus calls us. The question we must ask ourselves during any season of the year, including Ordinary Time, is: will we follow? Are there strings attached—like fishing nets—to our decision as to whether and how far and in what manner we will follow? Consider Jesus' first recorded encounter with his first disciples in Matthew 4. Notice that for Peter and Andrew, James and John, there were no strings attached to their determination when Jesus beckoned. They left everything to follow him, illustrated by leaving their nets, their boat(s), and their father(s) (Matt 4:18–22). At the outset of Jesus' ministry in which he calls people to repent for the kingdom of heaven is at hand (Matt 4:17), we find him calling his first disciples (read Matt 4:18–22). Notice their response: the disciples leave behind their allegiances to their families and their fishing businesses, the only way of life they had likely ever known, to become Jesus' apprentices in his work of fishing for people. These four knew nothing of the path laid out before them, only Jesus' call to follow. They followed unreservedly, no strings or nets attached. The only thing that they were attached to was Jesus' word in a spirit of total trust and obedience. I find such a response refreshing, though shocking and staggering given the all-too-human impulse in our day to hedge our bets, keep our relational options open, and play the perpetual cynic.

From the get go, Jesus' call is a call to die—to die to the old order of life, all they had ever known, to live anew according to his way of being. Thus, we find resonance with what Dietrich Bonhoeffer asserts in his volume on discipleship: "The cross is not the end of a pious, happy life. Instead, it stands at the beginning of community with Jesus Christ. Whenever Christ calls us, his call leads us to death."[24] While Jesus' disciples certainly did not understand all that stood before them on the path ahead, they understood that their past was dead to them in living in accordance with Jesus' future for them. Thus, there should have been no real surprise when Jesus exclaims later in the same Gospel: "If anyone would come after me, let him deny himself and take up his cross and follow me" (Matt 16:24). A few pages later in *Discipleship*, we find Bonhoeffer quoting Martin Luther, who urges us to "submerge" ourselves in a "lack of understanding" to gain Jesus'

---

in the typical way we think of it and infuses it with the sacred. See Warren, *Liturgy of the Ordinary*.

24. Bonhoeffer, *Discipleship*, 87.

VII—Ordinary Time: Follow Jesus in the Spirit to the End!

understanding.[25] Again, total trust and obedience in the face of death to new life is required. This requires unlearning to learn anew from Jesus.

No doubt, such total dependence and allegiance, and with it, new learning, can prove unnerving and disturbing to many. But from Jesus' vantage point, as well as that of his disciple Bonhoeffer, such dependence and allegiance is liberating and life-giving (read Matt 11:28–30). Jesus beckons those who are weary and weighed down with many burdens to come to him to find rest. How do they find such rest? By taking his yoke—which involves his cross—upon them! And how will that relieve them of their heavy burden? Jesus takes their burdens upon himself and replaces their burdens with his abiding presence involving his gentle and lowly spirit. Only then can they find rest for their souls, as they wear his easy yoke and light burden, of which he himself ultimately bears the brunt. Such a path of discipleship involves unlearning the old system of bearing their own burdens and learning as for the first time what it means to follow Jesus. So, he urges them to learn from him and to get to know him and his character and his good life-giving aims for their lives. The same holds true for us today.

Bonhoeffer explains why Jesus' burden is light and how his way for us is life-giving in the following manner:

> Those who follow Jesus' commandment entirely, who let Jesus' yoke rest on them without resistance, will find the burdens they must bear to be light. In the gentle pressure of this yoke they will receive the strength to walk the right path without becoming weary. Jesus' commandment is harsh, inhumanly harsh for someone who resists it. Jesus' commandment is gentle and not difficult for someone who willingly accepts it. "His commandments are not burdensome" (1 John 5:3). Jesus' commandment has nothing to do with forced spiritual cures. Jesus demands nothing from us without giving us the strength to comply. Jesus' commandment never wishes to destroy life, but rather to preserve, strengthen, and heal life.[26]

Jesus' call to us every day of the year, including during Ordinary Time, appears so unordinary, so counterintuitive. As has been argued in this entry, Jesus' call intends and invites a response of total trust and obedience, one that from its inception leads to death for the old order of our existence, but that from beginning to end also involves new and abundant life. May we submit ourselves to Jesus during Ordinary Time, and not just on Sundays or during Christmastide and Eastertide. May Jesus order our lives. Only his

---

25. Bonhoeffer, *Discipleship*, 91.
26. Bonhoeffer, *Discipleship*, 39.

May Jesus Order Our Steps During Ordinary Time

order brings true order out of the chaos of our daily existence. May we not be like those who experience the harsh reality of resisting Jesus' word, but like those first followers who experienced the gentle reality of obeying Jesus' life-giving command as they dropped their nets and left their family fishing boats to follow him.

JESUS ACTS EXTRAORDINARILY DURING ORDINARY TIME

In many church traditions, Ordinary Time constitutes two seasons in the church calendar. The first season or phase of Ordinary Time follows Christmas Time (the present volume treated Epiphanytide instead, as it overlaps with this first phase of Ordinary Time). The second season or period of Ordinary Time follows Easter Time or Eastertide. According to one site, Ordinary Time lead us "through the life of Christ. This is the time of conversion. This is living the life of Christ." The site goes on to state,

> Christmas Time and Easter Time highlight the central mysteries of the Paschal Mystery, namely, the incarnation, death on the cross, resurrection, and ascension of Jesus Christ, and the descent of the Holy Spirit at Pentecost. The Sundays and weeks of Ordinary Time, on the other hand, take us through the life of Christ. This is the time of conversion. This is living the life of Christ.
>
> Ordinary Time is a time for growth and maturation, a time in which the mystery of Christ is called to penetrate ever more deeply into history until all things are finally caught up in Christ. The goal, toward which all of history is directed, is represented by the final Sunday in Ordinary Time, the Solemnity of Our Lord Jesus Christ, King of the Universe.[27]

We see evidence of Jesus' mystery penetrating history and the world in his incarnate life, as he performs miracles of various kinds. For example, we find evidence of Jesus' penetration of history and the world in various ways and in quick succession in the following series of events recorded in Mark's Gospel. The winds and waves obey Jesus, as with the stilling of the storm (Mark 4:35–41). The demons also obey him, as when he casts out a

---

27. United States Conference of Catholic Bishops, "Ordinary Time."

legion of them from a wild and dangerous man and sends them into a herd of pigs (Mark 5:1–13). A little while later, according to Mark's Gospel, we find human bodies obeying him, as Jesus heals a woman of an issue of blood and raises a girl from the dead (Mark 5:21–43). But perhaps the greatest evidence of his presence is his long-suffering patience involving people's hard-heartedness, slowness to understand, and the transformation of the human heart, which takes place in Jesus' ministry through God's Spirit.

I find extraordinary those occasions when people do not believe in Jesus, though they know that he has performed mighty miraculous deeds. Take, for example, the brief transitional section in Mark 5:14–20 that stands between the event where Jesus casts out the demons into the herd of pigs, and the events where Jesus heals the woman with the issue of blood and raises a girl from the dead. There in between these events, we find the townspeople who are told by the herdsmen of the pigs what has happened. The townspeople rush out to find Jesus along with the formerly demon-possessed and crazed man sitting, clothed, and in his right mind. The text tells us that when they see the man sitting there, calm and collected, they are afraid. After being told in full what had occurred, they beg Jesus to depart, which he does. Certainly, one can understand their consternation if they are upset about the loss of the pig herd. But if Jesus could free a man from a legion of demons that their chains could not subdue, surely he could restore to them their herd of pigs, or more.

This is not the only extraordinary evidence of unbelief. After healing the woman with the issue of blood and raising the dead girl to life again, we find Jesus returning home to unbelieving Nazareth (read Mark 6:1–6). The only thing that matches the astonishing unbelief of the hometown crowd is Jesus' astonishment at their unbelief. Similarly, we find Jesus' own disciples later in this chapter going from observing Jesus feeding the five thousand to fearing for their lives in a boat sailing on a turbulent sea. Jesus approaches them, as he walks on the water, though they presume he is a ghost. After he assures them it is he, and tells them not to fear, he enters the boat. As in the case of the stilling of the storm in Mark 4, they are amazed, though so slow to understand (read Mark 6:48–52).

Jesus' patience with his disciples' slowness to understand and hardness of heart is extraordinary. If we did not have an awareness of his unfailing love, we would have a most difficult time believing that he did not abandon these first disciples to their unbelief. Yet, he called them—even them. How miraculous is his grace that he would call them to be his apostolic witnesses. And yet, they believe, as did the demons whom Jesus cast out on various occasions (see Mark 3:11). Jesus calls his apostles to himself (Mark 3:13–19) to replace the teachers and leaders of the people whose hardness of heart was

VII—Ordinary Time: Follow Jesus in the Spirit to the End!

so severe that they rejected Jesus outright and sought to destroy him for his miraculous mercy (Mark 3:5–6). Jesus entrusts the secret of the kingdom to the twelve (Mark 4:11).

Jesus acts in extraordinary ways during Ordinary Time. He performs miracles involving the stilling of storms and casting out of demons. He honors people's request for him to depart from their region. He even permits their unbelief to keep him from performing many miracles in their midst. Perhaps most extraordinary is his patience with his ordinary disciples—then and now—and his undying effort and effective call for them to follow and to transform their minds and hearts in order to minister through them in amazing ways. May the mystery of Jesus penetrate more fully not only history, but also our own minds, hearts, and actions as we seek to serve him as his equally ordinary followers until the end when all things are caught up in him. Come, Lord Jesus, come.

CHRONOS GOVERNS THE DAY. MAY *KAIROS* GOVERN OUR LIVES

"Ordinary Time" in the Christian calendar does not signify ordinary, but ordering according to Jesus' life, teaching, and call on our lives. It pertains to those times of the year beyond Christmastide and Eastertide. However, the distinction between Ordinary Time and Christmastide and Eastertide is porous. God's miraculous workings through Jesus and the Spirit during Christmastide and Eastertide permeate Ordinary Time in the Christian calendar. In fact, these events permeate and transform every day of the year. Of course, the secular calendar does not make any such distinction or connection between Christmastide, Eastertide, and Ordinary Time. The secular calendar operates only by way of *chronos* or quantitative and sequential time. All such time is mundane unless God's presence intersects and indwells it. *Kairos* or qualitative and opportune time—which in the Christian calendar is bound up with the events of the incarnation, crucifixion, resurrection, ascension, and Pentecost—should influence how we operate in *chronos* or quantitative time throughout the whole year.

Here is how Christopher Prowse discusses the difference between these two concepts derived from Greek words for different dimensions of time and as developed in the Christian context:

> When we think of time we think of hours and minutes, watches and clocks. We think of how time flies or drags.
>
> More recently, to respond to the perception that modern life means busyness and having no time, we use expressions such as time poor or time sensitive.
>
> Lack of sequential time worries us. It usually means we find it difficult to allocate time to pray and reflect and organise our time that truly reflects our deeply felt priorities. Failure to do this prudently places modern people into a dazed state of inattentiveness and unreflectiveness. This deeply worries us. This

VII—Ordinary Time: Follow Jesus in the Spirit to the End!

is time as "chronos" from the Greek word. We derive the word chronology from this.

Then comes biblical time. This is called "Kairos." It is not so much a matter of a clicking clock, but time as "the favourable time." It is the opportune or right time. It is a great and supreme moment to refresh ourselves and come back to what really is important in life.[28]

Chronos or quantitative time governs the day. But it should not govern our daily lives. Rather, we must prayerfully consider how to live in accordance with *kairos* in every moment. Unfortunately, we often frantically try and squeeze as much juice out of the turnip of chronological time before it's too late. Perhaps such turnip-of-time squeezing is on the increase the more we seek to displace eternity in our society and eclipse the Christian calendar with the secular calendar. It shows up when we fail to imagine the reality of Jesus' incarnation in time and the Spirit's descent at Pentecost.

We find the effects of the displacement and eclipse of sacred or *kairos* time in the Christian life on such occasions when waiting with agitation for someone to stop speaking so we can talk, when growing quickly impatient to the point of cutting in line at the store, or when riding someone's bumper or cutting off other drivers to get farther down the road.

Where are we going today with our increasing flurry of activity, as we race to our destinations? Anywhere meaningful? Once we get there, do we truly rest, or do we immediately begin thinking of our next move to make to fill the time of day?

The displacement of *kairos* in the Christian life entails that we have little time for others, since we and our time are priceless, not them or theirs. Time is money and time does not stand still for anyone. When we live like this, time becomes relationally void and meaningless no matter how much we fill up our moments with things to do. From this vantage point, we can never do enough with the time available to us since we know that it keeps slipping away, as do our relationships.

Having spoken of the failure to imagine the penetration of chronological time with *kairos*, such as the incarnation and Pentecost's permeation in

---

28. Prowse, "Lent 2017." Oscar Cullman treats such terms as *kairos*, *aiōn*, and *chronos* in their New Testament biblical context and also contrasts linear time in Christian Scripture with cyclical time in Hellenistic thought in *Christ and Time*. For *kairos* and related notions, see chapter 1. For linear versus cyclical time, see chapter 2. Note that, for Cullman, time as *chronos* in the New Testament context does not entail its problematic usage in Greek philosophical thought. Given that God grants us time and governs it, time is not viewed in the abstract. In the biblical context, it is used in relation to God's redemptive historical plan rather than merely as time in general. In fact, no word for "time" in the New Testament bears the sense of "time as an abstraction," 49.

time, we find that qualitative or sacred time permeates life in such a way that we can live meaningfully moment by moment. Let us consider briefly Jesus' life to unpack this reality.

Note how Jesus engaged others. He was not hurried, though people tried to hurry him along, as in the sequence of events involving Jairus's daughter and the woman with the issue of blood (Mark 5:21–43), or the account of Lazarus's death (John 11:1–44). In the case of the woman with the issue of blood, his presence healed her. Though she had "inconvenienced" him by touching his robe for healing on his way to Jairus's house, he did not push ahead. He paused and addressed her, humanizing and dignifying her in the eyes of others. Jesus then proceeded on his way and raised Jairus's daughter from the dead. Jesus' time or hour was not in accordance with others' time, as in the case of Jesus' brothers' exhortation for him to go showtime (John 7:1–39). Since Jesus came in the fullness of time (Gal 4:4), and knew his time was in God's hands, he did not worry that he would ever be late to fulfill his destiny and enter into his glory.

As we participate in Jesus' life through the Spirit, we enter the *kairos* time zone known as his hour of glory. It is not quantitative time, but qualitative time, as we live into his cruciform, resurrected glory. What does that entail?

Living into Jesus' hour of glory necessitates humbly serving others, which means we will consider others better than ourselves. What does that entail? Rather than rushing them to finish speaking so that we can talk, we will let them complete their ideas, listening attentively and inquisitively, realizing that listening is a form of love. Rather than cutting in line or cutting off others on the road, we will wait our turn in line and allow them to merge. We will allow people to "inconvenience" us at various points on life's journey when we discern it will affirm their dignity, knowing that our time and theirs is in God's hands.

We have written here of Jesus' hour of glory (see John 7:30; 12:23; 13:1; 17:1). In contrast to John's Gospel's emphasis on this *kairos* theme, 1960s pop cultural icon Andy Warhol spoke of how in the future people will be famous for fifteen minutes. Whether we are talking of fifteen minutes or fifteen hundred years, fame—which is often associated with the cultural elite—comes and goes like fleeting, sequential time. But God's glory—which favors humble service of others behind the scenes and defers to them in conversations and in checkout lines and on life's highways—remains forever. Which will it be for you and me? *Chronos* and fame govern the day. But may *kairos* and humble glory in service to God and others govern our lives forever.

CONQUER INORDINATE DESIRE DURING ORDINARY TIME

How might Ordinary Time's emphasis on ordering our lives according to Jesus' life and teaching bear upon inordinate desire today and every day of the year? A gospel text often chosen for Ordinary Time is Luke 12:13–21. The text addresses the subject of greed, avarice, inordinate desire for material gain (please read it now).

The account features a man begging Jesus to serve as an arbiter between him and his brother in dividing their inheritance. Jesus takes issue with the request and warns the man to guard against fixation on possessions. Then Jesus shares the story of a rich man whose wealth enslaves him. It is quite clear from this text that Jesus does not subscribe to the idea that those with the most toys win. Rather, Jesus calls the rich man (and those like him) a fool who will lose everything.

The rich person in question makes a poor judgment and decision. Just because his land produces plentifully does not mean that he has plenty of time. In fact, his time is up: "But God said to him, 'Fool! This night your soul is required of you'" (Luke 12:20). So much for his wishful thinking that he can "relax, eat, drink, be merry" for "many years" (Luke 12:19).

René Camilleri comments on this passage:

> Today we feel a deep sense of crisis in the collective conscience. The greed that governs us is just a symptom of this crisis. The greed to get at all costs what we don't have; the greed to keep what we have, whatever the price; the greed that makes us live above our means.
>
> This is avarice at its worst, with implications for our individual well-being and implications on the political level of a society constantly crucified with scandals and corruption. Little do we realise that Christian tradition ranks avarice, or greed, ahead of lust and second only to pride. It is what Thomas Aquinas called

"the immoderate desire for temporal possessions," the emphasis being on "immoderate." Avarice is among the most hidden and dangerous sins.[29]

One does not have to be Roman Catholic like St. Thomas Aquinas to get this point. Even though Protestantism has traditionally viewed every sin as mortal, such consideration should never minimize how deadly avarice or greed is. Moreover, one does not have to be rich in material wealth to struggle with greed. This inordinate desire for material gain can take root in all of us. In other words, greed is no respecter of traditions or persons.

This being the case, I am always struck by people who live in such a way that they steward their possessions relationally well before God and others. For example, I know a wealthy Christian philanthropist who looks at money in a unique way: "Money is like manure. It helps me grow things." This person seeks to honor God and invest in initiatives that serve the underserved in ways that sustain and strengthen them for their own long-term vitality and personal growth. It appears that this Christian philanthropist has taken to heart the message of Luke 12:13–21. From all that I know of him, he also cherishes his relationships with family and friends. He has done well to avoid a costly mistake that a mutual friend who is an estate attorney often finds when providing legal counsel to wealthy individuals: those who are possessed by their financial possessions are estranged from their families and they don't even know why.

In Luke 12, it appears that the man in the crowd who begs Jesus to tell his brother to divide their inheritance is not concerned for relationship given that Jesus tells this parable of the rich fool. Certainly, the rich fool is not concerned for relationship with God and others, but only his own well-being, "to relax, eat, drink, be merry" for "many years" (Luke 12:19). Jesus warns us to guard against being like this man with his inordinate desire for financial gain and material well-being. For everyone who is like this rich fool will end up with a similar fate: "So is the one who lays up treasure for himself and is not rich toward God" (Luke 12:21).

John Paul Thomas writes of this passage in Luke 12 for this Sunday in Ordinary Time that while not everyone is called to take the vow of poverty, every Christian must seek to live out poverty of spirit. Thus, we must guard our hearts in such a manner that we cherish and embrace only the great lifelong treasures of faith, hope, and love.[30] Only then can we move beyond the

---

29. Camilleri, "18th Sunday."

30. See Thomas, *Daily Reflections*, 7. This biblical text was chosen for the eighteenth week of Ordinary Time in year C of the church calendar.

VII—Ordinary Time: Follow Jesus in the Spirit to the End!

fear bound up with what Walter Brueggemann calls "the myth of scarcity" and live into "the liturgy of abundance."[31]

Speaking of liturgy, the liturgical year helps us not fall prey to the idea that time is on our side and that we will live this life as we know it forever. We must live ever mindful that our mortal existence could end this day or this night and that we will have to stand before God and give an accounting for what we did with our resources during our lifetime. While the IRS does not account for inordinate desires of greed, only that we have our financial records in good legal order, God's accounting addresses our heart's deepest values and whether we have invested relationally well with God and others. After all, as Jesus warns us, "Take care, and be on your guard against all covetousness, for one's life does not consist in the abundance of his possessions" (Luke 12:15). If Jesus' exhortation out of concern for our eternal and relational well-being does not cure inordinate desire during Ordinary Time, I don't know what will.

---

31. Brueggemann, "The Liturgy of Abundance."

MARY'S ASSUMPTION: AN UNASSUMING HEART AND HONOR

August 15 marks the assumption of the Blessed Virgin Mary according to official Roman Catholic teaching. What is the "assumption of Mary"? It is the Roman Catholic teaching that at the end of her life Mary was taken up in soul and in body to be present along with her Son Jesus in God's glory. While the Eastern Church and certain Anglican communities also reserve a special and elevated place for Mary, Protestantism in general takes issue with the teaching of Mary's assumption. It is also worth noting here that whereas the month of June is dedicated to honoring Jesus' sacred heart, the month of August is dedicated to honoring Mary's immaculate heart in Catholic circles. This essay will consider both Roman Catholic teachings—her immaculate heart and assumption into glory.

Devotion to Jesus' sacred heart centers on his divine love for humanity, which is all too often despised or dismissed, whereas devotion to Mary's heart centers on her human love for God in Jesus.[32] It is important to note that in official Catholic teaching Jesus' qualitatively greater status and distinction between him and Mary is secure. Here is one example of this distinction: "The physical heart of Mary is venerated (and not adored as the Sacred Heart of Jesus is) because it is united to her person: and as the seat of her love (especially for her divine Son), virtue, and inner life. Such devotion is an incentive to a similar love and virtue."[33]

We are not to adore or worship Mary, but venerate her, according to Catholic doctrine. The idea that her heart is immaculate or sinless signifies that she alone among humans (other than her Son, who is God) lives a

---

32. Catholic News Agency, "The Immaculate Heart of Mary." Refer also to Cross and Livingstone, eds., "Assumption of the BVM," 118–19, in *The Oxford Dictionary of the Christian Church*.

33. CatholicCulture.org, "Catholic Prayer."

VII—Ordinary Time: Follow Jesus in the Spirit to the End!

life that exemplifies what God desires—total, pure obedience. One Catholic article presents this teaching in the following manner:

> In an age of sensuality and materialism the Assumption points out the dignity and destiny of our human body, extols the dignity of womanhood, and turns our eyes to the true life beyond the grave. At Mass today ask Mary for the grace to keep your mind fixed on things above and to aspire continually to be united with her and to be brought to the glory of the Resurrection.[34]

At the close of this article, a few assertions will be made on Mary and her significance that hopefully Catholics and Protestants can affirm together. For now, it is worth highlighting some of the key points of contention that separate many Catholics and Protestants.

First, Protestants generally express suspicion about Mary's immaculate heart and assumption of her soul and body into heaven at the end of her life because they do not find the teaching explicitly taught in Scripture. In fact, the idea that Mary's heart is immaculate or sinless might suggest to some that she is not in need of salvation. Scripture is quite clear that all people (which would include Mary) are in need of salvation from sin through Jesus who alone is our mediator before God (see for example 1 Tim 2:4–5), as we are corrupt as a result of the universal fall and our fallen condition. Similarly, Protestants generally express severe caution about any sign of recognizing Mary in a unique manner in the church since they fear such recognition will make her a co-mediator with Jesus for our sins. The following statement will raise suspicions in many Protestant minds, namely, that Mary was/is "the Mother of God" and she alone is "called to share in and co-operate in his [Jesus'] redemptive sufferings."[35] While for Protestants generally, Mary does not "share in and co-operate in [Jesus'] redemptive sufferings," she does have theological significance in that Mary really is the Mother of God through whom the second person of the eternal Trinity came into this world and was made human (as is accounted for in the teaching of the *theotokos*). Those who deny this theological claim fail to safeguard the unity of Jesus' person against the threat of Nestorianism with its assertion that Jesus has two personal centers—one divine and one human. Moreover, while it is true that the teaching that Mary was assumed body and soul into heaven at the end of her life does not have clear biblical warrant, Catholics do make a theological point worth considering that is derived from the unique bond between Jesus and Mary. Here is one such articulation:

---

34. CatholicCulture.org, "Solemnity of the Assumption."
35. Catholic News Agency, "The Immaculate Heart of Mary."

Mary's Assumption: An Unassuming Heart and Honor

Even as incarnate Word, God does not want to grow in her in such a way that he uses her for a time and then drops her when he has achieved his purposes. He uses her wholly; therefore he uses her without temporal limits, and when he allows her to give him everything constantly in her human fashion, he also gives her everything in his divine, eternal fashion. The Mother is not separated from the fruit that she brings forth; after the birth she does not cease to be mother and bearer. Rather it is part of her fruit that she becomes the Mother of all Christians. Her own fruitfulness is the fruit of her assent; in this the Son shows her his gratitude. He does not want simply to proceed from her life the effect from the case; he also wants his Mother to be the effect of her own case, a cause whose beginning lies in the decree of grace decided upon between the Father and the Son.[36]

We all make theological assumptions that reflect presuppositions of various kinds regarding Mary. No doubt, the debate over Mary between Catholics and Protestants will continue, not simply on August 15, the day Catholics recognize Mary's assumption into heaven, but throughout the church year. Yet hopefully, in the midst of the clear and strong differences, both traditions can come together to recognize Mary's importance in various ways. While not exhaustive, here are a few such items of importance. God's selection of Mary highlights God's elevation of the humble and lowly and judgment on the proud and mighty in every age. Moreover, Mary's decision to obey God and accept the call to be the Mother of the Messiah reflects her pure devotion to God and her son—especially in our "age of sensuality and materialism," as already noted. Furthermore, Mary's special bond with Jesus, who also cherished her as his mother, reflects the special place awarded to womanhood here on earth and in eternity, as she is rightfully hailed as a great and foundational saint along with the apostles and worthy of recognition throughout time and in the age to come. We close by contemplating the *Magnificat*. No matter our theological take on the Catholic teaching of Mary's assumption and her immaculate heart, these words should unite all Christians in affirming her unassuming honor and dignity that also reflects the heart of God:

And Mary said,

> "My soul magnifies the Lord,
> and my spirit rejoices in God my Savior,
> for he has looked on the humble estate of his servant.
> For behold, from now on all generations will call me blessed;

---

36. Speyr, *Handmaid of the Lord*, 43.

VII—Ordinary Time: Follow Jesus in the Spirit to the End!

for he who is mighty has done great things for me,
and holy is his name.
And his mercy is for those who fear him
from generation to generation.
He has shown strength with his arm;
he has scattered the proud in the thoughts of their hearts;
he has brought down the mighty from their thrones
and exalted those of humble estate;
he has filled the hungry with good things,
and the rich he has sent away empty.
He has helped his servant Israel,
in remembrance of his mercy,
as he spoke to our fathers,
to Abraham and to his offspring forever." (Luke 1:46–55)

MARY'S DORMITION: WORTH LOSING SLEEP?

The last entry engaged the subject of Mary's assumption or exaltation to heaven at the end of her life. Mary's dormition, derived from the Latin word *dormire*, which means "to sleep," focuses on her death. The Orthodox honor the end of Mary's life on August 15. The date also marks for the Eastern Church Mary's subsequent resurrection and assumption. One source provides a good summary of Mary's dormition and how the Eastern (Byzantine) and Western (Latin) churches place emphasis on different aspects of Mary's life's culmination:

> Catholics of the Latin tradition often assume that Mary's final end has been sufficiently addressed by the dogma of the Assumption, that is, her translation, body and soul, into heaven as defined by Pius XII in 1950. But as glorious as the mystery of her Assumption is, it represents only one dimension of the mystery of the end of Mary's life. There is also her death and subsequent resurrection. On this subject, Pope Pius remained silent, choosing not to address the subject of Mary's mortality. The Byzantine tradition, however, as part of the universal and fully Catholic patrimony of the Church, is not silent on this topic. It guards a rich treasury of teaching, iconography, and liturgy concerning the end of Mary's life.
>
> According to the tradition of the Byzantine East, the Assumption was the final stage of Mary's transition into the glory of heaven. This Analepsis or "translation" of Mary to eternal life was preceded by what was called the Koimesis or "sleep" or Mary in death. These three events—her death, her resurrection, and her assumption into heaven—complete the mosaic of the holy end of Mary's life . . .[37]

---

37. Dozier, "Mary's Assumption."

VII—Ordinary Time: Follow Jesus in the Spirit to the End!

The interested observer may come away asking whether there is enough import with Mary's dormition to lose sleep over it. Considering the preceding account, the answer will likely vary depending on one's tradition and perspective.

As was stated in the last entry, many Protestants will lose sleep over any significant role being awarded to Mary other than her being a virgin and the mother of Jesus. They may not appreciate either the title "Mother of God" taken from *theotokos*, which can also be translated "God bearer." But as was briefly noted in the article on Mary's assumption, the claim that Mary is the Mother of God says as much about Jesus' identity as it does about Mary's status. The idea that she bore God signifies that Jesus' deity and humanity are not separate from one another, as with Nestorianism, which teaches that Jesus is constituted of two natures and two persons. Rather, as articulated in Chalcedonian Christology, there is one person, who has two natures—one divine and one human. Thus, *theotokos* signifies that Mary bore in her womb the second person of the eternal Trinity who became human.

Some Roman Catholics may lose sleep over the idea of Mary's dormition in keeping with Pope Pious XII's determination to remain silent on Mary's mortal state, as specified above in the quotation. These Catholics may wish to focus on her exalted state at the culmination of life, which they may feel is jeopardized by emphasizing to any degree her mortality.

For the Orthodox, the dormition is worth losing sleep over in that it is part and parcel of the culmination of Mary's life, and in the mind of some, key to maintaining the distinction between Jesus and his mother. According to Orthodox New Testament scholar John Breck,

> In our Orthodox tradition we are usually very careful to distinguish between the "Dormition" of the Mother of God and her "Assumption" into heaven. The former, we feel, is properly Orthodox, while the latter strikes us as a purely Western designation, derived from a Roman Catholic "misunderstanding" of the meaning of this feast, celebrated universally on August 15.
> It is true that some very genuine yet misguided interpretations of Mary's death and exaltation can be found both in Catholic spiritual writings and in contemporary Western icons: a tendency, for example, to exalt the Holy Virgin to a level of "divinity" that effectively erases the crucial and absolute distinction between human and divine life. Orthodox theologians will insist that the "deification" (*theôsis*) known by the Mother of God in no way involves an ontological transformation of her being from created humanity to divinity. She was and will always remain a human creature: the most exalted of all those who bear God's

image, yet always a human being, whose glory appears in her humility, her simple desire to "let it be" according to the divine will.[38]

While Roman Catholicism will certainly beg to differ with Fr. Breck's judgment of a "tendency" to erase the fundamental distinction between God and humanity in Mary's case, it is also worth noting that Breck along with other Orthodox also wish to highlight Mary's resurrection and exaltation to heaven by her Son Jesus. She becomes the "first fruits" of the eschatological fulfilment for the new humanity in Jesus.

In a discussion of this important day in the Orthodox Church, along with the icon representing the dormition, the Greek Orthodox Archdiocese of America claims:

> This great Feast of the Church and the icon celebrates a fundamental teaching of our faith—the Resurrection of the body. In the case of the Theotokos, this has been accomplished by the divine will of God. Thus, this Feast is a feast of hope, hope in Resurrection and life eternal. Like those who gathered around the body of the Virgin Mary, we gather around our departed loved ones and commend their souls into the hands of Christ. As we remember those who have reposed in the faith before us and have passed on into the communion of the Saints, we prepare ourselves to one day be received into the new life of the age to come.
>
> We also affirm through this Feast as we journey toward our heavenly abode that the Mother of God intercedes for us. Through Christ she has become the mother of all of the children of God, embracing us with divine love.[39]

Whether we fall asleep unto death to be raised later or transfigured if we are alive at the Lord's appearing, we can take hope in knowing that Jesus' mother awaits us as the mother of all the church. We can also take comfort in knowing that she along with others in the great cloud of witnesses (Heb 12:1) cheer us on until the day when our faith becomes sight.

Having reflected upon Mother Mary, who may be considered the greatest of saints, the next entry on the church calendar will address this great cloud of witnesses. This great cloud extends throughout time (diachronic) as well as across the globe in the form of a community of faithful witnesses at this time (synchronic).

---

38. Breck, "Dormition or Assumption?"
39. Greek Orthodox Archdiocese of America, "Dormition of the Theotokos."

THE CHURCH CALENDAR REORDERS US: COMMUNAL PAST AND PRESENT

The church calendar reorders us in time. How so? For example, the ecclesial calendar helps us see ourselves in communal relation to the saints who have gone before us over the span of the centuries and in communal relation to the saints dispersed across the expanse of the earth today. As it relates to the church of the ages and global church, the span of the centuries concerns "through time" (*diachronic*) and the time frame of all people alive today (or at any one period) across the earth concerns this time or "together time" (*synchronic*). As we consider the lives of saints who are honored during the church year, and as we recite the liturgy and pray in unison every week in churches across the earth, we find that the church calendar reorders our past and present to expand our sense of community. We are not alone. There is a great cloud of witnesses that surrounds us.

In the last two entries on the church calendar, we discussed the assumption (exaltation to heaven) and dormition (mortal sleep) of Mary, who in my estimation, is the first great patron saint of the church as Jesus' mother. Iconic paintings of Mary's mortal sleep picture her with the Apostles Peter and Paul at her head and feet and elders and bishops in the church standing around them (with Christ above them). We belong to this great cloud of witnesses, as I noted in the entry on Mary's dormition.

The biblical text for the "great cloud" imagery is found in Hebrews 12:1: "Therefore, since we are surrounded by so great a cloud of witnesses, let us also lay aside every weight, and sin which clings so closely, and let us run with endurance the race that is set before us . . ." This "great cloud of witnesses" hearkens further back than the apostolic community, as it includes the great cloud of witnesses pictured in Hebrews 11 that highlights the saints portrayed in the Hebrew Scriptures. They include Abel, Enoch, Abraham, Isaac, Jacob, Joseph, Moses, and Rahab. Whether or not they are conscious of us in their eternal abode, we are to be conscious of their

The Church Calendar Reorders Us: Communal Past and Present

faithful witness. Moreover, we should be mindful of other faithful witnesses to Christ throughout the centuries and in our world today.

It is so very easy for American Christians like myself to falsely think that the church began with my conversion and that the Christian faith is all about me. If we attend church, we may be inclined to think in terms of how the services and programs benefit us individually rather than how each of us integrate into the community of faith as vital parts or members of an even greater whole. Given such an individualistic focus, it is vitally important that we see ourselves as connected to the community of faith throughout the centuries and throughout the earth today. Hebrews 11 and 12:1 highlight the importance of the community of faith throughout time whereas Hebrews 10:24–25 highlights the importance of the community of faith in our time (read Heb 10:24–25). We will take up the subject of the temporal future, namely, the "day drawing near" (Heb 10:25) in the next entry on the church calendar. For now, consideration centers only on the past and present.

Protestants are often wary of awarding attention to saints, since Protestantism tends to view all Christians as saints. While we who are Protestants should certainly cherish the Reformation teaching of the priesthood of all believers (derived from such texts as 1 Pet 2:5), we all too easily slip into deferring to certain pastoral figures to act as priestly functionaries to do all the heavy lifting.

We who are Protestants may also easily point to the errors of those in other traditions who come close to worshiping saints. But that does not mean we should throw out the saints with the dirty practice bathwater. As with icons, saints are not meant to be worshiped, but to be viewed as windows through which we see God. As Paul writes to the Corinthians to "Be imitators of me, as I am of Christ" (1 Cor 11:1)—we are to imitate faithful witnesses to Christ to become more like Christ ourselves.

Saints like Polycarp (d. 155), Francis of Assisi (d. 1226), and Mother Teresa (d. 1997) have much to teach us. In his homily declaring Mother Teresa a saint, Pope Francis claimed:

> Mother Teresa, in all aspects of her life, was a generous dispenser of divine mercy, making herself available for everyone through her welcome and defence of human life, those unborn and those abandoned and discarded. She was committed to defending life, ceaselessly proclaiming that "the unborn are the weakest, the smallest, the most vulnerable." She bowed down before those who were spent, left to die on the side of the road, seeing in them their God-given dignity; she made her voice heard before the powers of this world, so that they might recognize their guilt

VII—Ordinary Time: Follow Jesus in the Spirit to the End!

for the crime—the crimes!—of poverty they created. For Mother Teresa, mercy was the "salt" which gave flavour to her work, it was the "light" which shone in the darkness of the many who no longer had tears to shed for their poverty and suffering.[40]

The pope goes on to state that Mother Teresa serves as a "model of holiness" for us. Here she resembles Mother Mary. Such modeling and ordering does not begin and end on days dedicated to their honor like August 15 for Mother Mary or September 5 for Mother Teresa. Their example shines bright every day of the year. Of course, there are other people past and present who operate in saintly ways as models of holiness and compassion for us each and every day. Such saintly people do not have to achieve official sainthood to make an indelible mark on our lives. Imitate them as they imitate Christ Jesus.

The church did not begin with us. Nor will it end with us. We are surrounded by a great cloud of witnesses that spans the entire history of the church and indeed salvation history, as well as spans the entire earth here and now. Such communal encouragement creates in us greater courage to model saintly lives as well for those who come after us. The church calendar with its pageantry of saintly models reminds and reorders us in our worship of God in unison through the ages and across the globe. We are not alone.

---

40. Francis, "Holy Mass and Canonization."

MARK YOUR CALENDARS DAILY FOR CHRIST'S RETURN

The church calendar has no singular day marking Christ's return to judge the nations, bring history as we know it to a close, and usher in the kingdom of God in its fullness. Rather, every Lord's Day or Sunday is intended to help us make preparations (in addition to the Advent season, as well as Christ the King Sunday at the close of the year). That's wise, since Christ himself said no one knows the day and the hour: "But concerning that day and hour no one knows, not even the angels of heaven, nor the Son, but the Father only" (Matt 24:36). With this point in mind, we must always remain ready for Christ's return, as the Lord exhorts his listeners: "Therefore you also must be ready, for the Son of Man is coming at an hour you do not expect" (Matt 24:44).

Having reflected last Sunday upon the significance of the church calendar for ordering our lives in relation to the past and present people of God, we now address how the future return of Christ should mark each Christian's life every day of the church year. Hebrews 10:24–25, which was referenced in last Sunday's entry, exhorts the saints to come together regularly to encourage one another increasingly in their lives of faith as the day of the Lord's second coming approaches: "And let us consider how to stir up one another to love and good works, not neglecting to meet together, as is the habit of some, but encouraging one another, and all the more as you see the Day drawing near" (Heb 10:24–25).

It is wise to be mindful at all times of the mighty acts of God in history as well as the eschatological future. After all, Jesus is the Alpha and Omega, the beginning and the end. His incarnation and resurrection mark the entry point into the eschatological future, which penetrates every instant of time so that it is possible for us to live every second as a *kairos* moment. John Paul II puts it this way in "Tertio Millennio Adveniente": "*Christ is the Lord of time;* he is its beginning and its end; every year, every day and

VII—Ordinary Time: Follow Jesus in the Spirit to the End!

every moment are embraced by his Incarnation and Resurrection, and thus become part of the 'fullness of time.'"[41]

Certainly, the global church takes to heart the liturgical calendar to remember the history of salvation centered in Jesus and to recall faithful witnesses to him over the centuries through the Spirit of Pentecost in order to prepare for Jesus' second coming. In addition to preparing for Jesus' second coming as the Advent season approaches at the end of Ordinary Time in late November, we also prepare throughout the year, as highlighted by the Lord's Day every given Sunday. John Paul II eloquently makes this point in his encyclical letter "Dies Domini," which exhorts God's people to keep the Lord's Day holy:

> As the Church journeys through time, the reference to Christ's Resurrection and the weekly recurrence of this solemn memorial help to remind us of *the pilgrim and eschatological character of the People of God.* Sunday after Sunday the Church moves towards the final "Lord's Day," that Sunday which knows no end. The expectation of Christ's coming is inscribed in the very mystery of the Church and is evidenced in every Eucharistic celebration. But, with its specific remembrance of the glory of the Risen Christ, the Lord's Day recalls with greater intensity the future glory of his "return." This makes Sunday the day on which the Church, showing forth more clearly her identity as "Bride," anticipates in some sense the eschatological reality of the heavenly Jerusalem. Gathering her children into the Eucharistic assembly and teaching them to wait for the "divine Bridegroom," she engages in a kind of "exercise of desire," receiving a foretaste of the joy of the new heavens and new earth, when the holy city, the new Jerusalem, will come down from God, "prepared as a bride adorned for her husband" (Rev 21:2).[42]

Every Sunday, we remember the Lord's life here on earth. Every Sunday, we recount his resurrection, realizing he is not dead, but alive and returning. Thus, Jesus' past is never really past. With every passing Sunday, we move forward to the ultimate Lord's Day that will never end.

William Faulkner penned the famous line "The past is never dead. It's not even past."[43] Similarly, salvation history is never dead. It's not even past. So, too, the eschatological future is never distant. It's already here. In fact, it's been here since Jesus' first coming. Jesus began his public ministry

---

41. John Paul II, "Tertio Millennio Adveniente," §10.
42. John Paul II, "Dies Domini," §37
43. Faulkner, *Requiem*, 73.

preaching, "Repent, for the kingdom of heaven is at hand" (Matt 4:17). Peter's first sermon includes words from Joel 2 to explain the meaning of the descent of the Spirit with the display of signs and wonders on the Day of Pentecost. From its inception, the church has been living "in the last days" (Acts 2:17).

Let's pause for a second. To be honest, it's not easy to remain ready since we've been living "in the last days" for a very long time. Rather, it's easy to get sluggish and slack off in staying alert and awaiting Christ's return as the liturgical season moves on through the various Sundays of Ordinary Time every given year. Easter and Pentecost seem so long ago now that we are in late August. Add to that two millennia since Jesus walked the earth.

Ordering our time according to Ordinary Time in the church calendar should help us stay the course. Rather than focus our attention only on the climactic events of Jesus' passion and resurrection, Ordinary Time trains our eye to view Jesus' entire life, teaching, and parables and what they entail for discipleship during our earthly sojourn. Part and parcel of this focus on Jesus' entire life and teaching involving parables is to help us when we come down from the mountain of the Epiphany and Easter seasons and walk about in the valleys below during Ordinary Time. Now more than ever, we need help liturgically in setting the spiritual clocks to be on time for Jesus.

Mention was made of parables. Jesus' parables include consideration of faithful service in view of the harvest at the end of the age. The liturgical calendar's emphasis on Jesus' teaching and parables during Ordinary Time helps us in our efforts to remain mindful of Jesus' coming to reward his harvest workers. August belongs to the harvest season, which extends through November. The harvest season falls within Ordinary Time, whose liturgical color is green for growth and development to maturation.

Here it is worth noting that the church celebrates the Season of Creation beginning on September 1. This season is a month in duration and will receive treatment in what follows. We are to be good stewards of creation as Jesus' disciples, just as we are to be faithful servants who invest the talents we have received from the Lord.

Speaking of creation, Jesus often draws attention to the creation in his parables. Take for example the parable of the Sower, Seed, and Soils. May we be like seed sown on good soil, the kind that hears God's word, understands and obeys it, the kind that makes possible growth and maturation bearing much fruit (Matt 13:18–23). Consider the Parable of the Wheat and Weeds. May we be like the harvested wheat gathered and stored in the Master's barn (Matt 13:24–30).

Jesus always instructs us to be vigilant. We are to be like wise virgins who fill their flasks with oil as they prepare to greet the bridegroom (Matt

VII—Ordinary Time: Follow Jesus in the Spirit to the End!

25:1–13). We are to be servants who are trustworthy with the talents the Lord gives us so that God will entrust us with stewarding much more at his return (Matt 25:14–30). Jesus moves from these parabolic exhortations to offer a mix of haunting and hopeful words about the great judgment and separation of the sheep and goats. Live to hear Jesus calling us his sheep, not goats (pray over Matt 25:34–40). In view of Jesus' parables and instructions on his return, let's mark our calendars daily to remain ready. The time is at hand.

PRAY FOR CREATION CARE TODAY

How often have you and your church prayed for the care of creation? If you can't recall ever praying for the care of creation, today would be a good day to start. September 1 marks the beginning of the Season of Creation in the church calendar with the World Day of Prayer for the Care of Creation.[44] Before delving deeper into this subject, let's further embed this day and month in its liturgical and salvation-historical context.[45]

It is worth noting that the Season of Creation extends for approximately a month's time, as it concludes on October 4 with the Feast of St. Francis. St. Francis is hailed in various ecclesial traditions as the patron saint of ecology. It is fitting that St. Francis's namesake, Pope Francis, declared in August 2015 that September 1 would be the World Day of Prayer for the Care of Creation,[46] an occasion celebrated by the Orthodox Church since 1989. Earlier in the same year, Pope Francis published his encyclical "Laudato Sí," which is focused "On Care for Our Common Home."[47]

It is also fitting that the Season of Creation begins in September, which is part of the harvest season. As we move toward the end of the calendar year in Ordinary Time, we also consider how best to prepare for the Lord's return at the end of the ages. Faithful service in this life, which includes the Genesis mandate at the beginning of the biblical narrative to have dominion as in care for the creation, is certainly part of what is entailed for the church to prepare for Jesus' return.

Our dominion in creation is subject to the Lord's sovereign care. Thus, we cannot do as we wish with the creaturely realm but must care for it wisely

---

44. Society of the Holy Child Jesus, "World Day of Prayer."

45. For liturgical resources of value for this season in the church life or for all seasons from an environmental or ecological perspective, see the following: Habel et al., eds., *The Season of Creation*; Rowthorn and Rowthorn, *God's Good Earth*. Refer also to the following resource: "Season of Creation."

46. O'Kane, "Pope's Appeal to Pray."

47. Francis, "Laudato Sí."

and moderately as tenants in God's vineyard. As Karl Barth remarked, we do not have ultimate dominion over the creation. Humans have dominion in the creation. God alone has ultimate dominion over the creation. When we separate our lordship in the creation from consideration of God's lordship over all, including humanity, we readily move toward subjecting the creation to idolatrous and abusive control.[48] Thus, we must be very careful not to treat spirituality in a completely otherworldly manner that views praying and caring for creation odd and irrelevant.

Such otherworldly separation manifests itself in various other ways. It may involve the separation of science and religion, or nature and grace, whereby we surrender reason to autonomous human control or discount reason in favor of blind, irrational faith. Hans Urs von Balthasar addresses the polarization of faith and reason, asserting that there is no place for the "dialectical opposition between 'knowledge' and 'faith.'" "God's sovereign freedom" does not fall "under the judgment of human reason." The worldly order and reason do not necessitate or make possible the cross. Rather, "the light of the Cross makes worldly being intelligible," as it shines a light on God's imprint of love throughout the whole of creation.[49] Whenever such integration involving the harmonious relation of nature and grace in keeping with knowledge and faith is lost, Balthasar writes,

> worldly being will necessarily fall under the sign of the constant dominion of "knowledge" and thus science, technology, and cybernetics will overpower and suffocate the forces of love within the world. The result will be a world without women, without children, without reverence for the form of love in poverty and humility, a world in which everything is viewed solely in terms of power or profit-margin, in which everything that is disinterested and gratuitous and useless is despised, persecuted, and

---

48. Harrison has critiqued White's famous claim that *orthodox* Christianity is at the ideological root of the current ecological crisis. See Harrison, "Subduing the Earth." See also White Jr., "The Historical Roots," 1203–7. One of the points Harrison makes is that the rendering of "dominion" as total mastery of the world so popular today does not arise from ancient and medieval (orthodox) readings of the biblical narrative, but from early modern interpretations: "In the seventeenth century we find practitioners of the new sciences, preachers of the virtues of agriculture and husbandry, advocates of colonization, and even gardeners explicitly legitimating their engagement with nature by appeals to the text of Genesis. The rise of modern science, the mastery of the world that it enabled, and the catastrophic consequences for the natural environment that ensued, were intimately related to *new* readings of the seminal Genesis text, 'Have dominion.'" Harrison, "Subduing the Earth," 96; italics added.

49. Balthasar, *Love Alone*, 141–42.

wiped out, and even art is forced to wear the mask and features of technique.[50]

This worldly system does not view the creation as God's handiwork to cherish and inhabit, but as a handy commodity to exploit and discard. From another angle, such separation leads to championing faith and discounting science, whereby the latter is perceived simply as another version of fake news. While there is good reason to be wary of scientific exploits that are bound up with efficiency and technique, economic profit margins, and political gains that undermine human flourishing, the solution is not to equate scientific exploration itself with fake news. Those who employ "fake news" rhetoric often do it for the very same reason: efficiency and technique, economic profit margins and political short-term gains that do not promote the long-term well-being of our planet and the human race.

So, let's pray for the creation today. Let's pray for wisdom in providing holistic and strategic care as humans in stewarding well the creation as tenants in God's vineyard. Let's pray for sacrificial love and prudence. Let's pray against greed and waste. Let's pray against the divorce of grace and nature, against the divorce of faith and knowledge, against the divorce of faith and science that involves disrespect and dismisses discourse that cherishes the distinctive contributions of each domain. Otherwise, the current ecological crisis that affects the most vulnerable human populations and other life forms will continue.

Contrary to what is often argued, orthodox Christianity was not responsible historically for the current environmental crisis (in contrast to Lynn White's claim referenced in a footnote earlier). However, if we who are Christians stand idly by and do nothing to combat environmental devastation presently, we will be held responsible along with others for the growing ecological crisis.[51] So, as we rest from our labors with Labor Day upon us, let's recall how God rested and looked upon all he created as good, indeed as very good (Gen 1:31). Let's pray during the Labor Day weekend Sabbath rest and throughout this liturgical season for creation's flourishing and act accordingly. May we realize that if we truly love the Creator, we will love the creation, protecting and nurturing our world until Christ, the high priest of creation, returns to reign from earth. With these points in mind, I end this reflection on the World Day of Prayer for the Care of Creation with the closing words of Pope Francis' prayer in "Laudato Sí":

---

50. Balthasar, *Love Alone*, 142.

51. For an evangelical treatment of global climate change, see my article, "Thinking Globally."

VII—Ordinary Time: Follow Jesus in the Spirit to the End!

God of love, show us our place in this world
as channels of your love
for all the creatures of this earth,
for not one of them is forgotten in your sight.
Enlighten those who possess power and money
that they may avoid the sin of indifference,
that they may love the common good, advance the weak,
and care for this world in which we live.
The poor and the earth are crying out.
O Lord, seize us with your power and light,
help us to protect all life,
to prepare for a better future,
for the coming of your Kingdom
of justice, peace, love and beauty.
Praise be to you!
Amen.[52]

---

52. Francis, "Laudato Sí," para. 246.

"LET THERE BE LIGHT!" —DON'T TAKE IT LIGHTLY

This is the second entry on the Season of Creation, which many ecclesial traditions celebrate every year. On September 1, which marks the start of the Season of Creation, we honored World Day of Prayer for the Care of Creation. Church liturgies for the Season of Creation vary from year to year in highlighting which aspects of creation to celebrate on particular Sundays. In light of such variance, I have decided to highlight certain dimensions of the creation featured in the Genesis creation account, beginning with light.

I often take light for granted day and night. All it takes for me to remember how much I need light is for a power outage to occur and the house to go dark. It can be very destabilizing, especially if one does not have a working flashlight to hand. The Genesis creation narrative portrays the world as formless and void, and without any light: "In the beginning, God created the heavens and the earth. The earth was without form and void, and darkness was over the face of the deep" (Gen 1:1–2). The closest I came to experience anything of this envisioned sort of darkness was during a summer vacation from college many years ago when several friends and I decided to stay overnight in a cave—far away from the cave entrance. The cave was cold, damp, and completely dark—once we turned off the flashlights. Of course, I was not alone, as my friends and some bats shared the cave with me. So, I cannot cross the infinity of difference between what I experienced in that cave and what the Genesis account suggests.

Given that cave man context, I greatly appreciate that the Genesis account of creation begins with God declaring "Let there be light." While I could turn on my flashlight, once I fumbled around to locate it in the dark, my light would eventually phase out due to the battery's limited lifespan. In my case, I was dependent on another source for light. In fact, I always am. In contrast, God is the source of all light and indeed all energy, according to Genesis. God made everything: "In the beginning, God created the heavens

VII—Ordinary Time: Follow Jesus in the Spirit to the End!

and the earth" (Gen 1:1). One might think that given our dependence on light from sources external to ourselves at every turn, whether it be a flashlight, a lamp plugged into an outlet, headlights, or the sun, moon, and stars in the sky, we would never take light for granted. But we so often do, that is, until our light sources burn out.

We read reports of how someday in the very, very distant future the sun will burn out.[53] I can only imagine what that would entail for life here on earth or elsewhere in our solar system. The sun is essential for illumining the day, not to mention that it casts its glow on the moon at night. We read other reports of how smog blocks the sun's rays, which impacts negatively our employment of solar energy.[54] We read still other reports of how air pollution has partly destroyed good ozone in the upper atmosphere: "Called stratospheric ozone, good ozone occurs naturally in the upper atmosphere, where it forms a protective layer that shields us from the sun's harmful ultraviolet rays. This beneficial ozone has been partially destroyed by manmade chemicals, causing what is sometimes called a 'hole in the ozone.'"[55]

As with the Son of God around which the Christian calendar revolves and who gives us life and makes it possible for us to flourish spiritually, we should not take the sun for granted. It provides illumination, heat, and is essential to growth and development. We should also be careful not to take the sun for granted when it comes to risks associated with such health problems as skin cancer and sun stroke. Along with the sun, we should be sure to treasure natural light that breaks through the darkness in so many ways.

Light features prominently in the Genesis account. Of course, we find God's declaration of "Let there be light" and "Let there be lights" on the first and fourth days respectively (read Gen 1:3–5; 14–19).

The declaration of light being the first of God's creative works is no doubt essential for the ordering of each day, including morning and evening. In other words, light refers to time in this creation narrative. This point on light's role in God's ordering each day bears repeating given that this essay falls within this book's treatment of Ordinary Time. We should never take light for granted during Ordinary Time, or any other season during the church year, given light's role in ordering life and creation, along with light's other important traits.

My daughter does not take light for granted. She loves a vibrant sundown and draws it to my attention. Often lost in my thoughts, I would easily miss the colorful pageantry of the night sky. I can learn a thing or two from

---

53. Wendel, "When Will the Sun Die?"
54. Zimmer, "Air Pollution."
55. "Ground-level Ozone Basics."

my daughter and from a NASA astrophysicist I know who does not take light for granted. She and other astrophysicists and astronomers I have met, no matter how scholarly and dignified, reflect the fervent and playful curiosity of children when they gaze in raptured wonder at stars in the night sky.

Then there's Vincent Van Gogh, whose post-impressionist art I cherish. His paintings boldly, vividly, and symbolically portray nature and even the night sky in ways that reflect something of the grandeur and mystery of the Genesis creation account. In a letter to his sister Willemien, Van Gogh expressed how he was "very sensitive to color and its particular language, its effects of complementaries, contrasts, harmony." As he wrote to his brother Theo, "Painters understand nature and love it, and *teach us to see*." Certainly, we find all these traits in his painting, *The Starry Night* (1889).[56]

Van Gogh presented symbolic imagery in his post-impressionist paintings. The Genesis creation account appears to express a fair degree of symbolism, too. St. Irenaeus of Lyons also made use of symbolism in affirming the creation. One of the Christian faith's premier theologians of creation, Irenaeus, did not take nature or creation for granted, but celebrated it robustly in his orthodox defense against Gnosticism. God is like a great artist and artisan who does everything through his two hands. For Irenaeus, these two hands signify the Son or Word and the Spirit.[57]

The early church with its symbolic and typological reading of the Hebrew Scriptures finds Trinitarian imagery in Genesis 1, where the Spirit of life hovers over the waters (Gen 1:2) and God brings into existence all of creaturely life through his word or Word (see Gen 1:3 for example: "And God said, 'Let there be light,' and there was light"). Surely, the opening verses of John's Gospel draw the alert reader's attention to the beginning words of Genesis: "In the beginning was the Word, and the Word was with God, and the Word was God. He was in the beginning with God. All things were made through him, and without him was not any thing made that was made. In him was life, and the life was the light of men. The light shines in the darkness, and the darkness has not overcome it" (John 1:1–5). We should take to heart Jesus as "the Sun of righteousness," as Clement of Alexandria highlighted. He confers great benefits on humanity through his appearance.[58]

In succeeding essays on the Season of Creation, we will have opportunity to draw attention to God's two hands—the Son and Spirit—and consider how a Trinitarian account of creation does not take the creation for

---

56. See MoMALearning.
57. Refer here for example: Irenaeus, *Against Heresies*, 531.
58. Clement, "How Great," 203–4.

VII—Ordinary Time: Follow Jesus in the Spirit to the End!

granted.[59] Just as we should not take light for granted, so we should not take the light of life (John 1:4), the light of the world (John 8:12), for granted. He who is the light, the solid rock, the one who through the Spirit pours out the water of life, he who is the lion and the lamb, who always works to bring us rest through the dove who is the Spirit of life, exhorts his people to cherish the creation during the Season of Creation and throughout the year.

---

59. Recent theological explorations that develop Irenaean trajectories concerning a triune doctrine of creation include Gunton's works: *The Triune Creator*; *The Christian Faith*.

HONOR GOD'S TEMPLE OF CREATION

This is the third reflection for the Season of Creation, which is part and parcel of church liturgy in many traditions. With this point on liturgy in mind, it is fitting that consideration be given to the creation narratives in Genesis 1 and 2 as liturgical texts. The creation as a whole, and specifically Eden, functions as God's temple over which God rules and humanity serves as priest.

We will discuss liturgy and temple in the context of addressing the second day of creation. On the first day, God declares that there be light. According to John Walton, "Day 1 speaks of time. Even if one thought it was about light, we cannot assume a physicist's concept of light—we have to think like ancient Israelites. Day 1 includes nothing material."[60] If the first day speaks of time, the second day speaks of inhabitable space (read Gen 1:6–8).

Here on Day 2, we find that God makes an expanse or firmament. Peter Enns claims: "The Hebrew word for this is *raqia* (pronounced *ra-KEE-ah*). Biblical scholars understand the *raqia* to be a solid dome-like structure. It separates the water into two parts, so that there is water above the *raqia* and water below it (v. 7). The waters above are kept at bay so the world can become inhabitable."[61]

According to Walton, Enns, and other biblical scholars, we need to embed our understanding of the creation narratives in their ancient context rather than view them with modern eyes. One scholar claims that in the biblical world and the surrounding context, a connection was often made between cosmology and temple liturgy. I will position this point in relation to the inhabitable space involving the canopy in what follows in this post. Jeff Morrow puts the matter about cosmology and temple liturgy in this way: "This association between Temple and creation is not unique to the

60. Walton, "Material or Function?"
61. Enns, "The Firmament."

VII—Ordinary Time: Follow Jesus in the Spirit to the End!

Genesis text... In fact, temples throughout the ancient Near East often had cosmological connotations. The building of a temple often accompanied creation, as we find in the *Enuma Elish* and elsewhere."[62] That does not mean that the Genesis story is enslaved to the ancient Near Eastern worldview. It challenges it at points. My colleague Karl Kutz, who has also written on the Genesis creation account,[63] shared with me that the canopy image in Genesis 1:6 demonstrates that God situates the biblical account against the backdrop of the pagan myths, but then reframes the canopy image so that it is viewed not as part of God (or as a god) as one finds in many myths, but as declared into being by God.

To return to the point on liturgy, temple, and inhabitable space, the ultimate aim in God forming the canopy and making the earth inhabitable is so that humanity can dwell and rule in the creation as an expression of worship. Morrow, to whom I referred above, claims that Eden is the Holy of Holies of God's temple of creation and humanity is its *Homo liturgicus*. He concludes his treatment of the creation account in this way:

> If Eden is the Holy of Holies in God's Temple of creation, the implication is that humanity, created for this inner sanctuary, is best understood as *Homo liturgicus*. Living in the Holy of Holies, humanity is called to give worship to God in all thoughts, words, and deeds. When we look at the Genesis account of Eden, we find other instances of people portrayed as created for worship. Adam, for example, is told to "till" (from the root 'bd) and "keep" (from the root šmr). When šmr and 'bd occur together in the OT (Num. 3:7–8; 8:25–26; 18:5–6; 1 Chr. 23:32; Ezek. 44:14) they refer to keeping/guarding and serving God's word and also they refer to priestly duties in the tabernacle. And, in fact, šmr and 'bd only occur together again in the Pentateuch in the descriptions in Numbers for the Levites' activities in the tabernacle. Such an association reinforces the understanding of Adam as a sort of priest-king, or even high priest, who guarded God's first temple of creation, as it were. In light of this discussion, therefore, what we find in Genesis 1–3 is creation unfolding as the construction of a divine temple, the Garden of Eden as an earthly Holy of Holies, and the human person created for liturgical worship.[64]

---

62. Morrow, "Creation," 7.
63. Kutz, "Genesis 1:1–2:3," 3–13.
64. Morrow, "Creation," 12–13.

Honor God's Temple of Creation

Against this backdrop, it appears fitting to view the canopy as containing God's tabernacle or temple where God meets with us and where we serve as priests in Eden and in creation.

As we will see when we get to the end of Genesis 1 and beginning of Genesis 2 in this series on the Season of Creation, God rests or rules from his temple. According to Walton, God ran the cosmos from the temple. For Walton, God resting (See Genesis 2:2) entailed God getting down to business and ruling over the creation he had ordered. It did not entail taking a break.[65]

God did not go off on holiday at the end of ordering the world and Eden for our habitation. God continues to rule. When we rest on the Sabbath, we are to remember that we ourselves are not God, and that the world is not God. We serve God who continues to rule over the entire temple of creation. We are to remember that we serve throughout the week and throughout life as royal priests in creation whereby we cherish and guard the creation as God's temple.

In keeping with Genesis's treatment of humanity serving as royal priests in creation, the New Testament instructs us that the church is a royal priesthood (1 Pet 2:9). The Season of Creation and the Sabbath or Lord's Day place reminders in our annual and weekly routines that we can and must break the apparently unending cycle of restless work, achievement, and consumption as a royal priesthood. The Sabbath urges us to say "no" to the unending cycle of business as busyness and craving for more.[66] Such restless striving keeps us from becoming whole and does not allow the creation to rest.

As difficult and as traumatic as the coronavirus pandemic has been for people across the globe at the time of this writing, hopefully we have taken the occasion to reassess our lives, drives, and what is most important—life itself as well as sound, loving relationships with God, other people, and the creation as a whole. Regardless, though, of whether we have taken this occasion to reflect carefully on what matters most, the pandemic shutdown has given rise not only to economic stimulus packages but also to environmental stimulus for the healing of the creation.[67]

We who are the church need to reset our spiritual clock in our service as a royal priesthood. We need to trust God who never stops working on our behalf to provide. After all, God is the creator of the entire universe and the risen Christ is the high priest and "firstfruits" of the new creation (1 Cor

---

65. Walton, "Understanding Genesis 1."
66. See for example Brueggemann, *Sabbath*.
67. Consider these reports: Nixdorf et al., "The Coronavirus"; Rogers, "LA's Skies."

VII—Ordinary Time: Follow Jesus in the Spirit to the End!

15:20, 23). In him, we are called to be a form of "firstfruits" of all that God created (Jas 1:18), which occurs when we manifest the fruit of the Spirit rather than the fruit of the flesh (Gal 5:19–26).

The Season of Creation and the Sabbath remind us that what is called nature is not divine. As God's creation, it requires rest from our labor, just as we do (see for example Lev 25:12; Exod 23:10–11). May it not take global pandemics to put a halt to our activity through fear, but in faith and gratitude may we stop and gather together each Sabbath to celebrate God's provision as Creator and Sustainer.[68] The God who reconciles all things to himself in the risen Christ who is the firstborn of all creation and head of his body the church (Col 1:15–20) will make all things new in heaven and on earth (Rev 21:5). The Spirit and Bride invite us to enter God's Sabbath rest and find nourishment (Rev 22:17) and bring an end to consumptive patterns of disorder during Ordinary Time.

---

68. See the insightful discussion of overlapping themes in Davis, *Scripture*, 78–79.

CONFESS TO GOD AND FELLOW HUMANS —BUT PLANTS?

This is the fourth entry dedicated to the Season of Creation. It is timely that we address plants this week, since it was around this time in 2019 that Union Theological Seminary students made public confession to plants during a chapel service. A Union Seminary tweet reads:

> Today in chapel, we confessed to plants. Together, we held our grief, joy, regret, hope, guilt and sorrow in prayer; offering them to the beings who sustain us but whose gift we too often fail to honor.
> What do you confess to the plants in your life?[69]

The tweet about confession drew strong reactions on Twitter, including the charge of "absolute theological bankruptcy."[70] For many conservative Christians, such symbolic actions signify New Age ways of thinking. The Twitter storm should cause us to seek shelter in Christian Scripture in search of nuanced understanding of our proper relation to the creation, including plants.

What does Christian Scripture have to say about creation? Scripture speaks of creation revealing and declaring God's glory (see for example Ps 19:1 and Rev 1:19–20). Scripture records Jesus' striking claim that the stones would cry out if people did not praise God in view of Jesus' miracles (Luke 19:40). The Law warns that the land will spit God's people out of the land if they defile it (Lev 18:28). The Bible also includes Paul's words that the whole creation groans waiting for humanity's redemption (Rom 8:22).

While the Bible says a great deal about creation, we should ask whether it includes mention of confession to plants. Certainly, Scripture exhorts us to make confession to God. Confession in public or in private should

---

69. Union Seminary, "Today in chapel."
70. Brown, "'Absolute Theological Bankruptcy.'"

VII—Ordinary Time: Follow Jesus in the Spirit to the End!

include confession of our sins to God (1 John 1:9). We are also to confess our sins to one another (Jas 5:16). But what about plants? As best as I can recall, no mention is made in the Bible of public or private confession of various kinds to plants, or other parts of the nonhuman creation.

Now, regardless of the theological rationale for the Union Seminary students or others making confession to plants, Scripture is quite clear that we have a responsibility as humans to care for the creation and not to sin against God by mistreating the creation. Such care includes the humane treatment of animals in the Hebrew Scriptures.[71] One Jewish source reads:

> Several commandments demonstrate concern for the physical or psychological suffering of animals. We may not plow a field using animals of different species (Deut. 22:10), because this would be a hardship to the animals. We are required to relieve an animal of its burden, even if we do not like its owner, do not know its owner, or even if it is ownerless (Ex. 23:5; Deut. 22:4). We are not permitted to kill an animal in the same day as its young (Lev. 22:28), and are specifically commanded to send away a mother bird when taking the eggs (Deut 22:6–7), because of the psychological distress this would cause the animal. In fact, the Torah specifically says that a person who sends away the mother bird will be rewarded with long life, precisely the same reward that is given for honoring mother and father (Ex. 20:12; Deut. 5:16), and indeed for observing the whole Torah (Deut. 4:40). This should give some indication of the importance of this law.[72]

Care for the creation extends to the land itself. God commanded Moses that Israel was to provide a Sabbath rest for the entire land. There was to be no sowing fields, pruning vineyards, harvesting or gathering in that seventh year (Lev 25:1–5).

The preceding remarks signify that Scripture is quite clear on humans having a responsibility to care for the creation, signifying that our dominion (see Gen 1:26, 28–29) does not permit us to treat creation in any way that we

---

71. Neither Judaism nor Christianity offer blood sacrifices. Certainly, the destruction of the Temple in AD 70 was a principal reason. Today, the Day of Atonement involves sacrifice in the form of intense prayer and fasting. For Christians, as the Epistle to the Hebrews makes clear, Jesus brings an end to the rationale for animal sacrifice. It is striking that the Day of Atonement, which the Jewish people celebrate this time of year, often falls during the month of September, which also marks the Season of Creation. While animal sacrifices were central to the Jewish Law and life of ancient Israel, there were important legal stipulations in place concerning the humane treatment of animals. See Sears's volume, *The Vision of Eden*.

72. Rich, "Treatment of Animals."

Confess to God and Fellow Humans—But Plants?

please. And yet, as those who alone are created in God's image according to the Genesis account (Gen 1:26–27), humanity is the pinnacle and center of creation. Moreover, the Genesis account makes quite clear that the creation is not divine, and that the God of Israel is the one who makes and orders all the creation. We find such divine singularity in forming/ordering the creation in day three when God brings order to the creation through plant life (read Gen 1:11–12).

Unlike other ancient creation stories that involved creating out of deities or that acknowledged celestial powers as deities,[73] the Genesis narrative proclaims that the God of lowly and little ancient Israel, not the gods of the superpowers, was responsible for creating and ordering the whole universe.[74]

Walton, who claims that the first three days of the Genesis 1 narrative are about functions (day one—time; day two—weather; day three—food)[75] and the last three days are about functionaries, reasons that the world functions for humankind's benefit and as a place for God to dwell with the divine image-bearers. Regarding the functional role of creation, Walton writes,

> As we actually read the text's account of each day, finding the focus on organization and ordering rather than the manufacture of material objects, we should be letting it shape our ideas about the narrator's intentions. God is articulating his vision for a world that will function for the benefit of humankind and as sacred space where God will dwell in relationship with them.[76]

Speaking of benefit for humankind, the Genesis 1 account makes clear that plant life was given to us and the animal creation for food (Gen 1:29–30).

The preceding reflections give us much food for thought. Whatever you think about the Union Seminary students' public confession to plants, we should all acknowledge that plants are very beneficial, indeed essential to our sustenance as God's image bearers and that we often fail to value them.[77] In the midst of the Twitter storm, we could learn a great deal not only from Scripture but also from St. Francis of Assisi (to whom we will return on the entry to close out the liturgical Season of Creation), whom Pope John

---

73. BioLogos, "How long are the days?"
74. Enns, "Genesis 1."
75. Erickson, "To Function." See also Walton, *The Lost World*.
76. Walton, "Material or Function."
77. Please note that the Union Seminary students sought to highlight the significance of valuing plants in providing sustenance for us and how we often fall short of proper regard for plant life. For a good, balanced article on the Union Seminary students' confession, refer to Huleatt, "Progressive Seminary Students."

VII—Ordinary Time: Follow Jesus in the Spirit to the End!

Paul II hailed as "heavenly Patron of the cultivators of ecology."[78] While I do not know if St. Francis ever spoke to plants, he did preach to animals and extolled the creation's worth to God. In his "Canticle of Creation," Francis praises God for creation, including plants, which, as noted above, the Genesis 1 account makes clear were given to us and the animal creation for food (Gen 1:29–30):

> Praised be You, my Lord, through our Sister Mother Earth,
>
> Who sustains and governs us,
>
> And who produces varied fruits with colored flowers and herbs.[79]

No good person harms their mother but cherishes her. Similarly, we should cherish the earth from which we come and to which we return (Gen 3:19). We should cherish fruit and vegetables of many kinds that sustain us, and flowers of many colors, that give us joy to strengthen us in the midst of life's struggles and sorrows. With these points in mind, it is worth tweeting Francis's Canticle of Creation during the Season of Creation. Why not make public confession and offer up praise to God by praying St. Francis' canticle today?

---

78. John Paul II, "Inter Sanctos."
79. Francis of Assisi, "Canticle of Brother Sun," 39.

HOW GODLIKE ARE HUMANS FUNCTIONING ON EARTH?

This is the fifth entry for the Season of Creation. Here we move from plant life to the animal creation and humanity as the pinnacle of creation. But how well are we humans functioning in our esteemed role of rule in the creation?

Speaking of function, biblical scholar Nancy Erickson reflects on her colleague John Walton's discussion of functions and functionaries in Genesis 1. Days 1 to 3 of the creation story deal with functions in Walton's account (days 1 to 3 are about time, weather, and food respectively). Days 4 to 6 deal with functionaries. Humanity's function is to operate in a "godlike capacity in relationship to the rest of creation." Here's Erickson:

> Following the normal literary structure of Genesis 1, Walton now explains days four through six as describing the installation of functionaries and their roles associated specifically with their inhabited space: celestial bodies in their sphere (day four), creatures and cosmic space (day five), and animals in terrestrial space (day six). The end of the chapter is devoted to the functions assigned humanity, rightly highlighting humankind as the climax of the creation account and whose functions, among procreating and subduing or ruling other creatures, includes functioning primarily in a godlike capacity in relationship to the rest of creation (i.e. in God's image).[80]

The question arises at this point: how godlike are we functioning as humans here on earth? Before going further, pause to read the Genesis 1 account of days 4 to 6, which for Walton depicts celestial bodies, sea creatures, animals, and humans functioning in their respective domains of space (Gen 1:14–31). Now that you have read the passage, let's focus attention

80. Erickson, "To Function."

VII—Ordinary Time: Follow Jesus in the Spirit to the End!

on humanity's particular functions in creation. In my estimation, central to humanity's godlike functions as being created in God's image is conscious reflection on the universe around us. While there is more to our relational constitution concerning our connection to God, to one another, and to the nonhuman creation, conscious reflection is certainly part of what makes us human. Such consideration of human uniqueness is not limited to the realm of biblical studies.

According to Br. Guy Consolmagno of The Vatican Observatory, one of the characteristic traits that makes us human is "the ability to look at the sky with wonder." Dr. Jeff Hardin at The University of Wisconsin says that whenever he looks through a microscope, he "cannot help but be struck with a sense of awe and wonder." Whether looking through a telescope or a microscope, a sense of "awe and wonder" pervades the human and scientific quest for understanding. As Dr. Jennifer Wiseman of the American Association for the Advancement of Science (AAAS) and NASA claims, it is our task as human societies, faith communities, and philosophers to "dig deep" and discover what the message is that is "beyond just what science is telling us."[81]

Humane reflection is godlike reflection—thinking God's thoughts after God. It does not involve that form of mundane mastery with our minds and then with our hands that simply aims to control the environment and use it merely to make a profit or to engage in mere sport. Rather, the sense of awe and wonder that makes us truly human involves a sacred regard for all life. Otherwise, we ourselves lose that dimension of existence that makes us distinctive. That is what happens when we try to play God rather than be like God.

The modern dismissal of the sacred with the rise of scientific positivism led to what Max Weber called the "disenchantment" of the world. Such disenchantment easily leads to alienation and opposition.

> Weber used the German word *Entzauberung*, translated into English as "disenchantment" but which literally means "de-magic-ation." More generally, the word connotes the breaking of a magic spell. For Weber, the advent of scientific methods and the use of enlightened reason meant that the world was rendered transparent and demystified. Theological and supernatural accounts of the world involving gods and spirits, for example, ceased to be plausible. Instead, one put one's faith in the ability of science to eventually explain everything in rational terms. But, for Weber, the effect of that demystification was that

---

81. For these reflections on the scientific quest, refer here to an excellent video: American Association for Advancement of Science, "Awe and Wonder."

the world was leeched of mystery and richness. It became disenchanted and disenchanting, predictable and intellectualized. In that sense, the disenchantment of the world is the alienating and undesirable flip side of scientific progress.[82]

Astronomers Wiseman and Consolmagno and biologist Hardin share none of this sense of disenchantment. While one does not have to be a person of faith to view the universe with wonder, and while one can argue for matter's enchantment from a purely naturalist orientation,[83] it is important for people of faith to pursue a constructive and mutually respecting alliance involving faith and reason, religion and science, nature and grace, as Balthasar (noted earlier) envisioned. Without such mutual respect in this shared pursuit involving faith and science communities, we will only go deeper into disenchantment, detachment, and disregard for the creation.

Those who explore the universe with a sense of awe and wonder not only grasp the grandeur of the universe, but also guard against grasping to exploit it. They realize that no matter how powerful and majestic nature is, life is very precious, and its harmonious balance on which we depend for our own existence is intricate and even fragile. So, may we look to the stars and skies, the seas and the dry land where abundant life teems, with a sense of awe and wonder rather than arrogant disregard. May we never take life in all its fecundity and mystery for granted. Otherwise, those who come after us may not be able to experience the goodness and beauty of our world, but rather face the very real threat of its destruction and our extinction as a race.

In closing, it is worth noting that while astrophysicists and astrobiologists go in search of life beyond earth,[84] a new study claims that it might be much harder to find advanced life than many scientists imagine. An AAAS article titled "New Study Dramatically Narrows the Search for Advanced Life in the Universe" includes a tag line that reads "Toxic gases limit the types of life we could find on habitable worlds." According to the study's lead researcher, Edward Schwieterman, "showing how rare and special our

---

82. Chua, "Disenchantment."

83. "The problem of meaninglessness arises only if 'matter' is conceived as inert, only as long as science deploys materialism whose physics is basically Newtonian." Bennett, *Enchantment*, 64. Bennett deploys "enchanted materialism," which involves conceiving matter as having "a liveliness, resilience, unpredictability, or recalcitrance that is itself a source of wonder for us." She contrasts her position with Weber's "disenchanted materialism" that opposes spirit to matter where matter is essentially "lifeless stuff" (64). For another work seeking to demonstrate a potent countertrend in modernity for providing forms of re-enchantment compatible with secular reason, see Landy and Saler, eds., *Re-Enchantment*.

84. Shreeve, "Life Probably Exists."

VII—Ordinary Time: Follow Jesus in the Spirit to the End!

planet is only enhances the case for protecting it." He continues, "As far as we know, Earth is the only planet in the universe that can sustain human life."[85] May we humans also be rare and special, even godlike, by protecting the masterpiece of creation. Only as we contemplate and cherish the world and universe in all its vibrant glory do we function well as humans created in God's image.

---

85. EurekAlert!, "New Study." See also the original study: Schwieterman et al., "Limited Habitable Zone."

CARE FOR THE CREATION: FEASTING WITH ST. FRANCIS AND ST. KATERI

This entry marks the conclusion to our feature treatment of the Season of Creation. The Season of Creation ends every year with the Feast Day of Saint Francis of Assisi on October 4. However, that does not mean our remembrance, celebration, and care for the creation should come to an end until the month of September next year. May we honor and cherish the creation every day of the year in worship and service to Jesus our Lord.

In the preceding entry for the Season of Creation, discussion centered on whether humanity functions well in the creation as a steward of all God's handiwork. God made humanity—male and female—to have dominion in the creation. Dominion does not suggest controlling and destroying nature but ruling in Eden as gardeners and caretakers.

One man and one woman who functioned well in relation to nature, and in relation to other humans, were St. Francis of Assisi and St. Kateri Tekakwitha. Separated by several centuries and thousands of miles, these two saints teach us how to live in relation to the entire creation not simply on their saint days but throughout the year. As many Christians celebrate this feast day, let's interact and learn from this honorable patron and matron.

St. Francis (d. 1226) is known as the Patron of Animals and Ecology. We know Francis as one who identified with the poor and who was a man of peace with all people (including his exchange with the Sultan of Egypt during the Crusades), not simply those belonging to Christendom. But his sense of family went even further than humanity. As one biographical sketch indicates, "Francis' brotherhood included all of God's creation. Much has been written about Francis' love of nature but his relationship was deeper than that. We call someone a lover of nature if they spend their free time in the woods or admire its beauty. But Francis really felt that nature, all

VII—Ordinary Time: Follow Jesus in the Spirit to the End!

God's creations, were part of his brotherhood. The sparrow was as much his brother as the pope."[86]

Many of us know the story of St. Francis turning a ferocious wolf that terrorized a community into its friend, or the tale of his preaching to animals. St. Francis is perhaps the most well-known saint in Christian history. Far less known is St. Kateri Tekakwitha. Earlier in the church calendar year, on July 14 to be exact, many Christians around the world now honor St. Kateri Tekakwitha, Lily of the Mohawks (d. 1680). In 2011, Pope Benedict named her a saint. She is the first Native American Catholic saint. According to one article, St. Kateri is the "patron of the environment, Native Americans, people in exile, and people ridiculed for their piety."[87] Another article (by the same author) refers to her as "Patron saint of ecology and ecologists. Patron saint of the environment, environmentalism, and environmentalists. Patron of exiles, and orphans. Patron for those ridiculed for their faith."[88]

St. Kateri's mother was an Algonquin and a Catholic. She was kidnapped by a Mohawk tribe, adopted into the tribe, and married the chief. Kateri was born to them, but then later her mother died. Kateri eventually became Catholic, like her mother. But the Mohawks were wary of her faith. She was an orphan and an exile and found spiritual solace in nature. How does this personal history bear upon Kateri being a patron saint of ecology and the environment? One of the articles on St. Kateri beautifully puts it this way:

> The intersection of ecology and environmentalism demands the vision of those who can look beyond the crowd, who can hear beyond the noise.
>
> And who is better suited to look and hear beyond the crowd than one who stands apart from it? By their very nature, the exile stands apart from society, and is able to observe and catalog it in ways those accepted by the greater group cannot. Then couple the exile status with that of orphan, one who longs for mother and father, and the tendency of an exile toward cynicism is tempered and softened with love and longing for the group. This paring, of exile and orphan, invites us to stand apart from the consensus, but not to grow unnecessarily callous toward it.[89]

---

86. Catholic Online, "St. Francis of Assisi." For a classic study of St. Francis, see Chesterton, *Saint Francis of Assisi*.

87. Donaldson, "St. Kateri Tekakwitha, Lily."

88. Donaldson, "St. Kateri Tekakwitha., Care of Creation"

89. Donaldson, "St. Kateri Tekakwitha., Care of Creation" For a study of St. Kateri, see Cavins, *Lily of the Mohawks*.

Care for the Creation: Feasting with St. Francis and St. Kateri

We can learn a great deal from patron saints Kateri and Francis, who lived in harmony with nature and who identified in different ways with the downtrodden and outcast. Rather than interacting with nature and fellow humans in a post-fallen manner, as in Genesis 3, where there is strife between all forms of life, they lived in keeping with the creation mandate in Genesis 1 that leads to the flourishing of all creation.

In addition to the creation mandate in Genesis 1, we should also account for the new creation envisioned in Colossians 1, which depicts Jesus as the firstborn of all creation, the firstborn from the dead, and head of the body—the church. Unlike Adam whose wife was Eve, Jesus is united to his church, which includes St. Francis and St. Kateri. Jesus transforms the creation, making all things new. Those who belong to the church should live in view of him who reconciles all things to himself through the peace of his life-giving blood shed on the cross (stop here to read Col 1:15–20).

The Christian calendar helps us to view all of time and space as endowed with the presence of him through whom and for whom all things were created. It is the church's task to remember Jesus and his lordship over all powers, in heaven and on earth, and throughout every season. After all, he is before all things in rank and time and he holds all things together. Like patron saints St. Francis and St. Kateri, may we honor, cherish, and protect the creation every day of the year in worship and service to Jesus our Lord. Also, like them, may we ensure that the orphans, the exiles, and those in poverty experience the spiritual solace and nourishment that God's creation provides.

THE CHRISTIAN LIFE: PILGRIMAGE THROUGH THE YEARS

Today marks the beginning of the Jewish pilgrimage festival known as Sukkot, the Feast of Tabernacles.[90] This feast lasts one week. It is one of three pilgrimage festivals in the Jewish tradition. The other two are Passover,[91] which Christians honor at the time of Jesus' death, and Shavuot,[92] which is also known as the Feast of Weeks or Pentecost, which Christians associate with the Spirit's descent. As Christians make their way through the church calendar, may we realize that the entire Christian life is one of pilgrimage throughout the years. We will focus on what is entailed by our distinctively Christian pilgrimage in this entry.

Before we go further, though, it would be good to provide a brief overview of these Jewish festivals and their historical backdrop.[93] Passover marks the momentous occasion when God commanded each Jewish household to sacrifice a lamb and brush the blood on the top and sides of the door frame of the home so the angel of death would pass over when he destroyed the firstborn offspring of Egypt and delivered Abraham's descendants from slavery in Egypt (Exod 12). Shavuot marks the landmark event when God gave Moses the Law at Mount Sinai (Exod 19–24). The Law signified the way of life the Jewish people were to honor in covenantal communion with God. The third pilgrimage festival, Sukkot, marks the dramatic wandering of Israel in the wilderness for forty years before entering the Promised Land (Num 32–33). These three occasions are called pilgrimage festivals because God's people were commanded to travel to God's dwelling place, ultimately Jerusalem, and celebrate them according to the instructions provided in

90. My Jewish Learning, "Sukkot."
91. My Jewish Learning, "Passover (Pesach) 101."
92. My Jewish Learning, "Shavuot 101."
93. For a detailed engagement of the Jewish calendar and holidays, see Telushkin, *Jewish Literacy*, part 13.

The Christian Life: Pilgrimage through the Years

the Law (see Num 28-29 for a list of these feasts along with other holy occasions).[94]

During the festival of Sukkot, the Jewish people were commanded to live in booths or huts. This tactile symbolism would help the generations to come to remember God's presence and provision during their wilderness wanderings. It is worth noting here that so much of biblical history focuses on pilgrimage and wandering, including the exodus and exile. Add to that how yearly, on three separate occasions, the people of Israel made their way to Jerusalem, the city where the temple stood, and which signified the location of God's presence.

How does the preceding discussion of Jewish pilgrimage feasts or festivals bear on the Christian life as one of pilgrimage? And what is distinctive about Christian pilgrimage? Regarding the first question, the church's story is not separate from Israel's story, but builds on and develops it.[95] Thus, we must account for Jewish holy days and festivals, including those pilgrimage holidays already mentioned, as well as Rosh Hashanah (Jewish New Year) and Yom Kippur (Day of Atonement), which are commemorated and celebrated this time of year. These two events are often considered the greatest Jewish religious holidays. Other holy days and festivals include Purim and Hanukkah.[96]

Some Christians may be quick to discount these holidays. But it is hard to make sound sense of Jesus and the church's mission when we remove the Christian faith from its Jewish roots and source. Jesus did not come to abolish the Law, which contains the underpinnings for these holy days and festivals, but to fulfill the Law (Matt 5:17). So, if we discount the Law, we unwittingly discount Jesus' context and make it impossible to grasp his complete story, which includes consideration of Israel's history.

---

94. Kohn, "Pilgrimage Festivals?"

95. Given how important time is to Israel, time must be important to the church as well. Abraham Heschel writes on the importance of time in the Jewish faith and way of life. See Heschel, *The Sabbath*. According to Heschel, "Judaism is a *religion of time* aiming at *the sanctification of time* . . . Judaism teaches us to be attached to *holiness in time*, to be attached to sacred events, to learn how to consecrate sanctuaries that emerge from the magnificent stream of a year" (8). Later Heschel writes, "The sanctity of time came first, the sanctity of man came second, and the sanctity of space last. Time was hallowed by God; space, the Tabernacle, was consecrated by Moses . . . The meaning of the Sabbath is to celebrate time rather than space. Six days a week we live under the tyranny of things of space; on the Sabbath we try to become attuned to *holiness in time*. It is a day on which we are called upon to share in what is eternal in time, to turn from the results of creation to the mystery of creation; from the world of creation to the creation of the world" (10).

96. My Jewish Learning, "Rosh Hashanah"; My Jewish Learning, "Yom Kippur"; My Jewish Learning, "Purim 101"; My Jewish Learning, "Hanukkah 101."

VII—Ordinary Time: Follow Jesus in the Spirit to the End!

The New Testament requires Christians to come to terms with the Jewish Scriptures. John's Gospel records three Passovers (John 2:13, 6:4, 13:1). Luke's Gospel records Jesus traveling to Jerusalem for the Passover when he was a child (Luke 2:41–42). John 8 alludes to Sukkot. In John 8, Jesus refers to himself as the Light of the world against the likely backdrop of scores of lights streaming from the booths and tents surrounding Jesus and illumining the night sky during the festival in Jerusalem. Hebrews 9–10 highlights the Day of Atonement. Acts 2 places the Spirit's descent on the Day of Pentecost or Shavuot, fifty days after Jesus' life-giving Passover offering.

Christians do not remember these days in isolation from Jesus. But we do well to remember that we only make proper sense of Jesus in relation to them. These pilgrimage festivals help us situate ourselves between our own exodus from bondage to slavery and sin in Egypt to wilderness wanderings between Egypt and Babylon involving exile and remnant life in the diaspora as we make our way by faith to the hoped-for Promised Land, which Jesus establishes for us.

Now we come to the second question: what is distinctive about Christian pilgrimage? The answer quite simply is Jesus. He is our ultimate Sabbath rest in the Promised Land (Heb 4). He is also our Passover Lamb who actualizes atonement for us as he takes away the sin of the world (John 1:29). Moreover, whereas Moses went up on the mountain to get the Law, Jesus went up on the mountain in the wilderness to give the Law. See Matthew 4 for the temptation and Matthew 5–7 for Jesus' delivery of the Law of his kingdom, that is, the Sermon on the Mount. Mention was already made of the festival of booths or tabernacles, which shows up in John 7 and 8. Jesus refers to himself there as the Light of the world, who lightens our path so we need not walk in darkness but experience the light of life.

The Passover celebration and Day of Atonement point to him, according to the entire biblical narrative, which for Christians includes the Old and New Testaments. Shavuot also points to him as the ultimate goal and embodiment of the Law (Matt 5–7). The Scriptures also point to him as the source of salvation (John 5:39–40). Even the temple and Jerusalem point to him. John 2 records that Jesus views his body as the ultimate temple where God dwells (John 2:18–22). Moreover, it is not on this or that mountain where God's people will worship. Rather, they can worship anywhere while on pilgrimage as they center their worship in Jesus in spirit and in truth (John 4:19–26).

So, where does all this discussion lead us as we seek to come to terms with Christian pilgrimage? For one, we need to know where we come from. Apart from Israel's history and story, we would be at a loss. Israel is part of the church's family tree. We must learn from their faithful commitment

The Christian Life: Pilgrimage through the Years

over the generations, which Hebrews 11 highlights, as well as their failures, as illustrated in the wilderness wanderings and later disobedience leading to exile. We also need to know where we are going. Abraham and the saints of old never received what they were looking for. Only together with us will they gain it—or rather, him—that is Jesus, our Sabbath rest: "And all these, though commended through their faith, did not receive what was promised, since God had provided something better for us, that apart from us they should not be made perfect" (Heb 11:39–40).

Until that time, we walk by faith, not by sight. And so, as a people on pilgrimage, we must never think we have arrived, get comfortable with where we are, or seek to return to Egypt. After all, we still have not found what or who we are looking for. We move forward, not simply to the close of the church calendar year, but to Jesus' return at the end of the age. During this week, when Jewish people celebrate Sukkot, may we, the apostolic community, see Jesus as our temple who is where God tabernacles with us (John 1:14). May we, the church, also see ourselves as God's temple community (1 Cor 3:16–17), not one that is stationary, but ever on the move, sharing life with others rather than hiding behind metal, wood, brick, and stained glass, longing for that day when we no longer "see through a glass, darkly," but see him "face to face" (1 Cor 13:12, KJV).

HONOR DISABILITY AWARENESS SUNDAY AND THE DIFFERENTLY ABLED

October is National Disability Employment Awareness Month.[97] Disability Awareness Sunday also falls in October in some church traditions. Different church traditions recognize Disability Sunday at various times of the year.[98] Given that Disability Month falls within Ordinary Time, which involves reordering us as believers in the pursuit of maturation in Christ Jesus, we need to grow in awareness and appreciation for the many ways those with disabilities can enrich society and the church and celebrate them. The Bible reorients us so that we move from disordered and distorted ways of viewing our fellow divine image bearers to see them as worthy of our time.

Rather than shut people with disabilities down, Jesus affirms their persons and their agency. Take for example the story of "Blind Bartimaeus" in Mark 10:46–52 (please read it). We find here that many in the crowd of people following Jesus tried to silence Bartimaeus when he cried out to Jesus to have mercy on him. Jesus, however, stopped in his tracks, called Bartimaeus to come to him, asked Bartimaeus what he wanted Jesus to do for him, and then affirmed his active faith after healing him. Bartimaeus, in turn, followed Jesus on his journey.

How often do we try explicitly or implicitly to silence people who want to recover their sight, or who desire to be able to walk? And if we do engage them, how often do we encourage them to take the first step toward recovery of sight or wholeness in some way? Jesus stops in his tracks. Jesus wants

---

97. What Can You Do?, "Celebrate National Disability Employment Awareness Month."

98. See for example: Reformed Church in America, "Disability Awareness Sunday Resources"; We Give: The United Methodist Church, "July 24—Disability Awareness Sunday"; DisAbility Ministries: The United Methodist Church, "Disability Sunday Order of Worship."

Honor Disability Awareness Sunday and the Differently Abled

Bartimaeus to come to him. How often do we ask them openly what they would like done, like Jesus did, rather than presume we always know best what they need or say it for them? How often do we affirm their agency in having the courage to cry out for help to be made whole so they don't have to continue begging based on fostered impositions of dependency? How often do we affirm their agency rather than point to our charity in aiding them? While Jesus obviously healed Bartimaeus of his blindness, Jesus does not take the credit, but credits Bartimaeus, affirming his agency and human dignity.

Numerous stories could be shared of Jesus healing people with disabilities. I will share a portion of one other account. Earlier in Mark's Gospel, we find the moving story of the man who was let down through an opening in a roof to receive healing (read Mark 2:1–5). Like the man who received assistance in getting to Jesus, sometimes those with disabilities simply need greater access. Sometimes those around them need to express agency and assist with providing access. Here those who carried the paralytic man on his bed did not allow the inaccessible room from street level to stop them, but creatively sought a solution to gain access, even if that meant taking the roof off the place! Jesus affirms their faith, not simply the paralytic's desire to be healed. How about us? Are we people of faith who creatively try to provide access for those with disabilities to flourish, or do we take overcrowded, inaccessible rooms as closed doors to solutions at home, in the workplace, the marketplace, or at church?

Now there may be times when God does not heal people of disabilities. How many of us have a disability that God has not healed? How many of us need glasses or contacts, or resort to having laser surgery on our eyes? How many have need of hearing aids? Some of our disabilities are so common that we no longer view them as disabilities or handicaps. They have been made acceptable, normal. Moreover, whether disabled now or not, all of us, given enough time, will deteriorate when our once supposedly able-bodied state becomes a state of disrepair.

Going beyond the preceding reflections on physical states, we often approach disabilities in merely physically and medical terms, or fixate on visible disabilities and do not account for invisible disabilities that also require careful attention and care beyond stigma (October also recognizes "Invisible Disabilities" as part of Disability Awareness Month.[99]) Going further, how many of us who are seemingly able-bodied beyond apparent visible and invisible disabilities account for the possibility of ourselves being emotionally or relationally disabled? Often those with physical disabilities

---

99. Allsup, "Invisible Disabilities."

VII—Ordinary Time: Follow Jesus in the Spirit to the End!

are "differently-abled," a striking phrase my friend Jimi Calhoun uses in his book *The Sounds of Love and Grace*.[100] These individuals have adjusted beautifully to their life situations where they cultivate other qualities of existence to a greater degree than the general population. Often their resilience, flexibility, and problem-solving skills, awareness of people's needs, and emotional intelligence far outweigh the challenges they face physically. Do our churches and workplaces account for their strengths or pity them based on our narrow-minded and imagined perceptions of what wholeness looks like?

Criticisms are sometimes left at the doorstep of Christian Scripture that the only role a disabled person has in the Bible is to be healed. I disagree based on numerous items, including inferences drawn from the lives of Paul and Jesus. We'll engage this subject briefly, starting with Paul.

Certainly, we find instances in Scripture where God works powerfully by healing people of disabilities. But God can also work powerfully through people's disabilities. Consider Paul's discussion of his thorn in the flesh in 2 Corinthians 12:8–10. Could it be that sometimes a disability functions as a thorn in the flesh to lead people to rely on God to work wonders in and through their lives rather than depend on themselves? Could it be that the thorn in the flesh to which Paul alluded was a disability? Whatever the case, Paul relied more fully on God and experienced more divine power on account of his weakness or thorn in the flesh than if he had operated in his own strength. Moreover, those with disabilities who like Paul rely on God's amazing power amid their apparent weaknesses can inspire us to be creative in our suffering as we deal with weaknesses and thorns in the flesh of various kinds.

If reflecting on Paul's situation is not enough, consider Jesus. In our culture of "body beautiful," Jesus challenges us to rethink what is truly beautiful. Take, for example, Isaiah 53's treatment of the Messiah or Suffering Servant, which the church believes is fulfilled in Jesus (read the chapter). There was nothing about the Messiah or Suffering Servant's physical state that would draw us to him. The description of the Suffering Servant, as applied to Jesus, does not appear to be isolated to Jesus' foreshadowed passion and crucifixion alone, but likely accounts for his entire life. Couple that with Revelation 5, where the Lord Jesus bears the marks of his passion in his glorified state as "a Lamb standing, as though it had been slain" (Rev 5:6). While we do not know what the marks left from his passion and death entail for Jesus' agency, could it be that God desires that Jesus retains those marks to lead us to see that true beauty goes far deeper than the surface

---

100. Calhoun, *The Sounds*, 10.

of one's skin? "Body beautiful" in the Christian community must undergo significant change to account for this eschatological reality and cruciform aesthetic.

During and beyond National Disability Employment Awareness Month and this or that Disability Awareness Sunday, may we approach disabilities differently and with greater awareness in view of Jesus. May we recognize people of various life experiences, whom we often view as handicapped, as "differently-abled." May we also consider our own need to move beyond our handicapped imaginations and become more creative in providing access to those we often shut out due to what we see as normalcy, which is sometimes nothing more than projecting onto society what we ourselves are.

May we take more than a designated Sunday or special month to celebrate how special and beautiful people are in the midst of all our collective challenges, and how special our own "able-bodied" needs are for Jesus to heal us in view of his cruciform glory, which truly makes his church body and the world beautiful. May we take time throughout our days to make more time for those with disabilities. God will teach us and transform our sense of time as we interact with these fellow humans created in God's image. Instead of trying to master and subdue time or leave the "differently-abled" behind to get ahead, God will speak through them to free us from enslavement to rush hour ways of thinking and find rest in the fullness of Jesus' time.[101]

---

101. An important theological work addressing concepts of time in relation to disabilities is Swinton, *Becoming Friends*. See also Brock's recent work on disability theology: *Wondrously Wounded*.

ALL SINNERS' DAY

On November 1, many Christians celebrate All Saints' Day. In this light, I am honoring repentant sinners this Sunday and calling it "All Sinners' Day." As a son of the Reformation (which will also be celebrated this week on October 31), I share Martin Luther's view that the believer is simultaneously righteous and sinful. We are always completely dependent on Jesus, who is our righteousness. Apart from him, we stand before God as guilty—in a desperate state of unrighteous despair. We are blessed when we live as repentant sinners, abiding in God's mercy.

One place where we find this emphasis in Luther is in an early Reformation treatise titled *The Freedom of a Christian*, which Luther dedicated to the pope. Here Luther speaks of our being righteous in relation to Christ, not in ourselves. Luther uses marital imagery to convey this notion of relational union:

> Who then can fully appreciate what this royal marriage means? Who can understand the riches of the glory of this grace? Here this rich and divine bridegroom Christ marries this poor, wicked harlot, redeems her from all her evil, and adorns her with all his goodness. Her sins cannot now destroy her, since they are laid upon Christ and swallowed up by him. And she has that righteousness in Christ, her husband, of which she may boast as of her own and which she can confidently display alongside her sins in the face of death and hell and say, "'If I have sinned, yet my Christ, in whom I believe, has not sinned, and all his is mine and all mine is his,' as the bride in the Song of Solomon (2:16) says, 'My beloved is mine and I am his.'"[102]

Protestants following Luther are not alone in drawing attention to our desperate need for God's mercy. A Catholic online publication marks this thirtieth Sunday in Ordinary Time by drawing attention to the parable of

---

102. Luther, *The Freedom*, 604.

the self-righteous Pharisee and repentant tax collector praying in the Temple.[103] (Pause to read this account in Luke 18:9–14.) As the account reveals, Jesus directs his parable to those who trusted in themselves and their supposed self-righteous standing before God, while looking down their noses at those around them. Jesus warns them and us today that those who exalt themselves will be humbled, while those who humble themselves will be exalted.

We find in this parable that the Pharisee's prayer is self-referential, paralleling his self-righteous attitude. In other words, he thanks God that he is worthy of God's favor given all his good deeds and his favorable standing in comparison with godless people, like this tax collector. In refreshing contrast, the tax collector does not praise himself or compare himself to others. He keeps his head down while beating his breast and crying out to God for mercy. Jesus declares that the tax collector goes home that day justified, but not the Pharisee.

We will return to this theme in the next essay on Reformation Day. For now, we would do well to remember always that God exalts those who humble themselves and humbles those who exalt themselves (Jas 4:6). May our trust ever be in God, not ourselves, and may we never play the comparative righteousness game with others.

In closing, as you go to church this Sunday in Ordinary Time, keep in mind that the church is both a sanctuary of saints and a hospital of sinners. In fact, these two groups are really one. That is, the church is made up of saints who are sinners and sinners who are saints. May we wear both name tags today simultaneously ("Righteous" and "Sinful") and introduce ourselves to others in good Lutheran fashion: "Hello, I'm ____, a repentant sinner and holy child of God saved by grace. So glad you're here!" Moreover, may we encourage one another to live godly lives of gratitude daily in view of God's amazing mercy and grace.

---

103. CatholicCulture.org, "Ordinary Time: October 27th."

WHO WILL YOU BE ON HALLOWEEN —A REPENTANT MONK?

In addition to Halloween, October 31 marks the anniversary of the Protestant Reformation. The story goes that the date marks the occasion when the Catholic monk Martin Luther nailed his Ninety-five Theses on a church door in Wittenberg, Germany.[104] Although the historicity of the event has been debated, there's no debate regarding the impact (positive or negative) of Luther's reforming zeal. His central concern was the sale of indulgences. As one site indicates, "The practice of buying indulgences, which quasi replaced confession and allowed people to buy their salvation, was completely repulsive to Luther. He strongly believed that one lived a life of humility in order to receive God's grace."[105] The same site indicates that in no way did he intend to dismantle the Catholic Church with his treatise, but to quicken a discussion in the hopes of bringing an end to the sale of indulgences.

There's no way in the world Luther could have foreseen the impact his Ninety-five Theses had on the future of ecclesial and societal life in Germany and beyond. Luther and his Reformation have been celebrated and/or blamed for a whole host of phenomena. Here's how one article frames the impact:

> To repeat, Luther did not intend to break from the Catholic Church, but to seek its reformation from within as a loyal critic. History is filled with accounts of Luther and his Protestant Reformation being praised and/or blamed for various matters. One article put it this way: Protestantism has been "credited for restoring Christian truth or blamed for church divisions," wrote Valparaiso University historian Thomas Albert Howard, author of the new book *Remembering the Reformation*.

---

104. Luther, *The Ninety-Five Theses*.
105. Luther, *The Ninety-Five Theses*.

Who Will You Be on Halloween—A Repentant Monk?

But beyond its strictly doctrinal content, Mr. Howard wrote, Protestantism "has been regarded as a cause of modern liberalism, capitalism, religious wars, tolerance, democracy, individualism, subjectivism, nationalism, pluralism, freedom of conscience, modern science, secularism, and so much else."[106]

A few of my favorite theses among the ninety-five are the first three:

1. When our Lord and Teacher Jesus Christ said, "Repent, etc.," he meant that the entire life of believers be a life of repentance.

2. Jesus' saying does not refer to the sacrament of penance (that is, confession and satisfaction as administered by priests).

3. And it does not mean inner repentance only—mere internal repentance is useless if it does not produce external self-control of one's selfish desires.[107]

Inner repentance that manifests itself outwardly in concrete actions of love of God and neighbor rather than love of the flesh is what is needed. No purchase of indulgences can take its place. So, too, for Luther, no ceremonial act on the part of a priest (*ex opere operato*) can take the place of Christ as vicar and the Spirit who alone create the needed repentant faith of salvation in the believer's life.[108]

In any event, Luther's point on the entirety of the Christian life being one of repentance applies to all of us—to Protestants, Catholics, Orthodox, and beyond. One cannot simply dress up and play the part of a repentant monk one day a year, as on Halloween or Reformation Day. Nor should one ever think one can discard the church like a relic from the past. Repentance and reformation should take place daily, and always occur for the sake of the whole of Christ's church. The problem is never simply other people, or this or that institution. The problem of sin exists in all of us. Therefore, after putting away the Halloween costume, tricks and treats, we should get back to business and confess our sins to one another, clergy and laypeople alike, so that we might be healed: "Therefore, confess your sins to one another and pray for one another, that you may be healed. The prayer of a righteous person has great power as it is working" (Jas 5:16).

---

106. Smith, "Luther's 95 Theses."
107. Luther, *The Ninety-Five Theses*.
108. On penance, see Bainton, *Here I Stand*, 39, 58, 67, 73. See also Bainton, *Reformation*, 10, 29, 30, 47, 195; Thornton, *Broken*; and Bilinkoff, *Related Lives*.

ALL SAINTS' SUNDAY

Last week, we paid tribute to what I termed "All Sinners' Day." The focus was on the need to identify with the repentant tax collector rather than the self-righteous pharisee in Jesus' parable recorded in Luke 18:9–14. This Sunday, which is generally referred to as "All Saints' Sunday," we will focus on the need to identify with saints like the Apostle Paul, imitate their godly lives, and set a good example for others to follow. With this point in mind, we must not allow our past failures or those of others to get in the way of modeling saintly lives presently and in the future. It is worth noting at the outset that St. Paul painfully believed he was the least of the apostles due to how he had persecuted the church prior to becoming a Christian (1 Cor 15:9). Moreover, he recognized that he still had not attained the goal of the Christian faith (Phil 3:12–14). Even so, Paul struggled hard to set a good example for his fellow Christians to follow: "Be imitators of me, as I am of Christ" (1 Cor 11:1). We should do the same.

Before proceeding to consider the importance of imitating saintly people old and new, we need to consider those impediments that stand in our way of honoring All Saints' Day and Sunday and/or following saintly examples.[109] Unfortunately, many low-church Protestants who place little emphasis on church tradition tend to discount All Saints' Day and All Saints' Sunday. Reasons can include the later association of All Saints' Day with Halloween and wariness of the Roman Catholic teaching on Purgatory, which comes into play with All Souls' Day on November 2 (one day after All Saints' Day),[110] as well as the fear that Catholics' celebration of saints takes away from the centrality of Jesus Christ in Christian devotion. There is perhaps a more recent concern that is not necessarily associated with

---

109. For a helpful perspective, see Bratcher and Stephenson-Bratcher, "All Saints Sunday."

110. For articles on "All Saints' Day" and "All Souls' Day," see Cross and Livingstone, eds., *The Oxford Dictionary of the Christian Church*, 42.

All Saints' Sunday

Protestantism, namely wariness of any claim to saintliness or affirmation of its pursuit given the epidemic of cynicism. In what immediately follows, we will consider this problem and how Paul's exhortation to imitate his example as he follows Jesus Christ takes on even more importance in our cynical age.

We hear often enough of priest and clergy scandals involving sexual and financial abuses. Such infamous stories leave a devastating impact on the church. It's almost as if the church becomes a Halloween haunted house throughout the year with ghouls and ghosts and skeletons in the closet. While it is certainly true that we who are Christians should make sure that Christ Jesus—who will never disappoint us—is our focus, we cannot help but be shaken when those who are called to lead the way in imitating Jesus falter badly.

I recall a shaky situation a few years ago. I was speaking to a small group of Christian lay leaders who had grown disillusioned with the need to set a good example for others based on the poor example of a pastor mentor. As I unpacked Paul's exhortation found in different places in his epistles to follow his example as he follows Christ, they pushed back and said it was not possible or even credible for them to imitate Christ and encourage others to imitate their example. They had become disillusioned based on their mentor's duplicity.

Reports of scandalous activity of Christian leaders not only serve to distract us from gazing on Christ but also can cause us to forget the examples of others who are incredibly credible followers of Jesus and leaders in the Christian community. It is not simply saints like Paul of Tarsus or Francis of Assisi or Teresa of Calcutta or John Wesley (who loved All Saints' Day) or Corrie ten Boom and her family[111] who are worthy of honor. Simple saints past and present who virtually no one knows about also merit consideration. I love what this article at a Methodist site has to say about the matter:

> Alongside the likes of Paul from the New Testament, Augustine, Martin Luther, and John and Charles Wesley, we tell stories of the grandmother who took us to church every Sunday. We remember the pastor who prayed with us in the hospital, and the neighbor who changed the oil in the family car. We give thanks for the youth leader who told us Jesus loved us, the kindergarten Sunday school teacher who showered us with that love, and the woman in the church who bought us groceries when we were out of work.

The meditation continues:

---

111. See for example Ten Boom, *The Hiding Place*.

VII—Ordinary Time: Follow Jesus in the Spirit to the End!

> Retelling these stories grounds us in our history. These memories teach us how God has provided for us through the generosity and sacrifice of those who have come before us. The stories of the saints encourage us to be all God has created us to be.[112]

Further to this point on simple saints, my own parents' unadorned faith and daily sacrificial love were instrumental in my own return to faith from disillusionment with churchianity in young adulthood. Perhaps similar saintly examples impacted you. Now the question is: what kind of saintly impact are we seeking to have?

Whatever our background and experience, we need to do everything possible to set a good example for others to follow. All Sinners' Day, to which I paid tribute last week, must never overshadow All Saints' Day and Sunday (which is often when high church Protestants honor the occasion, since Protestants generally only attend church on Sundays for services). Let us make every effort to imitate Jesus well for those entrusted to our spiritual care, and regardless of whether or not we become famous like some of the saints of old. Faithfulness, not fame, is valuable. May we pursue faithful witness, not fame, and may we guard with every ounce of energy against infamy. Moreover, in the midst of negative examples that often derail us from setting our gaze on Christ Jesus, take time to reflect on the lives of faithful Christians who inspire us to follow Jesus daily until the end of the age. May we also take to heart the example of saints like the Apostle Peter and later John Newton, who faltered terribly at points along the way, but who fervently repented and renewed their commitment to follow Christ and lead by exemplary witness.[113] Don't let your past example or that of others trip you up. Get up. Look up. Get going.

The end of the liturgical year is fast approaching with Christ the King Sunday. In view of Jesus' example here on earth, his anticipated return, and the faithful witness of others, let us not spiral downward and fall short. Rather, let us keep pressing forward and upward until we win the prize of our upward calling in Christ Jesus (read Philippians 3:12–21).

---

112. Lovino, "All Saints Day."
113. See *Christianity Today*, "John Newton."

ALIVE ON EARTH AND IN THE AFTERLIFE

What is the connection between people here on earth and those in the afterlife? People across the world, whether adherents of a religion or not, often wonder about this question. On October 31 through November 2, many people give greater attention to this theme due to Halloween (October 31), All Saints' Day (November 1), and All Souls' Day (November 2). I will return to the latter two days shortly.

As I noted above, people across the world ponder the connection between people here on earth and those in the afterlife. In Japan, where I once lived, families welcome back the spirits of their ancestors during Obon or Bon in mid-August of every year. The Romans celebrated the "Feast of the Lamures" or "Lemuria," which, I believe, originally occurred on May 9, 11, and 13.

The Roman Catholic Church originally celebrated All Saints' Day on May 13, but then later moved it to November 1. According to one Catholic source, "The choice of the day may have been intended to co-opt the pagan holiday 'Feast of the Lamures,' a day which pagans used to placate the restless spirits of the dead." The following day, November 2, the Roman Catholic Church, celebrates All Souls' Day. According to the same source, "All Saints' Day is a solemn holy day of the Catholic Church celebrated annually on November 1. The day is dedicated to the saints of the Church, that is, all those who have attained heaven. It should not be confused with All Souls' Day, which is observed on November 2, and is dedicated to those who have died and not yet reached heaven."[114] According to an Anglican source, the church on earth and the earth in heaven are one: "the Church on earth is united with the Church in heaven ('sanctorum communio'). They speak of the 'Church Militant here on earth' and the Church triumphant in heaven.

---

114. Catholic Online, "All Saints' Day."

VII—Ordinary Time: Follow Jesus in the Spirit to the End!

They worship God together with 'angels and archangels, and with all the company of heaven.'"[115]

Christian churches do not universally celebrate these two days. Certainly, the controversy surrounding indulgences stemming from Martin Luther's Nintety-five Theses and Reformation Day had an impact. Many Protestant denominations do not commemorate All Souls' Day. Generally, Protestants have rejected the teaching of Purgatory, which is often associated with All Souls' Day. It is worth noting that Protestant leader John Wesley cherished All Saints' Day, and his brother wrote worship music resonating with the idea that the church is made up not only of the living, but also departed saints.

What is the connection between the living and the dead? Christian Scripture (at least the Protestant Canon) is not completely clear.[116] First Samuel 28 records the witch of Endor summoning Samuel's spirit from the dead to speak with Saul. Matthew 17 records the transfiguration of Jesus, where the disciples witness the Lord speaking with Moses and Elijah. Luke 16 records the supposed parable of the rich man and Lazarus, where the rich man exhorts Abraham to send back the beggar Lazarus to warn his brothers of God's coming judgment, suggesting his awareness or concern for loved ones' eternal destiny. Still another text, Revelation 7, records martyred saints calling on God to judge those on earth who persecuted and killed them (Rev 6). At least in these texts, there is no mention of saints on earth praying for the dead. The same goes for David in 2 Samuel 12, when David's infant son dies. David fasts and prays (v. 16) before his son's death for his recovery, but not immediately following his death. After his son's passing, David says, "While the child was still alive, I fasted and wept, for I said, 'Who knows whether the LORD will be gracious to me, that the child may live?' But now he is dead. Why should I fast? Can I bring him back again? I shall go to him, but he will not return to me'" (2 Sam 12:22–23).[117]

The preceding discussion is not intended to address the subject of Purgatory, but more broadly, the relation of the living to those in the afterlife. One of my favorite texts in this regard is Hebrews 12:1–2: "Therefore, since we are surrounded by so great a cloud of witnesses, let us also lay aside every weight, and sin which clings so closely, and let us run with endurance the

---

115. Avis, *The Anglican Understanding*.

116. For more on this subject, see the following article on Purgatory in which consideration is given to 2 Maccabees 12:46. Maccabees is included in the Roman Catholic Church's canon: "It is therefore a holy and wholesome thought to pray for the dead, that they may be loosed from sins." Martin, "What About Purgatory?"

117. Refer to the following articles on 1 Corinthians 15:29 and baptisms for the dead: Doriani, "What Does Paul Mean?"; Carson, "Did Paul Baptize?," 63.

race that is set before us, looking to Jesus, the founder and perfecter of our faith, who for the joy that was set before him endured the cross, despising the shame, and is seated at the right hand of the throne of God." Regardless of our understanding of the great cloud of witnesses (departed saints? martyred saints? conscious or unconscious? humans or angels?), all Christians can take joy in knowing that we have not run the race alone. Others have gone before us who have run the race well, even in the face of great adversity, persecution, and martyrdom.

Misery loves company, but even in misery, there is joy, especially as we look to Jesus, who is the joyous founder and perfecter of our faith. The Lord Jesus himself endured the cross and despised its shame for the joy set before him (Heb 12:1–2). The risen and ascended Lord Jesus is certainly conscious of his followers here below, and of all people. In fact, we ourselves are already seated with him in the heavens, as Paul claims in Colossians 3:1–4. Stephen sees the ascended Jesus just before being martyred for his witness. He cries out to the Lord to receive his spirit as well as begs Jesus not to hold the sins of his persecutors against them (see Acts 7:54–60).

Where does this leave us? One does not have to be Roman Catholic to take seriously the saints in heaven or consider soberly the lives of all souls who have preceded us into the next life. The Bible instructs us that every person lives and dies only once, and after that faces judgment (Heb 9:27). With this point in mind, and mindful of our Lord Jesus' example, let us look to the Lord Jesus and consider the godly example of saints of old like Stephen. Let us run joyfully our race here below on sacred as well as secular days all the way to the finish line when we see Jesus face to face.

PURGATION OF SOULS AND SPOTLESS SHEEP, NOT GOATS

Beginning with All Saints' Day and All Souls' Day, the Catholic Church dedicates the month of November to Purgatory[118] and to consideration of the end times. Such end time reflection includes our personal end of life and the end of the age.[119] For centuries, Protestantism has, by and large, rejected the notion of Purgatory, though there has been some openness recently to the doctrine.[120] While the teaching has been the brunt of jokes as well as subject to abuse, as in the case of indulgences, its defenders often argue that the doctrine is comforting and highlights God's love. It is not a temporary hellish place, but more like an intermediate, preparatory state of existence to make the soul spotless in its transition to heaven. One source puts the matter this way:

> Purgatory is not, as many people think, one last trial; all of those who make it to Purgatory will one day be in Heaven. Purgatory is where those who have died in grace, but who have not fully atoned for the temporal punishments resulting from their sins, go to finish their atonement before entering Heaven. A soul in Purgatory may suffer, but he has the assurance that he will ultimately enter Heaven when his punishment is complete. Catholics believe Purgatory is an expression of God's love, His desire to cleanse our souls of all that might keep us from experiencing the fullness of joy in Heaven.[121]

Pope John Paul II claimed:

---

118. For a Roman Catholic treatment of purgatory, see Cevetello and Bastian, "Purgatory," in *New Catholic Encyclopedia*, 824–29.
119. CatholicCulture.org, "Month of the Souls in Purgatory."
120. See Gibson, "Does Purgatory?" and "Purgatory for Protestants."
121. Richert, "Prayers for November."

> Every trace of attachment to evil must be eliminated, every imperfection of the soul corrected. Purification must be complete, and indeed this is precisely what is meant by the Church's teaching on purgatory. The term does not indicate a place, but a condition of existence. Those who, after death, exist in a state of purification, are already in the love of Christ who removes from them the remnants of imperfection.[122]

Proponents of the doctrine also maintain that it is difficult logically to conceive that once life is over, one gets an express ticket to glory. Sanctification involves a process that in the case of most souls does not come to an end with the termination of our earthly existence.

Many Protestants will object to the teaching based on there being no explicit Scriptural support in the Protestant canon. Moreover, the idea that, in any way, one "has to finish their atonement before entering Heaven"—temporal or otherwise (as the first quotation above suggests)—proves problematic in that it appears to take away from Jesus' all-sufficient sacrifice. In the midst of these challenges, Catholicism and Protestantism agree on some things pertaining to the final state of salvation. Both traditions maintain that Jesus is the great high priest whose atoning work is the ultimate basis for our purification and sanctification. Moreover, as suggested earlier, both ecclesial traditions maintain that life continues for every human after death and the grave. Mortality will give way to immortality. Furthermore, Catholicism and Protestantism have historically concurred that there is no second chance after this life to change one's destiny from hell to heaven. In his teaching on Purgatory, Pope John II reasons that there is a finality to our destiny bound up with our mortal existence:

> It is necessary to explain that the state of purification is not a prol[o]ngation of the earthly condition, almost as if after death one were given another possibility to change one's destiny. The Church's teaching in this regard is unequivocal and was reaffirmed by the Second Vatican Council which teaches: "Since we know neither the day nor the hour, we should follow the advice of the Lord and watch constantly so that, when the single course of our earthly life is completed (cf. Heb 9:27), we may merit to enter with him into the marriage feast and be numbered among the blessed, and not, like the wicked and slothful servants, be ordered to depart into the eternal fire, into the outer darkness

---

122. John Paul II, "General Audience."

VII—Ordinary Time: Follow Jesus in the Spirit to the End!

where 'men will weep and gnash their teeth' (Mt 22:13 and 25:30).'"[123]

Lastly, each church tradition brings communal closure for people who mourn the loss of loved ones. For example, Catholicism and Protestantism alike provide comfort through established ritual (repetition is good for the soul) that keep the bereaved from having to start from scratch and create novel and unique ways of expressing grief and gratitude for the dead. Each church provides the faithful with a common language and expression of life's mystery through ritual, community bonds, and a shared sense of meaning as people try to make sense of their deceased loved ones' lives in the context of eternity.[124]

These are very appealing qualities that are often missing when spiritually eclectic individuals as well as secular people prepare to say their final goodbyes to their deceased loved ones. We will return to this concern shortly. For the moment, let's be honest and acknowledge that a strength of the spiritually eclectic is that they do not want their faith to become rote, nor do they approach faith passively. They want a lively and authentic encounter with God that requires their full participation. This leads them to engage in "unbundling," which involves "picking and choosing" from different contexts, though unfortunately quite possibly in a consumerist fashion.

An article that addresses this challenging subject in *Vox* suggested that nearly 30 percent of Americans envision having a secular funeral. Moreover, the author, Tara Isabella Burton, suggests that many otherwise individualistically minded secular people will likely build community structures to provide sustained care for the bereaved.[125] Secular humanists and the like are realizing that one of the enviable qualities of religious traditions is that

---

123. John Paul II, "General Audience."

124. Burton speaks more generally to these three characteristic traits as distinctive qualities of religious communities in providing care for the bereaved in "Dying and Mourning."

125. Burton, "Dying and Mourning." Burton also interviews Phillip Zuckerman, author of *Living the Secular Life*, as well as Brad Wolfe, founder of the Reimagine End of Life festival that helps nonreligious people come to terms with preparing for death. Refer here: https://letsreimagine.org/. Another striking endeavor is "Friendsgiving," which is a communal phenomenon replacing extended families and religious communities in more individualistic settings, as in urban America. In addition to Burton's article, the interested observer is encouraged to read her book *Strange Rites*. Lastly, a classic study that helps us account for the sociological import of religion is Émile Durkheim's *The Elementary Forms of the Religious Life*. Burton says that Durkheim viewed "religion primarily as a shared construction of identity." She then quotes from his work: "The most barbarous and the most fantastic rites and the strangest myths translate some human need, some aspect of life, either individual or social." Durkheim, *Elementary Forms*, 2.

Purgation of Souls and Spotless Sheep, Not Goats

they provide sustained support to those who grieve. But even if secular humanists foster religious-like communities, will it provide enough closure and sustained meaning? Not from a traditional Judeo-Christian framework, at least. Christ Jesus alone brings that ultimate sense of meaning to our lives as we are included in him and share in his family story with all who await his return in glory.

Without intending to demean in any way our secularist friends and neighbors, or those religious types who choose to "unbundle," Catholic and Protestant as well as Orthodox churches alike should make every effort to prepare their congregants to meet Christ in glory. May we draw upon time-tested rituals, which are conveyed in contemporary expression when appropriate, bind ourselves together in community, and set our spiritual clocks according to the church calendar that provides enduring meaning for those alive and dead in Christ as it shows us our place in the grand scheme of things. That grand scheme centers around Jesus, who with the Father and the Spirit is the Alpha and Omega, the one from whom we come and to whom we go.

As we prepare ourselves and others to meet Jesus, take to heart the Apostle Paul's words in 1 Corinthians 3 (a text that Pope John Paul II references in support of his defense of Purgatory) and take care in building on the masterful foundation of the apostolic faith with precious metals and stones (read 1 Cor 3:10–15). Be ever mindful of the fact that everyone will stand before Jesus Christ, who will judge the nations and separate the sheep from the goats (Matt 25:31–33). While those who trust in Jesus Christ "will be saved," those believers who do not build wisely, skillfully, and soberly will experience loss of reward. They will inherit glory, "but only as through fire" (1 Cor 3:15). Make every effort now to be found spotless, without blemish, worthy of our calling in light of that day when we will stand before the Lord, as the Apostle Peter urges us (meditate on 2 Pet 3:13–14).

During the remaining days of November, which closes out the church calendar, let's take to heart the importance of living pure lives as we await the Lord's appearance as Savior and Judge and the dawning of the new heavens and earth. Let's live as spotless sheep, namely as those who seek to please the Lord here and now.

We await Jesus' coming in visible glory by caring for him now as he appears in hidden form in those around us who are hungry and thirsty, those who are aliens and strangers, those who are naked, sick, and in prison (Matt 25:35–36). We await him by looking after their well-being rather than being fixated on ourselves and our own presumed state of righteousness. After all, what seems to differentiate the sheep and goats in Matthew 25 is not simply what they did, but their perception of what they were: the sheep's

VII—Ordinary Time: Follow Jesus in the Spirit to the End!

surprise that they cared for the Lord suggests that they did not know they were sheep, while the goats' surprise that they did not care for the Lord suggests that they thought they were sheep! (Read Matt 25:37–39, 44.)

Regardless of our stance on Purgatory, all Christians should take to heart St. Peter's words about the need to live pure lives daily—without blemish. Metaphorically speaking, we should live like spotless sheep. Will we prepare now during the remaining days of November and beyond for the Lord Jesus' second advent? Or will we simply coast to the end of the year and enter the advent season wrongly assuming the church calendar cycles endlessly? Wake up! Jesus is coming!

DEALING WITH UNMET EXPECTATIONS OF JESUS AT LIFE'S END

The approach of year's end leads many people to review what transpired over the preceding months and, in many cases, their entire lives. Unfulfilled resolutions and unmet expectations often come to mind, including disappointment with Jesus. As we look forward, may we examine our lives and rightful from wrongful expectations and renew hope that the next year or even next life will be better. May we take careful stock of what we need to do to prepare to meet Jesus face to face.

The church calendar designates November as a time dedicated to careful consideration of life's end—for us personally and for the world. According to one source,

> During November, as in all of Ordinary Time (Time After Pentecost), the Liturgy signifies and expresses the regenerated life from the coming of the Holy Spirit, which is to be spent on the model of Christ's Life and under the direction of His Spirit. As we come to the end of the Church year we are asked to consider the end times, our own as well as the world's. The culmination of the liturgical year is the Feast of Christ the King. "This feast asserts the supreme authority of Christ over human beings and their institutions.... Beyond it we see Advent dawning with its perspective of the Lord's coming in glory."[126]

As we approach the end of the church liturgical year, let's consider our life's end or telos in Christ through the Spirit and reflect upon unmet expectations and how they can stand in the way of our relationship with God.

Unmet expectations can really hurt relationships in any season, including at life's end. Speaking of life's end, let's consider the last days of John the Baptist and how he apparently struggled with expectations of Jesus.

---

126. Dalmais et al., *The Liturgy and Time*, 107.

VII—Ordinary Time: Follow Jesus in the Spirit to the End!

John was one of the most righteous individuals who ever lived. But as John languished in prison, no doubt aware that his life was nearing its end, he appeared to question whether he had mistakenly hoped in Jesus to deliver Israel and usher in God's kingdom.

In Luke 7, we find John receiving reports of Jesus' miracles from his disciples. John then sends his disciples to ask Jesus whether he is indeed the Messiah in whom John himself has hoped. A question arises at this point: why might this passage suggest that John has doubts even in the face of Jesus' astounding miracles?

Consider that previously John the Baptist displays great confidence that Jesus is the Messiah. Luke 3 highlights Jesus' baptism, which was performed by John, according to Matthew's Gospel. In Luke's Gospel, we find a voice from heaven declaring Jesus as God's Son while the Spirit descends on him during his baptism (Luke 3:21–22). In parallel fashion, the other canonical Gospels indicate that John clearly recognizes and identifies Jesus as the Son of God and Lamb of God who takes away the world's sins as a result of God confirming to him Jesus' identity based on the Spirit's descent on Jesus during his baptism (John 1:29–34; see also Matt 3:13–17 and Mark 1:1–11).

But then we come to Luke 7. It appears that John is not so confident anymore that Jesus is the Messiah. Perhaps he is wondering: *Why am I languishing in prison if I am the forerunner of the Messiah? Why isn't Jesus freeing Israel from the pagan reign of Rome and its proxy rulers like the corrupt Herod who has put me behind bars?*

Take time right now to read Luke 7:18–30. Reflect upon the healthy dose of realism, including John's honesty and vulnerability. Consider Jesus' measured though still staggering response. From this passage, it appears that even the great John the Baptist has doubts and possibly experiences disillusionment with Jesus. If unchecked, his unrealized expectations will hurt his relationship with God. Any unrealized expectations about Jesus' mission would be mistaken, though, since Jesus as the Lamb of God (as John called him; John 1:29) first has to offer himself up as the sacrifice for cleansing from sin before returning to reign on the earth. Still, regardless of John's perceptions, Jesus does not scold him. Rather, he provides an answer to John's disciples to take back to John: the miraculous works he performs and the word he declares on behalf of the needy are signs that he is indeed the Messiah. John has not hoped in him in vain.

Jesus goes on to praise John. Jesus goes even further and affirms us. How so? While affirming John as the greatest of those born of women, Jesus asserts that anyone who belongs to his kingdom is greater than John. How can that be? Given Jesus' superiority as the very one John proclaimed as

Dealing with Unmet Expectations of Jesus at Life's End

the Messiah, even the least who belongs to Jesus' kingdom community of disciples is greater than John. After all, Jesus is the point of reference. He is the one around whom they and John rotate, just like the church calendar.

We have no idea how John processed Jesus' words that John's disciples relayed to him. What we do know is that sometime later Herod has John beheaded (see Luke 9:7–9). We should also know that so many people have unrealized expectations of Jesus based on an overly realized eschatology with such mantras as attaining the "best life now." Just as with John the Baptist or Jesus' disciples, who expected immediate deliverance from persecution and oppression, we often expect Jesus to take all our problems away and conquer all forms of evil right now and instantly.

The preceding discussion should not be taken to convey that there is no ground for hopeful expectations of what Jesus inaugurates and eventually consummates. As noted in Luke 7, Jesus provides signs of his future reign of peace and wholeness through his miraculous interventions on behalf of the blind, deaf, lame, and poor. While these occasions provide some level of comfort and basis for sustained hope, they do not erase the fact that there will still be trouble and sorrow along life's path. John's head will soon come off. Jesus will die on a cross. His people will continue to suffer in this life. The creation will keep on groaning until he makes all things new.

Jesus never promises to shield us from various relational, financial, physical, mental, emotional, and vocational disappointments.[127] He does promise to be with us, though, to deliver us amid these challenges, and someday make all things new. We must not allow unrealized expectations that are unrealistic expectations in the here and now to stand in the way of coming to terms with Jesus as he really is and what he promises to do now and in the future. As we examine our expectations, it will help us examine our own lives and discern how to prepare for the end of the liturgical year, the end of our lives, and the end of the age. Remember that as great as John the Baptist was, those who are least in the kingdom are greater than John. May we take to heart John's message, as he prepared the way for us to follow Jesus. Let's make sure that we ourselves are doing everything possible to meet the real Jesus and help others prepare to meet him—free of unrealistic expectations—face to face.

---

127. Christians have struggled with disappointments, doubts, and darkness. Two works that address aspects of these themes are Philip Yancey, *Disappointment* and Saint John of the Cross, *John of the Cross*. The Christian tradition does not hide from doubt and struggles with God but encourages us to wrestle with God in pursuit of greater wisdom and deeper relationship with our Lord.

CELEBRATE CHRIST THE KING, NOT SECULAR CREEP

"Christmas creep" has nothing to do with the spread of Christianity. Rather, it refers to merchandisers featuring Christmas decorations and Christmas sale promotions prior to the start of the holiday season for shoppers, which officially begins the day after Thanksgiving or Black Friday. It is only fitting given the spread of secularism and consumerism that the church celebrates "Christ the King Sunday" today, which was established almost one hundred years ago in response to secular creep, or the global spread of secularization.

Christ the King Sunday is the newest day in the liturgical year. It is also the last Sunday of the Christian Year. Established in 1925 by the decree of Pope Pius XI,[128] it originally took place on the final Sunday of October in advance of All Saints' Day. Now it falls on the Sunday just prior to the Advent Season. Advent begins next Sunday. Further to what was stated above, the occasion for the addition of Christ the King Sunday was to combat increasing secularization worldwide. Moreover, the day was marked to pay tribute to the plight of Mexican Christians who stood firm against their government's demands for their ultimate allegiance. Let's just call it "government creep."

The church pays tribute to these Mexican Christians, and those persecuted for their faith worldwide, as we celebrate Christ the King. As one publication reads, "So today our voices come alongside those persecuted for their faith in all times and places, including in Mexico in the early twentieth century and the thousands facing persecution all over the world this very day, and with them we all proclaim in many languages, 'Christ is King!'"[129]

Whether the world around us increases in secular appetites and ambitions, it's important that Christians make sure nothing takes us captive.

128. Pius XI, "Quas Primas: On the Feast of Christ."
129. Church Office, "Worship."

Celebrate Christ the King, Not Secular Creep

Rather, we are to take every thought captive to the obedience of Christ in the Christian community, as Paul exhorts us: "We destroy arguments and every lofty opinion raised against the knowledge of God, and take every thought captive to obey Christ" (2 Cor 10:5). All too often, the secular calendar eclipses our sense of sacred time and how God's presence permeates all creation through Jesus' life story on earth as the Alpha and Omega (the first and last letters of the Greek alphabet). Jesus marks the beginning and end of the year, of time, and life, as the Ancient of Days and Lord of all.

Amid the furious flurry this Christmas season involving shopping and various festivities, it is important to note the significance of Jesus' life for time. He controls time as the one who enters history and lives forever as the Alpha and Omega. Thus, time does not ultimately control us, for he sets history's clock and offers time to us as a gift. The liturgical calendar helps us come to terms with this reality:

> Our Liturgical seasons present a way to receive time as a continual gift and change the way we actually live our daily lives. Our choice to celebrate them helps us to grow in the life of grace as we say "yes" to their invitations. They invite us to walk in a new way of life which becomes infused with supernatural meaning; to enter into the mystery of living in the Church as the New World and thereby become leaven in an age which has lost its soul. Human beings have always marked time by significant events. The real question is not whether we will mark time, but how we will mark time? What events and what messages are we proclaiming in our calendaring? What are we saying with our lives in an age which needs the witness of God's loving plan?[130]

The church calendar assists us with seeing time as our friend rather than as our foe. Such is the significance of the Sabbath or Lord's Day. Scripture makes clear that we are not to allow anyone to judge us according to a festival or new moon or Sabbath laws (see Col 2:16). After all, the Sabbath was made for us. We were not made for the Sabbath (Mark 2:23–27). Still, special days like Sunday can help us rest, remember, and reimagine. Just as we are to come together to meet on the Lord's Day and at other times to encourage one another as we await the Lord's appearing (Heb 10:24–25), the liturgical calendar assists us in reorienting our lives and expanding our imaginations so that shopping mall religion and secular creep do not take us captive.

Don't think for a moment that the shopping mall fails to offer us religion. In fact, it's so religious that many churches have been designed to look

---

130. Fournier, "Every End."

VII—Ordinary Time: Follow Jesus in the Spirit to the End!

like them. The shopping mall shapes our sense of time as well as space.[131] As noted in the book's introduction, you won't find clocks, only mirrors, in most department stores. The subliminal message, whether or not accompanied by store music, is "Forget time. Forget where you need to be. Immerse yourself in our products. Worship!"

James K. A. Smith writes on shopping mall religion:

> The genius of mall religion is that actually it operates with a more holistic, affective, embodied anthropology (or theory of the human person) than the Church tends to assume! Because worldview-thinking tends to focus on ideas and beliefs, the formative cultural impact of sites like the mall tends to not show up on our radar. Such a heady approach focused on beliefs, is not really calibrated to see the quasi-liturgical practices at work . . . In order to recognize the religious power and formative force [of sites like the mall], we need to adopt a paradigm of cultural critique and discernment that thinks even deeper than beliefs or worldviews and takes seriously the central role of formative practices.[132]

Yes, we need to be more attentive to formative, liturgical practices, such as those found on Black Friday just prior to Advent. Shopping mall religion flows from the dynamic that humans are liturgical beings. One liturgy or another will shape us. Which one will it be? Take everything—including the secular society's liturgy, including Black Friday weekend—captive to Jesus Christ. Everything pales in comparison to him: "Therefore let no one pass judgment on you in questions of food and drink, or with regard to a festival or a new moon or a Sabbath. These are a shadow of the things to come, but the substance belongs to Christ" (Col 2:16–17).

With liturgies firmly in mind, and as people flock to churches and malls today, consider this liturgical account excerpted from the *Companion to the Book of Common Worship* to mark Christ the King Sunday:

> The festival of Christ the King (or Reign of Christ) ends our marking of Ordinary Time after the Day of Pentecost, and

---

131. Gretchen T. Buggeln makes the following point on sacred space and consumerism: "We are perhaps too close to the architecture of our era to decipher its meanings so completely. Nonetheless, we should be aware of the messages our churches communicate about the place of religion in our lives and in our communities. Consider the megachurch. How honest are buildings that rely on sophisticated sound systems to mask dismal acoustics? Can a church built in the idiom of a secular consumer society effectively counter that culture's influences?" Buggeln, "Sacred Spaces," 20–25. Refer also to my article titled "Walls Do Talk," 20–23.

132. Smith, *Desiring*, 24.

Celebrate Christ the King, Not Secular Creep

moves us to the threshold of Advent, the season of hope for Christ's coming again at the end of time.[133]

This day centers on the crucified and risen Christ, whom God exalted to rule over the whole universe. The celebration of the lordship of Christ thus looks back to Transfiguration Sunday, Easter, and Ascension Sunday, and points ahead to his appearing in glory as the King of kings and Lord of lords. Christ reigns supreme. Christ the Truth judges falsehood. As the Alpha and Omega, the beginning and the end, Christ is the center of the universe, the ruler of all history, the judge and deliverer of all peoples. In Christ all things began, and in Christ all things will be fulfilled. In the end, Christ will triumph over the forces of evil.

Such concepts as these cluster around the affirmation that Christ is King or Christ reigns! As sovereign ruler, Christ calls us to a loyalty that transcends every earthly claim to the human heart. To Christ alone belongs the supreme allegiance in our lives. God's Spirit calls us to stand with those who in every age confess, "Jesus Christ is Lord!" In every generation, demagogues emerge to claim an allegiance that belongs only to God. But Christ alone has the right to claim our highest loyalty. The blood of martyrs, past and present, witnesses to this truth. Behold the glory of the eternal Christ! From the beginning of time to its ending, Christ rules above all earthly powers!

---

133. Bower, ed., *Companion*, 151.

CONCLUSION: OUT OF JOINT AND TIME? RESET THE SPIRITUAL CLOCK

Today marks the end of "Ordinary Time" in the Christian calendar. Tomorrow marks the first Sunday in Advent and beginning of the liturgical year. It is important for the Christian and church to set their spiritual clocks, just like we do with time changes in the spring and autumn, or when we change the date on the checks that we write at the beginning of the secular calendar year.

As has been stated at different points in this book, Ordinary Time in the Christian calendar is very different from ordinary time in the secular calendar. When the secular calendar year is past, it is simply past. There is nothing important about one moment versus another in the secular calendar, except what we might assign to it as individuals and societies.

Things are very different in the liturgical or sacred calendar which operates in accordance with *illo tempore*—"at that time," namely, when Christ walked the earth. Given that Jesus is God incarnate, he brings eternity to bear on history and infuses it with his divine fullness. Paul gets at this idea in Galatians 4:4 when he states that Jesus is born in the fullness of time. Jesus' time on earth "participates in God's eternity," as Charles Taylor argues. If this is the case, we need to set our clocks here on earth according to that eternal pattern that we find in Jesus' time on earth. To the extent our timeframe follows this pattern, it will be more in sync—in step with God's Spirit. To the extent our time frame does not follow this pattern, it will be out of joint. Taylor develops this theme in *A Secular Age*.

> "Secular" time is what to us is ordinary time, indeed, to us it's just time, period. One thing happens after another, and when something is past, its past. . . . Now higher times gather and re-order secular time. . . . [For example] Good Friday 1998 is closer in a way to the original day of the Crucifixion than mid-summer's day 1997. . . . [T]he Church, in its liturgical year,

Conclusion: Out of Joint and Time? Reset the Spiritual Clock

remembers and re-enacts what happened in illo tempore when Christ was on earth. Which is why this year's Good Friday can be closer to the Crucifixion than last year's mid-summer day. And the Crucifixion itself, since Christ's action/passion here participates in God's eternity, is closer to all times than they in secular terms are to each other. . . . A time which has fallen away from the eternal paradigm of order will exhibit more disorder. A time-place which is closer to God's eternity will be more gathered. At the pilgrimage center on the saint's feast day, it is the time itself which is hallowed. When Hamlet says that "the times are out of joint," we could take this remark literally . . . "Out of joint" means things don't fit together in proper fashion, as they do in times which are closer to the ordering paradigms of eternity.[134]

For those who wish to be in sync, they need to be in immediate proximity to what Taylor calls "the ordering paradigms of eternity." For those who go to the beat of their own drum, or better, tick of their own clock, they will find themselves "out of joint."

The church calendar helps orient us as it circles the Son in all his glory. When we circle him throughout the year, time is on our side since time belongs to him. Following the church calendar proves instructive for those who follow Jesus. It involves praying with the psalmist as he beseeches God, who is from everlasting to everlasting (Ps 90:2), who is the Alpha and Omega (Rev 22:13), to teach us to number our days so we might have a heart of wisdom (Ps 90:12).

Take heart. He who came in the fullness of time will give fullness to our lives. Jesus is the reason for the seasons, not just Advent, but every season in the Christian calendar, including Ordinary Time. No day is ordinary, no soul is out of joint, no life is out of time, when we order our heartbeat and footsteps to the rhythm of his life and teaching throughout the ecclesial year. So, let's set our spiritual clocks according to the liturgical calendar, which circles the glorious Son as he breaks through the secular eclipse.

---

134. See Taylor, *A Secular Age*, 55–58.

APPENDIX

How to Read This Book

MANY READERS MAY WISH to approach the entries in this volume in accord with the liturgical seasons and days they represent. Just as Easter does not fall on the same date annually, the relationship of the liturgical calendar to the civic calendar is not static; the dates of the seasons and days vary by year. This appendix places notes into the table of contents outline of this book. The notes are designed to help you schedule the readings to best fit the seasons of any particular year, should you choose to utilize this book in such a manner. The alternative is simply to read this book at your own pace from front to back.

INTRODUCTION

I. ADVENT: JESUS IS COMING!

The Advent season begins four Sundays prior to Christmas and concludes on Christmas Eve. The following entries follow the themes for the respective weeks in their chronological order. Read one on each of the four Sundays of Advent in the order shown here. While there are fewer essays here than for any other section of the book, note that we do not simply meditate on Jesus' first coming during Advent, but also his second coming. Appearances in length can be deceiving, though not Jesus' appearing at the end of the age.

    Jesus Is Coming! Are We Waiting for Him?

    Looking for Jesus in the Least Likely of Places—Bethlehem

    "Joy to the World!" But Why?

    God's Peace Defies Circumstances

Appendix

II. CHRISTMASTIDE: JESUS IS BORN!

The Christmas season or Christmastide begins on the close of Christmas Eve, the beginning of Christmas Day. However, its ending varies depending on the church tradition. Technically, it ends on February 2, which marks forty days from Christmas. It can also be taken to refer to the twelve days of Christmas, which ends on January 5. For our purposes in honoring the Epiphany season, which begins on Epiphany Sunday, January 6, this volume uses the latter dating. While more entries could certainly have been included to feature each of the twelve days of Christmas, due to spatial limits, we highlighted central themes and also accounted for the Jewish holiday known as Hanukkah, which the church once celebrated. Read and reflect on the following five entries in this order over these twelve days.

Christmas Day Is Finally Here! What's the Big Deal?

Christmas Day Is Over, But Jesus' Life Has Only Just Begun!

Remember Hanukkah—Celebrate Religious Liberty

New Year's Eve and Day: Foolish Feasting or Joyful Solemnity?

Mother Mary Stands at the Crossroads of the New Year

III. EPIPHANYTIDE: GOD IS WITH US!

Epiphany Season begins on the Feast of Epiphany (January 6) and ends on the Tuesday preceding Ash Wednesday. The number of weeks vary (from four to nine weeks) depending on when Easter falls in a given year. I am striking a happy medium with six lessons! The pace for reading the essays will vary based on the number of weeks for this season in a given year. It would be best to read these essays on Sundays after discerning how many weeks one has before Lent. In some years, you will need to read more than one in a given week (if there are fewer than six weeks from Epiphany to Lent), while in other years, you have more time to read one or more again (if there are more than six weeks from Epiphany to Lent). Just be sure to start with Epiphany on Epiphany Sunday and end with the Transfiguration on Transfiguration Sunday. You won't want to miss it!

Epiphany: What We Worship Is Quite Revealing

Epiphany, Baptismal Theophany, and Jesus' Life as a Rich Tapestry

Epiphanytide: Seeing Jesus Is Believing and Following

How to Read This Book

Epiphanytide: Jesus' Signs Aim at Faith, not Fanfare

Jesus' Baby Dedication Reveals the New World Order

Transfiguration: Transitioning to Lent and Later

IV. LENT: DIE TO SELF TO GAIN JESUS!

The Lenten season begins on Ash Wednesday and lasts forty days, excluding Sundays. It ends three days before Easter in many contexts. Those days from Thursday evening to Saturday evening are often referred to as the Easter Triduum. In this book, we have decided to feature Holy Week as a distinct time frame. It begins on Palm Sunday and ends on Holy Saturday. For this Lenten season, begin with the essay for Ash Wednesday on that day rather than Thursday or Friday. The remainder of entries should take you all the way until Holy Week, the Sunday before Easter.

Ash Wednesday: Lament Indifferent Faith

Lent and Black History Month: Liturgies of Lament and Celebration

Forty Days of Lenten Purpose

Esther's Fast, Purim, Lent, and International Women's Day

What Did God Give Up for Lent?

Lent: Giving Up Vice to Gain the Savior

Lenten Extravagance

V. HOLY WEEK: JESUS DIES TO BRING NEW LIFE!

This book features Holy Week as a distinct time frame. Actually, it overlaps with two seasons in the church calendar—Lent and the Easter Triduum. Holy Week begins by featuring Jesus' triumphal entry into Jerusalem on Palm Sunday and ends with his entombment on Holy Saturday. Read each of the essays on the days of the week that bear the titles' names. Given that there is a gap from Palm Sunday to Maundy Thursday, consider returning to the Palm Sunday entry on Monday through Wednesday and reflect upon what is said there pertaining to other events beyond the Triumphal entry, such as Jesus' cleansing of the Temple and weeping over Jerusalem.

Palm Sunday, Holy Week, and Holy War

Appendix

Maundy Thursday: Jesus' Last Stand Is Everlasting

Don't Pass Over the Passover on Good Friday

Holy Saturday: Wholly in the Dark?

VI. EASTERTIDE: JESUS IS RISEN!

The Easter season begins on Easter Sunday and ends fifty days later at Pentecost. I provide essays for such themes and Mother's Day and Memorial Day, which occur during this season. The basis for this decision was to offer a lens to view these holidays in light of the sacred calendar rather than be eclipsed by the secular calendar in the church setting. It is best to read the meditations related to the ecclesial calendar on the Sundays designated for them. Easter Sunday goes first, as expected, followed by Divine Mercy Sunday for the second Sunday of Eastertide. Several of the essays following Easter and Divine Mercy Sunday reflect on the post-resurrection appearances of Jesus. So read them in order following Divine Mercy Sunday. Given that there are more entries than Sundays during the Eastertide season, one can double up if necessary. One could also read the articles that discuss Ascension and Pentecost together during the week that connects Ascension Sunday and Pentecost Sunday. Only make sure to read the Ascension Sunday entry before the Pentecost Sunday entry. Otherwise, the Son and Spirit will not be working in sync in your imagination, which may cause Ordinary Time to appear to be nothing other than a disordered mess.

Easter: New Creation and Vocation in the Promised Land

Thank God It's Divine Mercy Sunday

We See Jesus When Breaking Bread Together

Jesus' Resurrection Doesn't Depend on Faith, But Deepens It

Sometimes Doubt Is Devotion

Post-Resurrection Appearances—Faith Resuscitation

A Mother's Day Tribute: The Pierced Heart

On Memorial Days, Honor the Dead, Not Religious Propaganda

The Ascension: Jesus Has Some Serious Hang Time

Ascension and Pentecost: Above the Fray Yet on the Ground

Pentecost Sunday: Happy Birthday to the Missional Church!

How to Read This Book

VII. ORDINARY TIME: FOLLOW JESUS IN THE SPIRIT TO THE END!

Here we treat the longest season of the liturgical year. Depending on how one presents the Christian calendar, the entries for Ordinary Time could be far greater in number. As with the entries for Mother's Day and Memorial Day, which occur during Eastertide, there are entries for Father's Day and the Fourth of July. Once again, the point is to bring sacred time to bear upon secular calendar themes rather than sacred time being eclipsed in the church's imagination. The aim is to ensure that the church rotates in its thinking and sense of time around the glorious Son.

The first Sunday of Ordinary Time is Trinity Sunday. The last Sunday in Ordinary Time and the Christian calendar year is Christ the King Sunday. In total, there are somewhere between twenty-three to twenty-eight Sundays during Ordinary Time following Eastertide. So your reading rhythm will vary based on the year. In addition to reading the Trinity Sunday essay and Christ the King Sunday essay on the first and last Sundays in Ordinary Time, as the following list shows, it would be good to read the Corpus Christi Sunday entry on the Sunday immediately following Trinity Sunday, followed by those for Father's Day and the Fourth of July on or around the Sundays on which churches often reference them. One can read the essays specifically focused on the theme of Ordinary Time on Sundays or other days of the week. But make the attempt to read the entries for Mary's Assumption and Dormition close together on or around the Sunday closest to August 15, which is the date designated for commemorating them. Also, be sure to read the essay on praying for the creation on the first Sunday of September, marking the beginning of the Season of Creation. Read the piece honoring St. Francis and St. Kateri on or around the Sunday closest to October 5 as possible. This entry brings an end to the treatment of the Season of Creation in this book. Read the entry for Disability Sunday on the Sunday designated for it in a given year. The Reformation entry ("Repentant Monk") could be read during the week following "All Sinners' Sunday" and preceding "All Saints' Sunday." All Saints' Day occurs on November 1. Pace yourself in how you wish to read the essays that follow "All Saints' Sunday." Just be sure to save the last week in Ordinary Time to celebrate Christ the King Sunday, which is the culmination of the church year. Unless Christ tarries, it is time to reset the clock that week and get back in sync with the Spirit during the holiday shopping season rush. Advent will begin again the very next Sunday.

Appendix

The Trinity Is Not Just for Trinity Sunday, But the Whole Year

Corpus Christi Sunday: Discerning Christ's Real Presence

What Would Father's Day Be Like for Jesus?

A Fourth of July Reflection: Taking Exception to American Exceptionalism

May Jesus Order Our Steps During Ordinary Time

Jesus Acts Extraordinarily During Ordinary Time

Chronos Governs the Day. May *Kairos* Govern Our Lives

Conquer Inordinate Desire During Ordinary Time

Mary's Assumption: An Unassuming Heart and Honor

Mary's Dormition: Worth Losing Sleep?

The Church Calendar Reorders Us: Communal Past and Present

Mark Your Calendars Daily for Christ's Return

Pray for Creation Care Today

"Let There Be Light!"—Don't Take It Lightly

Honor God's Temple of Creation

Confess to God and Fellow Humans—But Plants?

How Godlike Are Humans Functioning on Earth?

Care for the Creation: Feasting with St. Francis and St. Kateri

The Christian Life: Pilgrimage through the Years

Honor Disability Awareness Sunday and the Differently Abled

All Sinners' Day

Who Will You Be on Halloween—A Repentant Monk?

All Saints' Sunday

Alive on Earth and in the Afterlife

Purgation of Souls and Spotless Sheep, Not Goats

Dealing with Unmet Expectations of Jesus at Life's End

Celebrate Christ the King, Not Secular Creep

CONCLUSION

BIBLIOGRAPHY

Adam, Adolf. *The Liturgical Year: Its History and Its Meaning After the Reform of the Liturgy*. Translated by Matthew J. O'Connell. Collegeville, MN: Liturgical, 1981.
Aledo United Methodist Church. "Ash Wednesday." February 26, 2020. https://aledoumc.org/events/details/2020/02/26/ash-wednesday/.
Allen-Ebrahimian, Bethany. "Evangelicals Side with Israel. That's Hurting Palestinian Christians." *Washington Post*, December 23, 2016. https://www.washingtonpost.com/posteverything/wp/2016/12/23/evangelicals-side-with-israel-thats-hurting-palestinian-christians/.
Allsup. "Invisible Disabilities Recognized During Disability Awareness Month in October." https://www.allsup.com/allsup-place/disability-awareness-month-in-october.
American Association for the Advancement of Science (wwwAAASorg). "Awe and Wonder." YouTube video. February 4, 2019. https://www.youtube.com/watch?v=DKate5pTx-Q.
The American Yawp Reader. "John Winthrop Dreams of a City on a Hill, 1630." https://www.americanyawp.com/reader/colliding-cultures/john-winthrop-dreams-of-a-city-on-a-hill-1630.
Aquinas, Thomas. *Opusculum 57*. In *Corpus Christi, lect.* 1–4. The Liturgy of the Hours. Vol. 3. New York: Catholic, 1975.
Araque, Nelson. "St. Francis of Assisi and Church Teachings on the Environment." *Let's Talk*, October 4, 2011. https://www.miamiarch.org/CatholicDiocese.php?op=Blog_11925151340998.
Ashton, Dianne. *Hanukkah in America: A History*. Goldstein-Goren Series in American Jewish History. New York: New York University Press, 2013.
Aslanoff, Catherine, ed. *The Incarnate God: The Feasts of Jesus Christ and the Virgin Mary*. Translated by Paul Meyendorff. Crestwood, NY: St Vladimir's Seminary Press, 1995.
Athanasius. *On the Incarnation*. Popular Patristics 44. Yonkers, NY: St Vladimir's Seminary Press, 2011.
Augustyn, Adam, managing ed. "Hanukkah." In *Encyclopedia Britannica*. https://www.britannica.com/topic/Hanukkah.
Avis, Paul. *The Anglican Understanding of the Church: An Introduction*. London: SPCK, 2000.
Bacevich, Andrew. *American Empire: The Realities and Consequences of U.S. Diplomacy*. Cambridge, MA: Harvard University Press, 2002.

Bibliography

Bainton, Roland H. *Here I Stand: A Life of Martin Luther*. Nashville: Abingdon, 2013.
———. *The Reformation of the Sixteenth Century*. Boston: Beacon, 1985.
Balthasar, Hans Urs von. *Love Alone Is Credible*. Translated by D. C. Schindler. San Francisco: Ignatius, 2004.
Barth, Karl. *The Christian Life. Church Dogmatics*, vol. IV. Grand Rapids: Eerdmans, 1981.
Basil the Great. *On the Holy Spirit*. Popular Patristics Series. Translated by David Anderson. Crestwood, NY: St Vladimir's Seminary Press, 2001.
Bauckham, Richard. *Jesus and the Eyewitnesses: The Gospels as Eyewitness Testimony*. 2d ed. Grand Rapids: Eerdmans, 2017.
Bennett, Jane. *The Enchantment of Modern Life: Attachments, Crossings, and Ethics*. Princeton, NJ: Princeton University Press, 2001.
Bigelow, Gordon. "Let There Be Markets: The Evangelical Roots of Economics." *Harper's* 310.1860 (May 2005) 33–38.
Bilinkoff, Jodi. *Related Lives: Confessors and Their Female Penitents, 1450–1750*. Ithaca, NY: Cornell University Press, 2005.
BioLogos. "How long are the days of Genesis 1?" *Common Questions*. https://biologos.org/common-questions/how-long-are-the-days-of-genesis-1/.
Bird, Michael. "N. T. Wright: The Church Continues the Revolution Jesus Started." *Christianity Today*, October 13, 2016. https://www.christianitytoday.com/ct/2016/october-web-only/n-t-wright-jesus-death-does-more-than-just-get-us-into-heav.html.
Bonhoeffer, Dietrich. *Christ the Center*. Translated by Edwin H. Robertson. New York: Harper and Row, 1978.
———. *Discipleship*. Bonhoeffer Works, vol. 4, edited by Geffrey B. Kelly and John D. Godsey. Translated by Barbara Green and Reinhard Krauss. Minneapolis, MN: Fortress, 2003.
Borchard, Therese. "5 Ways to Survive January—The Most Depressing Month of the Year." *Every Day Health*, January 7, 2015. https://www.everydayhealth.com/columns/therese-borchard-sanity-break/ways-survive-january-most-depressing-month-year/.
Bower, Peter C., ed. *Companion to the Book of Common Worship*. Louisville: Geneva, 2003.
Braaten, Carl E., and Robert W. Jenson, eds. *In One Body Through the Cross: The Princeton Proposal for Christian Unity*. Grand Rapids: Eerdmans, 2003.
Bratcher, Dennis, and Robin Stephenson-Bratcher. "All Saints Sunday: A Service of Worship." *The Voice*, 2016. http://www.crivoice.org/allsaints.html.
———. "The Seasons of the Church Year." *The Voice*. 2018. http://www.crivoice.org/chyear.html.
Breck, John. "Dormition or Assumption?" *Life in Christ*, August 1, 2008. https://www.oca.org/reflections/fr.-john-breck/dormition-or-assumption.
Brock, Brian. *Wondrously Wounded: Theology, Disability, and the Body of Christ*. Studies in Religion, Theology, and Disability. Waco, TX: Baylor University Press, 2019.
Brooks, Philip. "O Little Town of Bethlehem." In *The Hymnal of the Protestant Episcopal Church in the United States of America 1940*. New York: Church Pension Fund, 1961.
Brown, Joe. "'Absolute Theological Bankruptcy': Union Theological Seminary Students Confess Climate Sins to Plants." *Washington Examiner*, September 18, 2019.

Bibliography

https://www.washingtonexaminer.com/news/absolute-theological-bankruptcy-union-theological-seminary-students-pray-to-plants.

Brown, Raymond E. *The Birth of the Messiah: A Commentary, on the Infancy Narratives in Matthew and Luke*. Garden City, NY: Doubleday, 1979.

———. *The Gospel According to John (I–XII): Introduction, Translation, and Notes*. The Anchor Bible 29. New York: Doubleday, 1966.

Brueggemann, Walter. "The Liturgy of Abundance, The Myth of Scarcity." *Christian Century*, March 24–31, 1999. https://www.religion-online.org/article/the-liturgy-of-abundance-the-myth-of-scarcity/.

———. *Names for the Messiah: An Advent Study*. Louisville: Westminster John Knox, 2016.

———. *Peace*. St. Louis: Chalice, 2001.

———. *Sabbath as Resistance: Saying No to the Culture of Now*. Louisville: Westminster John Knox, 2014.

———. *Way Other Than Our Own: Devotions for Lent*. Louisville: Westminster John Knox Press, 2016.

Buckley, Michael J., SJ *At the Origins of Modern Atheism*. New Haven, CT: Yale University Press, 1987.

Buggeln, Gretchen T. "Sacred Spaces." *The Christian Century*, June 15, 2004, 20–25. https://www.religion-online.org/article/sacred-spaces/.

Burge, Gary M. *Jesus and the Jewish Festivals*. Ancient Context, Ancient Faith. Grand Rapids: Zondervan, 2012.

Burton, Tara Isabella. "Christianity Gets Weird: Modern Life Is Ugly, Brutal and Barren. Maybe You Should Try a Latin Mass." *New York Times*, May 8, 2020. https://www.nytimes.com/2020/05/08/opinion/sunday/weird-christians.html.

———. *Strange Rites: New Religions for a Godless World*. New York: Public Affairs, 2020.

———. "What Does Dying—and Mourning—Look Like in a Secular Age?" *Vox*, December 4, 2018. https://www.vox.com/identities/2018/12/4/18078714/death-secular-age-funeral-end-of-life-reimagine.

Cahill, Thomas. *How the Irish Saved Civilization: The Untold Story , and Ireland's Heroic Role from the Fall of Rome to the Rise of Medieval Europe*. The Hinges of History. New York: Anchor, 1996.

Caird, G. B. *Principalities and Powers: A Study in Pauline Theology*. Eugene, OR: Wipf and Stock, 2003.

Calhoun, Jimi. *The Sounds of Love and Grace: Ten Sounds that Will Save the World*. Eugene, OR: Cascade, 2020.

Camilleri, René. "18th Sunday in Ordinary Time: Greed, Vicious Malaise." *Times of Malta*, August 3, 2019. https://timesofmalta.com/articles/view/18th-sunday-in-ordinary-time-greed-vicious-malaise.726853.

Carson, D. A. "Did Paul Baptize for the Dead?" *Christianity Today*, August 10, 1998. https://www.christianitytoday.com/ct/1998/august10/8t9063.htm.

———. *God with Us: Themes from Matthew*. Eugene, OR: Wipf and Stock, 1995.

———. *The Gospel According to John*. Grand Rapids: Eerdmans, 1991.

———. "Matthew." In *Matthew, Mark, Luke*, edited by Peter E. Gaebelein, 1–599. The Expositor's Bible Commentary 8. Grand Rapids: Zondervan, 1984.

Bibliography

Catholic Church. *English Translation Catechism of the Catholic Church for the United States of America*. 2nd ed. Washington, DC: United States Conference of Catholic Bishops, 1997.

CatholicCulture.org. "Advent, December 3rd First Sunday of Advent." December 9, 2017. https://www.catholicculture.org/culture/liturgicalyear/calendar/day.cfm?date=2017-12-03.

———. "Catholic Prayer: Immaculate Heart." https://wwwcatholicculture.org/culture/liturgicalyear/prayers/view.cfm?id=761.

———. "Feast of the Baptism of the Lord." January 9, 2017. https://www.catholicculture.org/culture/liturgicalyear/calendar/day.cfm?date=2017-01-09.

———. "Month of the Souls in Purgatory." https://www.catholicculture.org/culture/liturgicalyear/overviews/months/11_1.cfm.

———. "November 2019—Overview for the Month." https://www.catholicculture.org/culture/liturgicalyear/overviews/months/11.cfm.

———. "Ordinary Time: October 27th." https://www.catholicculture.org/culture/liturgicalyear/calendar/day.cfm?date=2019-10-27.

———. "Solemnity of the Assumption." Excerpted from *The One Year Book of Saints*, Clifford Stevens. Huntington: Our Sunday Visitor, 2002. https://www.catholicculture.org/culture/liturgicalyear/calendar/day.cfm?date=2019-08-15.

———. "Solemnity of the Most Holy Body and Blood of Christ." June 23, 2019. https://www.catholicculture.org/culture/liturgicalyear/calendar/day.cfm?date=2019-06-23.

Catholic News Agency. "The Immaculate Heart of Mary." https://www.catholicnewsagency.com/resources/mary/popular-marian-devotions/the-immaculate-heart-of-mary.

Catholic Online. "All Saints' Day." https://www.catholic.org/saints/allsaints/.

———. "All Souls' Day." https://www.catholic.org/saints/allsouls/.

———. "Feast of the Epiphany." https://www.catholic.org/advent/advent.php?id=42.

———. "Nature." In *Catholic Encyclopedia*. https://www.catholic.org/encyclopedia/view.php?id=8348.

———. "Relationship." In *Catholic Encyclopedia*. https://www.catholic.org/encyclopedia/view.php?id=9931.

———. "St. Francis of Assisi." https://www.catholic.org/saints/saint.php?saint_id=50.

———. "Time." In *Catholic Encyclopedia*. https://www.catholic.org/encyclopedia/view.php?id=11571.

Catholic University of America. *New Catholic Encyclopedia*. 2nd ed. 15 vols. Detroit: Thomson/Gale, 2003.

Cavanaugh, William T. *Migrations of the Holy: God, State, and the Political Meaning of the Church*. Grand Rapids: Eerdmans, 2011.

———. *The Myth of Religious Violence: Secular Ideology and the Roots of Modern Conflict*. New York: Oxford University Press, 2009.

Cavins, Emily. *Lily of the Mohawks: The Story of Kateri*. Cincinnati, OH: Franciscan Media, 2013.

Chabad.org. "The Fast of Esther: What, Why and How." https://www.chabad.org/holidays/purim/article_cdo/aid/644314/jewish/The-Fast-of-Esther-What-Why-and-How.htm.

———. "What is Purim?" https://www.chabad.org/holidays/purim/article_cdo/aid/645309/jewish/What-Is-Purim.htm.

Bibliography

Chapman, John. "Council of Ephesus." In *The Catholic Encyclopedia*, vol. 5. New York: Robert Appleton Company, 1909. http://www.newadvent.org/cathen/05491a.htm.

Chesterton, G. K. *Advent and Christmas Wisdom from G. K. Chesterton*. Liguori, MO: Liguori, 2007.

———. *Saint Francis of Assisi*. New York: Image, 2001.

Chittister, Joan. *The Liturgical Year: The Spiraling Adventure of the Spiritual Life*. The Ancient Practices Series. Nashville: Thomas Nelson, 2010.

Christensen, John. "Did He Really Post His 95 Theses? And How Did He Manage to Stay Alive?" CNN.com. http://edition.cnn.com/SPECIALS/1999/millenium/16/histories/inner1.exclude.html.

Christianity Stack Exchange. "Did Martin Luther Accept or Reject the Existence of Purgatory?" https://christianity.stackexchange.com/questions/43994/did-martin-luther-accept-or-reject-the-existence-of-purgatory.

———. "How Did Luther View 'Confessing Intentional Sins' to a Priest For Forgiveness?" https://christianity.stackexchange.com/questions/9655/how-did-luther-view-confessing-intentional-sins-to-a-priest-for-forgiveness.

Christianity Today. "John Newton: Reformed Slave Trader." https://www.christianitytoday.com/history/people/pastorsandpreachers/john-newton.html.

Chua, Eu Jin. "Disenchantment." *Encyclopedia Britannica*. https://www.britannica.com/topic/disenchantment-sociology.

Church Office. "Worship: Christ the King Sunday." St John XXIII Catholic Church, November 22, 2017. https://johnxxiii.net/2017/11/nov-26th-2017-the-23rd-times/.

Claiborne, Shane, et al. *Common Prayer: A Liturgy for Ordinary Radicals*. Grand Rapids: Zondervan, 2010.

Clapp, Rodney. *Families at the Crossroads: Beyond Traditional and Modern Options*. Downers Grove, IL: InterVarsity, 1993.

———. "Our First Family: If Anything Remains Sacred in Our Culture, It's the Family. Yet Jesus Challenged the Family's Ultimacy." *Christian Century*, April 20, 2012. https://www.christiancentury.org/article/2012-04/our-first-family.

Clement of Alexandria. "How Great are the Benefits Conferred on Man Through the Advent of Christ." In *Exhortation to the Heathen*. Translated by William Wilson. Ante-Nicene Fathers 2, edited by Alexander Roberts, et al. Buffalo, NY: Christian Literature, 1885.

Coleman, Robert E. *Singing with the Angels*. Grand Rapids: Fleming H. Revell, 1980.

Cone, James H. *A Black Theology of Liberation*. Twentieth Anniversary Edition. Maryknoll, NY: Orbis, 1990.

Connell, Martin. *Eternity Today: On the Liturgical Year*. 2 vols. New York: Continuum, 2006.

Cooper, Richard T. "General Casts War in Religious Terms." *Los Angeles Times*, October 16, 2003. https://www.latimes.com/archives/la-xpm-2003-oct-16-na-general16-story.html.

Corrie Ten Boom House. "The History of the Museum." https://www.corrietenboom.com/en/information/the-history-of-the-museum.

Cox, Harvey. *The Feast of Fools: A Theological Essay on Festivity and Fantasy*. Cambridge, MA: Harvard University Press, 1969.

Crawford, Sidnie White. "Esther: Bible." *Jewish Women: A Comprehensive Historical Encyclopedia*. Jewish Women's Archive. https://jwa.org/encyclopedia/article/esther-bible.

Bibliography

Crosby, Cindy, ed. *Ancient Christian Devotional Lectionary Cycle A–C.* Downers Grove, IL: InterVarsity, 2007–2011.

Cross, F. L., and E. A. Livingstone, eds. *The Oxford Dictionary of the Christian Church.* 3rd ed., revised. New York: Oxford University Press, 2005.

Cullman, Oscar. *Christ and Time: The Primitive Christian Conception of Time and History.* 3rd ed. Eugene, OR: Wipf and Stock, 2018.

Cunningham, Genevieve. "Christmastide: The Celebration Has Just Begun!" *Get Fed: Feed Your Faith* (blog), December 20, 2018. https://www.getfed.com/celebrating-christmastide-6242/.

Dalmais, I. H., et al. *The Liturgy and Time.* The Church at Prayer, vol. 4, edited by A. G. Martimort. Translated by Matthew J. O'Connel. Collegeville, MN: Liturgical, 1986.

D'Angelo, Mary Rose. "Abba and 'Father': Imperial Theology and the Jesus Traditions." *Journal of Biblical Literature* 111.4 (Winter, 1992) 611–30.

Davis, Ellen F. *Scripture, Culture, and Agriculture: An Agrarian Reading of the Bible.* Cambridge: Cambridge University Press, 2009.

Delaware-Maryland Synod. "Disabilities Awareness Sunday." https://demdsynod.org/connectedness/definitely-abled-advocacy-and-resource-team/disability-awareness-sunday/.

DisAbility Ministries: The United Methodist Church. "Disability Sunday Order of Worship." https://umcdmc.org/worship/disability-sunday-order-of-worship/.

Dodd, C. H. *The Interpretation of the Fourth Gospel.* Cambridge: Cambridge University Press, 1953.

Donaldson, Cari. "St. Kateri Tekakwitha and The Care of Creation." *Catholic Exchange*, July 14, 2016. https://catholicexchange.com/st-kateri-tekakwitha-care-creation.

———. "St. Kateri Tekakwitha, Lily of the Mohawks." *Catholic Exchange*, July 14, 2015. https://catholicexchange.com/st-kateri-tekakwitha-lily-of-the-mohawks.

Doriani, Dan. "What Does Paul Mean by 'Baptism for the Dead'?" *Bible and Theology*, November 2, 2015. https://www.thegospelcoalition.org/article/what-does-paul-mean-by-baptism-for-the-dead/.

Dostoevsky, Fyodor. *The Brothers Karamazov.* Translated by Constance Garnett. New York: Modern Library, 1996.

Dozier, Daniel G. "Mary's Assumption in the Eastern Tradition." *Catholic Answers*, August 14, 2019. https://www.catholic.com/magazine/online-edition/marys-assumption-in-the-eastern-tradition.

Drucker, Malka. *The Family Treasury of Jewish Holidays.* Boston: Little, Brown, and Company, 1994.

Durkheim, Émile. *The Elementary Forms of the Religious Life.* Translated by Joseph Ward Swain. Mineola, NY: Dover, 2008.

Eliade, Mircea. *The Sacred and Profane: The Nature of Religion.* Translated by Willard R. Traske. New York: Harcourt, 1987.

Elliot, Elisabeth. *Shadow of the Almighty: The Life and Testament of Jim Elliot.* Reissue ed. New York: HarperCollins, 2009.

Enns, Peter. "The Firmament of Genesis 1 is Solid, but That's Not the Point." *BioLogos*, January 14, 2010. https://biologos.org/articles/the-firmament-of-genesis-1-is-solid-but-thats-not-the-point.

———. "Genesis 1 and a Babylonian Creation Story." *BioLogos*, May 18, 2020. https://biologos.org/articles/genesis-1-and-a-babylonian-creation-story.EPA.

Bibliography

Erickson, Nancy. "To Function or Not to Function." *BioLogos*, February 19, 2015. https://biologos.org/articles/series/reflections-on-the-lost-world-of-genesis-1-by-john-walton/to-function-or-not-to-function.

Esler, Philip Francis. *Community and Gospel in Luke-Acts: The Social and Political Motivations of Lucan Theology*. Cambridge: Cambridge University Press, 1987.

EurekAlert!: AAAS. "New Study Dramatically Narrows the Search for Advanced Life in the Universe: Toxic Gases Limit the Types of Life We Could Find on Habitable Worlds." June 10, 2019. https://www.eurekalert.org/pub_releases/2019-06/uoc-nsd060719.php.

Farrow, Douglas. *Ascension and Ecclesia: On the Significance of the Doctrine of the Ascension for Ecclesiology and Christian Cosmology*. Grand Rapids: Eerdmans, 2009.

———. *Ascension Theology*. New York: T. & T. Clark International, 2011.

Faulkner, William. *Requiem for a Nun*. New York: Vintage, 2001.

Fee, Gordon. *The First Epistle to the Corinthians*. The New International Commentary on the New Testament, vol. 7. Grand Rapids: Eerdmans, 1987.

Fee, Gordon, and Douglas Stuart. *How to Read the Bible for All Its Worth*. 2d ed. Grand Rapids: Zondervan, 1993.

Fenelon, Marge. "5 Things You Might Not Know About January 1st." *Aleteia*, December 30, 2014. https://aleteia.org/2014/12/30/5-things-you-might-not-know-about-january-1st/.

Filz, Gretchen. "Does Christmas End on Epiphany?" *Get Fed: Feed Your Faith* (blog), January 6, 2017. https://www.getfed.com/does-christmas-end-on-epiphany-5962/.

Fisher, Max. "The Jerusalem Issue, Explained." *New York Times*, December 9, 2017. https://www.nytimes.com/2017/12/09/world/middleeast/jerusalem-trump-capital.html.

Fortescue, Adrian. "Liturgy." In *The Catholic Encyclopedia*, vol. 9. New York: Robert Appleton Company, 1910. http://www.newadvent.org/cathen/09306a.htm.

Fournier, Keith. "Every End is a Beginning. Christ the King, Thanksgiving and Advent." *Catholic by Choice*. https://www.beliefnet.com/columnists/catholicbychoice/2010/11/every-end-is-a-beginning-christ-the-king-thanksgiving-and-advent.html.

———. "Mother of God (Theotokos)." Catholic Online. https://www.catholic.org/mary/theo.php.

Fox, Michael V. "The Women in Esther." *TheTorah.com*, 2015. https://www.thetorah.com/article/the-women-in-esther.

———. *Character and Ideology in the Book of Esther*. 2d ed. Columbia, SC: University of South Carolina Press, 1991. Reprint ed.: Eugene, OR: Wipf and Stock, 2010.

France, R. T. *The Gospel of Matthew*. The New International Commentary on the New Testament. Grand Rapids: Eerdmans, 2007.

Francis. "Message of His Holiness Pope Francis for Lent 2015." Vatican website. October 4, 2014. http://w2.vatican.va/content/francesco/en/messages/lent/documents/papa-francesco_20141004_messaggio-quaresima2015.html.

———. "Holy Mass and Canonization of Blessed Mother Teresa of Calcutta: Jubilee for Workers of Mercy and Volunteers." Vatican website. September 4, 2016. https://w2.vatican.va/content/francesco/en/homilies/2016/documents/papa-francesco_20160904_omelia-canonizzazione-madre-teresa.html.

Bibliography

———. "Laudato Sí." Vatican website, 2015. http://w2.vatican.va/content/francesco/en/encyclicals/documents/papa-francesco_20150524_enciclica-laudato-si.html.

Francis of Assisi. "The Canticle of Brother Sun." In *Francis and Clare: The Complete Works*, edited by Regis J. Armstrong and Ignatius Brady, 37–39. The Classics of Western Spirituality. Mahwah, NJ: Paulist, 1982.

———. "The Canticle of Creation." Catholic Online. https://www.catholic.org/prayers/prayer.php?p=3188.

Francis, Mary, trans. *The Festal Menaion*. 3rd ed. Waymart, PA: St Tikhons Monastery, 1990.

Fredriksen, Paula. "When Jesus Celebrated Passover." *Wall Street Journal*, April 19, 2019. https://www.wsj.com/articles/when-jesus-celebrated-passover-11555685683.

Frei, Hans W. *The Eclipse of Biblical Narrative: A Study in Eighteenth and Nineteenth Century Hermeneutics*. New Haven, CT: Yale University Press, 1980.

French, Tia. "Christmastide: A Rookie Anglican Guide to the 12 Days of Christmas." *Anglican Compass*, December 16, 2019. https://anglicancompass.com/christmastide-a-rookie-anglican-guide-to-the-12-days-of-christmas/.

Geist, Tania M. "Benedict XVI's Theology of Holy Saturday." *First Things*, March 30, 2013. https://www.firstthings.com/web-exclusives/2013/03/benedict-xvis-theology-of-holy-saturday.

George, Timothy. "The Blessed Evangelical Mary: Why We Shouldn't Ignore Her Any Longer." *Christianity Today*, December 1, 2003. https://www.christianitytoday.com/ct/2003/december/1.34html.

———. *The Blessed Evangelical Mary: Why We Shouldn't Ignore Her Any Longer*. Nashville: Thomas Nelson, 2020.

Giallanza, Joel. *The Seven Sorrows of Mary: A Meditative Guide*. Notre Dame, IN: Ave Maria, 2008.

Gibbon, Edward. *The Decline and Fall of the Roman Empire*. 3 vols. New York: The Modern Library, 1995.

Gibson, David. "Does Purgatory Have a Prayer with Protestants?" *Religious News Service*, October 29, 2014. https://religionnews.com/2014/10/29/purgatory-prayer-protestants/.

———. "Purgatory for Protestants." *Commonweal*, October 31, 2014. https://www.commonwealmagazine.org/purgatory-protestants.

Gillet, Lev. *The Year of Grace of the Lord: A Scriptural and Liturgical Commentary on the Calendar of the Orthodox Church*. Yonkers, NY: St. Vladimir's Seminary Press, 1980.

Goldsworthy, Adrian. *Pax Romana: War, Peace and Conquest in the Roman World*. New Haven, CT: Yale University Press, 2016.

González, Justo L. "April 7, Fifth Sunday of Lent (John 12:1–8), Judas Is Right: What Mary Does Makes No Sense." *Christian Century*, March 5, 2019. https://www.christiancentury.org/article/living-word/april-7-fifth-sunday-lent-john-121-8.

Greek Orthodox Archdiocese of America. "Dormition of the Theotokos." https://www.goarch.org/dormition.

———. "Presentation of Christ to the Temple." https://www.goarch.org/presentation.

Green, Emma. "Hanukkah, Why? Cultural Critics Often Blame Christmas for the Festival's Commercialized Kitsch. The Real Story is Much More Complicated." *The Atlantic*, December 9, 2015. https://www.theatlantic.com/business/archive/2015/12/hanukkah-sucks-amirite/419649/.

Bibliography

Green, Joel B. *The Gospel of Luke*. The New International Commentary on the New Testament. Grand Rapids: Eerdmans, 1997.

Greenacre, Roger, and Jeremy Haselock. *The Sacrament of Easter*. Grand Rapids: Eerdmans, 1995.

Griffith, Daniel. "The Feast of the Circumcision of the Lord." Antiochian Orthodox Christian Archdiocese of North America. http://ww1.antiochian.org/node/22776.

Gross, Bobby. *Living the Christian Year: Time to Inhabit the Story of God*. Downers Grove, IL: InterVarsity, 2009.

"Ground-level Ozone Basics." https://www.epa.gov/ground-level-ozone-pollution/ground-level-ozone-basics.

Gunton, Colin E. *Act and Being: Toward a Theology of the Divine Attributes*. London: SCM, 2002.

———. *The Christian Faith: An Introduction to Christian Doctrine*. Oxford: Blackwell, 2002.

———. *The Triune Creator: A Historical and Systematic Study*. Edinburgh Studies in Constructive Theology. Edinburgh: Edinburgh University Press, 1998.

Habel, Norman C., et al., eds. *The Season of Creation: A Preaching Commentary*. Minneapolis: Augsburg Fortress, 2011.

Hallström, Lasse, dir. *Chocolat*. Los Angeles: Miramax, 2000.

Harper, Brad, and Paul Louis Metzger. *Exploring Ecclesiology: An Evangelical and Ecumenical Introduction*. Grand Rapids: Brazos, 2009.

Harris, Max. "Feast of Fools." *Oxford Bibliographies*, October 29, 2013. https://www.oxfordbibliographies.com/view/document/obo-9780195396584/obo-9780195396584-0078.xml.

Harrison, Peter. "Subduing the Earth: Genesis 1, Early Modern Science, and the Exploitation of Nature." *The Journal of Religion* 79.1 (January 1999) 86–110.

Hassett, Maurice. "Martyr." In *The Catholic Encyclopedia*. Vol. 9. New York: Robert Appleton Company, 1910. https://www.newadvent.org/cathen/09736b.htm.

Hauptman, Judith. *Rereading the Rabbis: A Woman's Voice*. Boulder, CO: Westview, 1998.

Hawn, C. Michael. "Spirit of the Living God." Written by Daniel Iverson. *The UM Hymnal*, no. 393, The United Methodist Church, 1989.

Heady, Chene. *Numbering My Days: How the Liturgical Calendar Rearranged My Life*. San Francisco: Ignatius, 2016.

———. "What is the Liturgical Calendar?" *Simply Catholic*. https://simplycatholic.com/what-is-the-liturgical-calendar/.

Heiberg, Jeanne. *The Twelve Days of Christmas*. Collegeville, MN: Liturgical, 1955. https://www.catholic.org/advent/advent.php?id=1.

Heschel, Abraham Joshua. *The Sabbath*. New York: Farrar, Strauss, and Giroux, 2005.

Hickman, Hoyt L., et al. *The New Handbook of the Christian Year*. 2d ed. Nashville: Abingdon, 1992.

Hofer, Andrew, OP, ed. *Divinization: Becoming Icons of Christ Through the Liturgy*. Chicago: Hillenbrand, 2015.

Holy Trinity Episcopal Church. "What is Epiphany?" January 6, 2017. http://holytrinityhillsdale.org/event/what-epiphany.

Hopkins, Denise. *Journey Through the Psalms*. St Louis: Chalice, 2002.

Hopko, Thomas. "Easter Sunday." https://www.oca.org/orthodoxy/the-orthodox-faith/worship/the-church-year/easter-sunday-the-holy-pascha.

Bibliography

———. *The Orthodox Faith*. 4 vols. Crestwood, NY: St Vladimir's Seminary Press, 2016.

Huleatt, Veery. "Progressive Seminary Students Offered a Confession to Plants. How Do We Think About Sins Against Nature?" *The Washington Post*, September 18, 2019. https://www.washingtonpost.com/religion/2019/09/18/progressive-seminary-students-offered-confession-plants-what-are-we-make-it/.

Iovino, Joe. "All Saints Day: A Holy Day John Wesley Loved." UMC.org. October 25, 2018. https://www.umc.org/en/content/all-saints-day-a-holy-day-john-wesley-loved.

Irenaeus. *Against Heresies*, 5.6. Translated by William Rambaut and Alexander Roberts. In Ante-Nicene Fathers 1. Edited by Alexander Roberts, et al. Buffalo, NY: Christian Literature, 1880.

Ireton, Kimberlee Conway. *The Circle of Seasons: Meeting God in the Church Year*. Downers Grove, IL: InterVarsity, 2008.

Irving-Stonebraker, Sarah. "How Oxford and Peter Singer Drove Me From Atheism to Jesus." *Veritas*, May 22, 2017. http://www.veritas.org/oxford-atheism-to-jesus/.

Jenkins, Philip. *Crucible of Faith: The Ancient Revolution That Made Our Modern Religious World*. New York: Basic, 2017.

———. "Hanukkah and National Myths." *Anxious Bench*, December 23, 2019. https://www.patheos.com/blogs/anxiousbench/2019/12/hanukkah-and-national-myths/.

Jeremias, Joachim. "Abba." In *Studiem zur Neutestamentlichen Theologies und Zeitgeschichte*, 15–67. Gottingen: Vandenhoeck & Ruprecht, 1966. Translated by John Bowden in *The Prayers of Jesus*. SBT Second Series 6. Naperville, IL: Alec R. Allenson, 1967.

———. *The Eucharistic Words of Jesus*. 3rd ed. London: SCM, 1966.

John of the Cross. *John of the Cross: Selected Writings*. Edited and Translated by Kieran Kavanaugh. The Classics of Western Spirituality. Mahwah, NJ: Paulist, 1987.

John Paul II. "Address of His Holiness John Paul II to the Bishops of Western Canada on Their 'Ad Limina' Visit." Vatican website. October 30, 1999. http://www.vatican.va/content/john-paul-ii/en/speeches/1999/october/documents/hf_jp-ii_spe_30101999_ad-limina-west-canada.html.

———. "Dies Domini." Vatican website. July 30, 1998. http://www.vatican.va/content/john-paul-ii/en/apost_letters/1998/documents/hf_jp-ii_apl_05071998_dies-domini.html.

———. "General Audience." Vatican website. August 4, 1999. http://w2.vatican.va/content/john-paul-ii/en/audiences/1999/documents/hf_jp-ii_aud_04081999.html.

———. "Inter Sanctos: Proclamation of San Francisco De Asís as a Patron of Ecology." Vatican website. November 29, 1979. http://www.vatican.va/content/john-paul-ii/es/apost_letters/1979/documents/hf_jp-ii_apl_19791129_inter-sanctos.html.

———. "Tertio Millennio Adveniente." Vatican website. November 10, 1994. http://www.vatican.va/content/john-paul-ii/en/apost_letters/1994/documents/hf_jp-ii_apl_19941110_tertio-millennio-adveniente.html.

———. *Veritatis Splendor*. Vatican website. August 6, 1993; http://www.vatican.va/content/john-paul-ii/en/encyclicals/documents/hf_jp-ii_enc_06081993_veritatis-splendor.html.

Jones, Cheslyn, et al., eds. *The Study of Spirituality*. New York: Oxford University Press, 1986.

Bibliography

Jugie, Martin. "Purgatory: And the Means to Avoid it." Catholicism.org, March 1, 2011. https://catholicism.org/purgatory-and-the-means-to-avoid-it.html.
KDG Wittenberg. "The 95 Theses and their Results (1517–1519)." 1997. https://www.luther.de/en/anschlag.html.
Keller, Timothy. *Hidden Christmas: The Surprising Truth Behind the Birth of Christ*. New York: Viking, 2016.
Killgrove, Kristina. "How the Ancient Romans Gave Us 'Bones of the Dead' Cookies for Halloween." *Forbes*, October 31, 2015. https://www.forbes.com/sites/kristinakillgrove/2015/10/31/how-the-ancient-romans-gave-us-bones-of-the-dead-cookies-for-halloween/#7196a8c2438a.
Kirby, Jeffrey F. "Pentecost, its Teachings and Context, Can Still Inspire Believers Today." *Crux*, June 4, 2017. https://cruxnow.com/commentary/2017/06/pentecost-teachings-context-can-still-inspire-believers-today/.
Klawans, Jonathan. "Was Jesus' Last Supper a Seder?" *Bible History Daily*, April 19, 2019. https://www.biblicalarchaeology.org/daily/people-cultures-in-the-bible/jesus-historical-jesus/was-jesus-last-supper-a-seder/.
Kohn, Daniel. "What Are Pilgrimage Festivals?" *My Jewish Learning*. https://www.myjewishlearning.com/article/pilgrimage-festivals/.
Kowalska, Maria Faustina. *Diary: Divine Mercy in My Soul*. Stockbridge, MA: Congregation of Marians of the Immaculate Conception, 1987.
Kozlowski, Matthew. "Epiphany And The Baptism of Our Lord." *Building Faith*, January 2, 2017. https://buildfaith.org/epiphany-baptism-of-our-lord/.
Kutz, Karl. "Genesis 1:1–2:3—Letting the Text Speak for Itself." *Cultural Encounters* 13.1 (Winter 2017) 3–13. https://www.ingentaconnect.com/search;jsessionid=1xs77vktwxy3v.x-ic-live-02?option2=author&value2=Kutz,+Karl.
Ladd, George Eldon. *The Gospel of the Kingdom: Scriptural Studies in the Kingdom of God*. Grand Rapids: Eerdmans, 1990.
Landy, Joshua, and Michael Saler, eds. *The Re-Enchantment of the World: Secular Magic in a Rational Age*. Stanford, CA: Stanford University Press, 2009.
Lewis, Alan E. *Between Cross and Resurrection: A Theology of Holy Saturday*. Grand Rapids: Eerdmans, 2003.
Lewis, C. S. *God in the Dock*. Reprint ed. Edited by Walter Hooper. Grand Rapids: Eerdmans, 1972.
———. *The Lion, the Witch and the Wardrobe*. New York: HarperTrophy, 1998.
Lilje, Hanns. *The Last Book of the Bible*. Translated by Olive Wyon. Philadelphia: Muhlenberg, 1957.
Lincoln, Abraham. "Address Delivered at the Dedication of the Cemetery at Gettysburg." In *Lincoln Speeches*, edited with an introduction by Allen C. Guelzo, 149–50. New York: Penguin, 2012.
———. "Second Inaugural Address." In *Lincoln Speeches*, edited with an introduction by Allen C. Guelzo, 156–58. New York: Penguin, 2012.
Longenecker, Dwight. "Looking at the Jewish Roots of Pentecost." *Crux*, June 3, 2017. https://cruxnow.com/commentary/2017/06/looking-jewish-roots-pentecost/.
Lovino, Joe. "All Saints Day: A Holy Day John Wesley Loved." United Methodist Church. http://www.umc.org/en/content/all-saints-day-a-holy-day-john-wesley-loved.
Luther, Martin. *The Freedom of a Christian*. In *Martin Luther's Basic Theological Writings*, edited by Timothy F. Lull, 585–629. Minneapolis: Fortress, 1989.
———. "The 95 Theses." https://www.luther.de/en/95thesen.html.

Bibliography

———. *The Ninety-Five Theses and Other Writings*. Translated and edited by William R. Russell. New York: Penguin, 2017.

MacIntyre, Alasdair. *After Virtue: A Study in Moral Theory*. 3rd ed. Notre Dame, IN: University of Notre Dame Press, 2007.

Martin, Dennis. "What About Purgatory? The Doctrinal Grounding of Dante's Mysterious Mountain." *Christian History*, April 1, 2001. https://www.christianitytoday.com/history/issues/issue-70/what-about-purgatory.html.

Matson, David Lertis. "Breaking the Bread, Breaking the Veil: Recognition of Jesus at Emmaus." *Leaven* 3.3 (1995) 8–12. https://digitalcommons.pepperdine.edu/cgi/viewcontent.cgi?article=1977&context=leaven.

McGowan, Andrew. "How December 25 Became Christmas." *Bible History Daily*, December 10, 2019. https://www.biblicalarchaeology.org/daily/biblical-topics/new-testament/how-december-25-became-christmas/#note15.

Mershman, Francis. "Feast of Corpus Christi." In *The Catholic Encyclopedia* 4. New York: Robert Appleton Company, 1908. https://www.newadvent.org/cathen/04390b.htm.

Metzger, Marcel. *History of the Liturgy: The Major Stages*. Translated by Madeleine Beaumont. Collegeville, MN: Liturgical, 1997.

Metzger, Paul Louis. *Consuming Jesus: Beyond Race and Class Divisions in a Consumer Church*. Grand Rapids: Eerdmans, 2007.

———. *The Gospel of John: When Love Comes to Town*. Downers Grove, IL: InterVarsity, 2010.

———. "Thinking Globally on Global Climate Change: An Evangelical Reflection." *Oregon State Bar, Sustainable Future Section*, 2015. https://sustainablefuture.osbar.org/files/2015/08/2q15.pdf.

———. "Walls Do Talk." *Christianity Today*, September 22, 2009. https://www.christianitytoday.com/pastors/2009/fall/wallsdotalk.html.

Meyer, Lester. "A Lack of Laments in the Church's Use of the Psalter." *Lutheran Quarterly* (Spring, 1993) 67–78.

Mills, David. "The Nation with the Soul of a Church." *First Things*, August 20, 2010. https://www.firstthings.com/blogs/firstthoughts/2010/08/the-nation-with-the-soul-of-a-church.

Minear, Paul Sevier. *To Heal and To Reveal: The Prophetic Vocation According to Luke*. New York: Seabury, 1976.

———. "Luke's Use of the Birth Stories." In *Studies in Luke-Acts*, edited by L. E. Keck and J. L. Martyn, 111–30. Philadelphia: Fortress, 1980.

Molnar, Paul D. *Divine Freedom and the Doctrine of the Immanent Trinity: In Dialogue with Karl Barth and Contemporary Theology*. London: T. & T. Clark, 2002.

Moltmann, Jürgen. *The Crucified God: The Cross of Christ as the Foundation and Criticism of Christian Theology*. Minneapolis: Fortress, 1993.

MoMALearning. "Vincent van Gogh: Emotion, Vision, and A Singular Style." https://www.moma.org/learn/moma_learning/vincent-van-gogh-the-starry-night-1889/.

Morrow, Jeff. "Creation as Temple-Building and Work as Liturgy in Genesis 1–3." Paper, Seton Hall University. http://www.wisdomintorah.com/wp-content/uploads/Creation-as-Temple-Building-and-Work-as-Liturgy-in-Genesis-1-31.pdf.

Mounce, Robert H. *The Book of Revelation*. Rev. ed. The New International Commentary on the New Testament. Grand Rapids: Eerdmans, 1998.

Bibliography

My Jewish Learning. "Hanukkah 101: From Candle-Lighting to Maccabees and Latkes to Dreidels." https://www.myjewishlearning.com/article/hanukkah-101/.
———. "Passover (Pesach) 101." https://www.myjewishlearning.com/article/passover-pesach-101/.
———. "Purim 101." https://www.myjewishlearning.com/article/purim-101/.
———. "Rosh Hashanah." https://www.myjewishlearning.com/article/rosh-hashanah-101.
———. "Shavuot 101." https://www.myjewishlearning.com/article/shavuot-101/.
———. "Sukkot." https://www.myjewishlearning.com/article/sukkot-2019/.
———. "Yom Kippur." https://www.myjewishlearning.com/article/yom-kippur-2019/.
National Archives. "2019 Federal Holidays and Research Room Closings." *National Archives News*. https://www.archives.gov/news/federal-holidays-2019.
Nazianzus, Gregory. *On God and Christ: The Five Theological Orations and Two Letters to Cledonius*. Translated by Lionel Wickham. Crestwood, NY: St Vladimir's Seminary Press, 2002.
Newbigin, Lesslie. *The Open Secret: An Introduction to the Theology of Mission*. Rev. ed. Grand Rapids: Eerdmans, 1995.
———. "Religion for the Marketplace." In *Christian Uniqueness Reconsidered: The Myth of a Pluralistic Theology of Religions*, edited by Gavin D'Costa, 135–48. Faith Meets Faith Series in Interreligious Dialogue. Maryknoll, NY: Orbis, 1990.
———. "The Trinity as Public Truth." In *The Trinity in a Pluralistic Age: Theological Essays on Culture and Religion*, edited by Kevin J. Vanhoozer, 1–8. Grand Rapids: Eerdmans, 1997.
Newman, John Henry. *Waiting for Christ: Meditations for Advent and Christmas*. Edited by Christopher O. Blum. Greenwood Village, CO: Augustine Institute, 2018.
Niebuhr, Gustav. "More Than a Monument: The Spiritual Dimension of These Hallowed Walls." *The New York Times*, November 11, 1994. https://www.nytimes.com/1994/11/11/us/more-than-a-monument-the-spiritual-dimension-of-these-hallowed-walls.html.
Nietzsche, Friedrich. *The Antichrist*. In *The Portable Nietzsche*, edited by Walter Kaufmann, 565–656. New York: Viking, 1968.
Nixdorf, Katie, et al. "The Coronavirus is Giving the Environment a Break—But Experts Say it's Unlikely to Stay that Way." *Business Insider*, April 17, 2009. https://www.businessinsider.com/coronavirus-environment-impact-pollution-climate-quarantine-2020-4.
Nouwen, Henri J. M. *Advent and Christmas Wisdom from Henri J. M. Nouwen: Daily Scripture and Prayers Together with Nouwen's Own Words*. Liguori, MO: Liguori, 2004.
Oakley, Mark, ed. *A Good Year*. London: SPCK, 2016.
O'Connell, John P. and Jex Martin. *The Prayer Book*. Chicago: The Catholic, 1954. https://www.catholicculture.org/culture/liturgicalyear/prayers/view.cfm?id=761.
O'Kane, Lydia. "Pope's Appeal to Pray, Reflect, and Act to Safeguard Creation." *Vatican News*, September 1, 2019. https://www.vaticannews.va/en/pope/news/2019-09/pope-s-appeal-to-pray-reflect-and-act-to-safeguard-creation.html.
Onion, Amanda, et al. "Rosh Hashanah." History.com, October 27, 2019. https://www.history.com/topics/holidays/rosh-hashanah-history.
Orbis. *Bread and Wine: Readings for Lent and Easter*. Maryknoll, NY: Orbis, 2005.

Bibliography

Orr, Peter C. *Exalted Above the Heavens: The Risen and Ascended Christ*. New Studies in Biblical Theology 47, edited by D. A. Carson. Downers Grove, IL: IVP Academic, 2019.

Orthodox Church in America. "Feast of the Theophany of Our Lord and Saviour Jesus Christ." https://www.oca.org/saints/lives/2020/01/06/100106-feast-of-the-theophany-of-our-lord-and-savior-jesus-christ.

———. "Pentecost: The Descent of the Holy Spirit." https://www.oca.org/orthodoxy/the-orthodox-faith/worship/the-church-year/pentecost-the-descent-of-the-holy-spirit.

O'Sullivan, Kevin. *The Sunday Readings Cycle*, 3 vols. Quincy, IL: Franciscan Herald, 1971.

Patapios, Hieromonk, trans. "The Feast of the Circumcision of Our Lord Jesus Christ. Humble Comments and Suggestions." *Orthodox Tradition* XVI.2 (1999) 2–3. http://orthochristian.com/50952.html.

Pauw, Amy Plantinga. *Church in Ordinary Time: A Wisdom Ecclesiology*. Grand Rapids: Eerdmans, 2017.

Pease, Donald E. "American Exceptionalism." *Oxford Bibliographies*. https://www.oxfordbibliographies.com/view/document/obo-9780199827251/obo-9780199827251-0176.xml.

Pemberton, Glenn. *Hurting with God: Learning to Lament with the Psalms*. Abilene, TX: Abilene Christian University Press, 2012.

The People of the United Methodist Church. "What is Lent and Why Does it Last Forty Days?" Ask The UMC. https://www.umc.org/en/content/ask-the-umc-what-is-lent-and-why-does-it-last-forty-days.

Perowne, Henry Stewart. "Herod King of Judaea." In *Encyclopedia Britannica*. https://www.britannica.com/biography/Herod-king-of-Judaea.

Peterson, Eugene H. *Practice Resurrection: A Conversation on Growing Up in Christ*. Grand Rapids: Eerdmans, 2010.

Pius XI. "Quas Primus: On the Feast of Christ the King." Vatican website. December 11, 1925. http://www.vatican.va/content/pius-xi/en/encyclicals/documents/hf_p-xi_enc_11121925_quas-primas.html.

Prowse, Christopher. "Lent 2017—Biblical Time: Chronos or Kairos?" The Catholic Archdiocese of Canberra and Goulburn. https://cgcatholic.org.au/catholic-voice/blog/lent-2017-biblical-time-chronos-kairos/.

Rah, Soong-Chan. *Prophetic Lament: A Call for Justice in Troubled Times*. Resonate Series. Downers Grove, IL: InterVarsity, 2015.

Ratzinger, Joseph. *The Spirit of the Liturgy*. San Francisco: Ignatius, 2000.

Reformed Church in America. "Disability Awareness Sunday Resources." Disability Concerns. https://www.rca.org/resources/disability/disability-awareness-sunday-resources.

Rich, Tracey R. "Treatment of Animals." Judaism 101. http://www.jewfaq.org/animals.htm.

Richert, Scott P. "Prayers for November: Month of Holy Souls in Purgatory." Learn Religions. March 28, 2019. https://www.learnreligions.com/prayers-for-november-4590136.

Rogers, Taylor Nicole. "LA's Skies are Smog-free and Peacocks are Roaming the Streets of Dubai. Photos Show How Nature Has Returned to Cities Shut Down." *Business

Bibliography

Insider, April 20, 2020. https://www.businessinsider.com/photos-show-nature-is-reclaiming-urban-areas-amid-coronavirus-2020-4.

Rohr, Richard. *Wondrous Encounters*. Cincinnati: St Anthony Messenger, 2011.

Rothman, Lily. "How MLK Day Became a Holiday." *Time*, January 19, 2015. https://time.com/3661538/mlk-day-reagan-history/.

Rowthorn, Anne, and Jeffrey Rowthorn. *God's Good Earth: Praise and Prayer for Creation*. Collegeville, MN: Liturgical, 2018.

Sacks, Jonathan. "Markets and Morals." *First Things*, August, 2000. https://www.firstthings.com/article/2000/08/markets-and-morals.

———. "The Therapeutic Joy of Purim." *The Office of Rabbi Sacks*, March 1, 2015. http://rabbisacks.org/therapeutic-joy-purim-purim-5775/.

Schillebeeckx, Edward. *Jesus: An Experiment in Christology*. Translated by Hubert Hoskyns. New York: Seabury, 1974.

Schweitzer, Albert. *The Quest of the Historical Jesus: A Critical Study of Its Progress from Reimarus to Wrede*. Translated by W. Montgomery. London: A&C Black, 1910.

Schwieterman, Edward W., et al. "A Limited Habitable Zone for Complex Life." *Astrophysical Journal* 878.1 (June 10, 2019) 1–9. https://iopscience.iop.org/article/10.3847/1538-4357/ab1d52.

Sears, David. *The Vision of Eden: Animal Welfare and Vegetarianism in Jewish Law and Mysticism*. Spring Valley, NY: OROT, 2003.

Season of Creation. https://seasonofcreation.org.

———. "About the Season of Creation." https://seasonofcreation.org/about/.

———. "Liturgies." https://seasonofcreation.com/worship-resources/liturgies/.

Senn, Frank C. *New Creation: Elements of a Liturgical Worldview*. Minneapolis: Augsburg Fortress, 2000.

Shepherd, Massey H. "Church Year." In *Encyclopedia Britannica*. https://www.britannica.com/topic/church-year.

Shreeve, Jamie. "Life Probably Exists Beyond Earth. So How do We Find It?" *National Geographic*, March, 2019. https://www.nationalgeographic.com/magazine/2019/03/extraterrestrial-life-probably-exists-how-do-we-search-for-aliens/.

Smith, Christian. "'On 'Moralistic Therapeutic Deism' as U.S. Teenagers' Actual, Tacit, De Facto Religious Faith." *The 2005 Princeton Lectures on Youth, Church, and Culture: With Imagination and Love: Leadership in Youth Ministry*, 46–58. https://youthlectures.ptsem.edu/?action=tei&id=youth-2005-05.

Smith, James K. A. *Desiring the Kingdom: Worship, Worldview, and Cultural Formation*. Cultural Liturgies. Grand Rapids: Baker Academic, 2009.

———. "Homo Liturgicus: On the Persistence of Ritual in Contemporary Fiction." *Image*, Issue 98. https://imagejournal.org/article/homo-liturgicus-on-the-persistence-of-ritual-in-contemporary-fiction/.

———. *How (Not) to Be Secular: Reading Charles Taylor*. Grand Rapids: Eerdmans, 2014.

Smith, Ralph. "Jesus' Transfiguration: The Context." Theopolis. September 27, 2018. https://theopolisinstitute.com/jesus-transfiguration-the-context/.

Smith, Peter. "Martin Luther's 95 Theses Explained, in 95 Parts." *Pittsburgh Post-Gazette*, October 26, 2017. https://www.post-gazette.com/local/region/2017/10/26/Protestant-Reformation-explanation-martin-luther-95-parts/stories/201810190001.

Bibliography

Society of the Holy Child Jesus. "World Day of Prayer for the Care of Creation." https://www.shcj.org/european/world-day-of-prayer-for-the-care-of-creation-is-sept-1/.

Smolensky, Michael, and Lynne Lamberg. *The Body Clock Guide to Better Health: How to Use Your Body's Natural Clock to Fight Illness and Achieve Maximum Health.* New York: Henry Holt and Company LLC, 2000.

Soulen, R. Kendall. "'Go Tell Pharaoh,' Or, Why Empires Prefer a Nameless God." *Cultural Encounters: A Journal for the Theology of Culture* 1.2 (Summer 2005) 49–59.

Speyr, Adrienne von. *Handmaid of the Lord.* 2d ed. San Francisco: Ignatius, 2017.

Stathis, Stephen W. "Federal Holidays: Evolution and Application." CRC Report for Congress. Congressional Research Service, The Library of Congress. February 8, 1999. https://www.senate.gov/reference/resources/pdf/Federal_Holidays.pdf.

Stauffer, Ethelbert. *Christ and the Caesars.* London: SCM, 1955.

Steenwyk, Carrie, and John D. Witvliet. *The Worship Sourcebook.* 2d ed. Grand Rapids: Faith Alive, 2013.

Stookey, Laurence Hull. *Calendar: Christ's Time for the Church.* Nashville: Abingdon, 1996.

Swinton, John. *Becoming Friends of Time: Disability, Timefulness, and Gentle Discipleship.* Studies in Religion, Theology, and Disability. Waco, TX: Baylor University Press, 2018.

Tabor, James. "Jesus Died on a Thursday, Not a Friday." *Taborblog* (blog), March 20, 2016. https://jamestabor.com/jesus-died-on-a-thursday-not-a-friday/.

Tait, Edwin, and Jennifer Woodruff. "The Real 12 Days of Christmas." *Christian History*, August 8, 2008. https://www.christianitytoday.com/history/2008/august/real-twelve-days-of-christmas.html.

Taylor, Charles. *A Secular Age.* Cambridge, MA: The Belknap of Harvard University Press, 2007.

Telushkin, Joseph. *Jewish Literacy: The Most Important Things to Know About the Jewish Religion, Its People, and Its History.* Revised ed. New York: HarperCollins, 2008.

Ten Boom, Corrie. *The Hiding Place: The Triumphant True Story of Corrie Ten Boom.* New York: Bantam, 1971.

Theopedia. "Council of Ephesus." https://www.theopedia.com/council-of-ephesus.

Thomas, John Paul. *Daily Reflections for Ordinary Time: Weeks 18–34.* Washington, DC: My Catholic Life!, 2016.

Thornton, Sharon G. *Broken Yet Beloved.* Nashville: Chalice, 2002.

ThoughtCo. "What Ordinary Time Means in the Catholic Church and Why Is It Called That?" Learn Religions. https://www.learnreligions.com/ordinary-time-in-the-catholic-church-542442.

Thurston, Herbert. "Feast of Fools." In *The Catholic Encyclopedia*, vol. 6. New York: Robert Appleton Company, 1909. http://www.newadvent.org/cathen/06132a.htm.

Tickle, Phyllis. *The Divine Hours.* 3 vols. New York: Image/Doubleday, 2000.

———. *Eastertide: Prayers for Lent Through Easter.* New York: Image/Doubleday, 2004.

———. *Christmastide: Prayers for Advent Through Epiphany from The Divine Hours.* New York: Image/Doubleday, 2003.

Tierney, John. "Feast of the Circumcision." In *The Catholic Encyclopedia* 3. New York: Robert Appleton Company, 1908. http://www.newadvent.org/cathen/03779a.htm.

Bibliography

Tierney, Kendra. *The Catholic All Year Compendium: Liturgical Living for Real Life*. San Francisco: Ignatius, 2018.

Time and Date. "Corpus Christi in the United States." Timeanddate.com. https://www.timeanddate.com/holidays/us/corpus-christi.

Tkach, Joseph. "Speaking of Life—Birthday Candles." *Grace Communion International*. Video File. https://www.gci.org/media/videos/birthday-candles/.

Torrance, James B. *Worship, Community and the Triune God of Grace*. Downers Grove, IL: IVP Academic, 1997.

Twain, Mark. *The War Prayer*. With drawings by John Groth. New York: HarperCollins, 2002.

Union Seminary (@UnionSeminary). "Today in chapel, we confessed to plants . . ." Twitter, September 17, 2019. https://twitter.com/UnionSeminary/status/1174000941667880960?ref_src=twsrc%5Etfw%7Ctwcamp%5Etweetembed%7Ctwterm%5E1174000941667880960&ref_url=https%3A%2F%2Fwww.washingtonpost.com%2Freligion%2F2019%2F09%2F18%2Fprogressive-seminary-students-offered-confession-plants-what-are-we-make-it%2F.

United States Conference of Catholic Bishops. "Advent Season." http://www.usccb.org/prayer-and-worship/liturgical-year/advent/.

———. "Ordinary Time." http://www.usccb.org/prayer-and-worship/liturgical-year/ordinary-time.cfm.

Walton, John H. *The Lost World of Genesis 1*. Downers Grove, IL: InterVarsity, 2009.

———. "Material or Function in Genesis 1? John Walton Responds." BioLogos, April 3, 2015. https://biologos.org/articles/series/reflections-on-the-lost-world-of-genesis-1-by-john-walton/material-or-function-in-genesis-1-john-walton-responds.

———. "Understanding Genesis 1—Resting in the Temple of God." YouTube Video, 2:43. Posted by BioLogos, February 10, 2010. https://www.youtube.com/watch?v=o26Ad-WdjOw&feature=youtu.be.

We Give: The United Methodist Church. "July 24—Disability Awareness Sunday." *Mission Moments and More*. http://www.umcgiving.org/mission-moments/july-24-disability-awareness-sunday.

Warren, Tish Harrison. *Liturgy of the Ordinary: Sacred Practices in Everyday Life*. Downers Grove, IL: InterVarsity, 2016.

Waskow, Arthur. "The Renewal of Purim and the Fast of Esther." The Shalom Center, September 8, 2001. https://theshalomcenter.org/node/247.

Watts, Craig M. *Bowing Toward Babylon: The Nationalistic Subversion of Christian Worship in America*. Eugene, OR: Cascade, 2017.

Webber, Robert E. *Ancient-Future Faith: Rethinking Evangelicalism for a Postmodern World*. Grand Rapids: Baker, 1999.

———. *Ancient-Future Time: Forming Spirituality Through the Christian Year*. Grand Rapids: Baker, 2004

Weber, Max. *The Protestant Ethic and the Spirit of Capitalism and Other Writings*. Penguin Twentieth Century Classics. New York: Penguin, 2002.

Wendel, JoAnna. "When Will the Sun Die?" *Space.com*, August 7, 2019. https://www.space.com/14732-sun-burns-star-death.html.

What Can You Do? "Celebrate National Disability Employment Awareness Month." https://www.whatcanyoudocampaign.org/celebrate-ndeam/.

Bibliography

Whelchel, Hugh. "How the Sacred-Secular Divide Impacts the Church." Institute for Work & Economics, March 20, 2019. https://tifwe.org/how-the-sacred-secular-divide-impacts-the-church/.

White, Lynn, Jr. "The Historical Roots of Our Ecological Crisis." *Science* 155.3767 (March, 1967) 1203–7.

White, Sidnie Ann. "Churches Militant, Penitent, and Triumphant." https://en.wikipedia.org/wiki/Churches_Militant,_Penitent,_and_Triumphant.

———. "Esther: A Feminist Model for Jewish Diaspora." In *Gender and Difference in Ancient Israel*, edited by Peggy Day, 161–77. Minneapolis: Fortress, 2000.

Williams, Rowan. "The Church: God's Pilot Project." Dr. Rowan Williams, 104th Archbishop of Canterbury, April 5, 2006. http://aoc2013.brix.fatbeehive.com/articles.php/1779/the-church-gods-pilot-project.

———. *Resurrection: Interpreting the Easter Gospel*. Cleveland, OH: Pilgrim, 2003.

Winthrop, John. "A Model of Christian Charity. In *A Library of American Literature: Early Colonial Literature, 1607–1675*, edited by Ellen Mackay Hutchinson and Edmund Clarence Stedmann, 304–7. New York: Charles L. Webster and Co., 1892.

Woolf, Christopher, producer. "Why Is the Yasukuni Shrine So Controversial?" Audio. *The World*, December 26, 2013. https://www.pri.org/stories/2013-12-26/why-yasukuni-shrine-so-controversial.

Wright, N. T. *The Challenge of Jesus: Rediscovering Who Jesus Was and Is*. Downers Grove, IL: InterVarsity, 1999.

———. "Christian Origins and the Resurrection of Jesus: The Resurrection of Jesus as a Historical Problem." *Sewanee Theological Review* 41.2 (1998). https://ntwrightpage.com/2016/07/12/christian-origins-and-the-resurrection-of-jesus-the-resurrection-of-jesus-as-a-historical-problem/.

———. *The Day the Revolution Began: Reconsidering the Meaning of Jesus's Crucifixion*. New York: HarperOne, 2016.

———. "God in Private and Public." Sermon at the Maundy Thursday Sung Eucharist, March 20, 2008. https://ntwrightpage.com/2016/03/30/god-in-private-and-public/.

———. "On Palm Sunday, Jesus Rides into the Perfect Storm." *ABC Religion & Ethics*, April 11, 2014. https://www.abc.net.au/religion/palm-sunday-jesus-rides-into-the-perfect-storm/10095900.

———. *Paul: A Biography*. New York: HarperOne, 2018.

———. "The Royal Revolution: Fresh Perspectives on the Cross." *Calvin College January Series*, January 24, 2017. https://ntwrightpage.com/2017/01/30/the-royal-revolution-fresh-perspectives-on-the-cross/.

———. *Simply Jesus: A New Vision of Who He Was, What He Did, and Why He Matters*. New York: HarperOne, 2011.

———. *Surprised by Hope: Rethinking Heaven, the Resurrection, and the Mission of the Church*. New York: HarperOne, 2008.

———. "The Uncomfortable Truth of Easter." A Sermon at the Sung Eucharist in Durham Cathedral, Easter Day, 2008. https://ntwrightpage.com/2016/03/30/the-uncomfortable-truth-of-easter/.

Wynne, John. "Feast of the Ascension." In *The Catholic Encyclopedia*, vol. 1. New York: Robert Appleton Company, 1907. https://www.newadvent.org/cathen/01767b.htm.

Bibliography

Yale University Press. "*Pax Romana: War, Peace and Conquest in the Roman World.*" https://yalebooks.yale.edu/book/9780300178821/pax-romana.

Yancey, Philip. *Disappointment with God: Three Questions No One Asks Aloud.* Grand Rapids: Zondervan, 1997.

Zimmer, Katarina. "Air Pollution Is Choking Solar Energy Around the World: Capitalizing on the Sun's Rays, Countries Like China Need to Part the Smog." *Popular Science*, December 11, 2018. https://www.popsci.com/smog-reduces-solar-energy/.

Zirker, Jack B. *Total Eclipse of the Sun.* Expanded ed. Princeton, NJ: Princeton University Press, 1995.

Zuckerman, Philip. *Living the Secular Life: New Answers to Old Questions.* New York: Penguin, 2014.

SCRIPTURE INDEX

GENESIS

1–3	203–6
1	201, 203, 205, 209, 210, 211, 217
1:1–2	152, 199–201
1:1	200
1:2	152, 201
1:3–5	200
1:3	152, 201
1:6–8	203
1:6	152, 204
1:9	152
1:11–12	209
1:11	152
1:14–31	197, 211
1:14–19	200
1:14	152
1:20	152
1:24	152
1:26–27	209
1:26	152, 208
1:28–29	208
1:29–30	209–10
1:31	197
2	203, 205
2:2	205
2:7	152
3	217
3:19	210
12:1–3	20
15:7	20
17	20
17:10–13	40
27:41—28:22	57
49.10	20

EXODUS

12	107, 218
12:11	112
12:29–42	112
13:12–15	34
14:14	137
19–24	218
20:12	208
23:10–11	206
23:5	208
34:22	146

LEVITICUS

12:1–8	34
16	107
18:28	207
22:28	208
23:15–21	146
25:1–5	208
25:12	206

NUMBERS

28–29	219
28:26–31	146
32–33	218

DEUTERONOMY

3:22	137
4:40	208
5:16	208
10:18	120
16:16	8, 107
22:4	208
22:6–7	208

JOSHUA

5:13–15	165
10:12–14	137

RUTH

2:4	20

1 SAMUEL

16:7	19
28	234

2 SAMUEL

12:22–23	234

ESTHER

1–10	73–75, 83–86
1:10–12	84
1:13–22	84
2:1–18	84
2:8–18	84
2:5–18	84
2:10	84
2:20	84
4:8–17	84
4:8	84
4:10–14	84
4:11	85
4:15–17	84, 85
5:1–4	85
5:9–14	85
7–8	84
9:20–22	86

PSALMS

19:1	207
89:27	53, 54
90:2	249
90:12	xiii, 249
127	136

ECCLESIASTES

3:1–8	153
3:11	153

SONG OF SOLOMON

2:16	226

ISAIAH

53	224
53:3	79

JOEL

2	193

MICAH

5:2–3	27
5:2	19, 20

MATTHEW

1:1–17	44
1:5–6	20
1:18–25	161
1:21	32
1:23	17, 20, 33, 52, 54, 55, 156
2	47, 49, 56
2:1–12	52, 56
2:1–3	26
2:2	26, 53, 54
2:3–6	27
2:6	17, 19, 50
2:8	50
2:10–11	54
2:11	53
2:12	50
2:13–18	49–50
2:13–15	26, 161
2:16–18	26
3	56
3:11–12	54
3:13–17	52–54, 242
3:14	52–53
3:15	53, 54
3:16–17	53, 54, 81, 162
4	220
4:1–11	80, 90
4:17–22	169
4:17	169, 193
4:18–22	169
5–7	220
5	77
5:17	219
6:9–13	163
6:9–10	163
6:11–13	163

11:28–30	33, 170
12:8	9
12:49	135
13:18–23	193
13:24–30	193
16	66–68
16:13–28	66
16:22	68
16:23	68
16:24	169
16:27–28	66
16:28	67
17	66, 234
17:1–13	55
17:1–3	66
17:4–5	68
17:9	68
17:14–24	69
19	50
21	108
21:1–11	99
21:8	99
21:9	99, 100
21:12–17	99–102
21:14–15	100
21:15	99
21:45–46	99–100
22:15–22	101
22:34–40	156
24:36	191
24:44	191
24:50–53	140
25:1–40	193–94
25:1–13	193–94
25:14–30	194
25:31–33	239
25:34–40	194
25:35–36	239
25:37–39	240
25:44	240
26:1–5	99–100
26:14–16	93
26:39	81
26:40–41	112
26:57–68	140
27:15–31	99–100
27:62–66	111
28:4	111
28:18–20	146, 155
28:20	156, 156n9

MARK

1:1–11	242
1:1	162
2:1–5	223
2:23–27	245
2:27–28	9
3:5–6	174
3:11	173
3:13–19	173–74
3:20–21	45
3:31–35	45
4:11	174
4:35–41	172
5:1–13	172–73
5:14–20	173
5:21–43	173, 177
6:1–6	173
6:48–52	173
10:46–52	222
16:7–8	127
16:10–11	127
16:12–13	127

LUKE

1:1–4	125
1:29	44
1:34–35	44
1:38	44
1:42	134
1:46–55	23, 44, 183–84
1:48	134
1:50–55	135
1:51–53	23, 65
1:52	23
2	22–24, 35, 63
2:1–7	20, 26
2:1–2	23
2:3	64
2:8–21	27
2:8–14	22
2:9	24
2:10	22
2:13–14	26
2:14	24, 25, 27
2:15–20	22

LUKE (continued)

2:19	22
2:21	40
2:22–42	161
2:22–38	34
2:25	63
2:26	63
2:27	63
2:29–35	64
2:29–32	35
2:31	65
2:32	65
2:34	64, 65
2:35	45, 134
2:38	35
2:41–52	45, 161
2:41–42	220
2:48	162
2:49	64, 81, 135, 162
2:50–51	64
2:50	162
2:51	162
3	242
3:21–22	242
4.16–30	65
5:1–11	132–33
5:10	133
5:12–14	65
5:27–32	65
6	77
6:20–23	22
6:20	65
6:24	65, 77–78
7	94, 242–43
7:18–30	242
7:36–50	94
8:19–21	64
8:21	135
9:7–9	243
9:16	124
10:20	25
10:38–42	93
10:40	93
11:27–28	64
12:13–21	178–80
12:15	180
12:19	178, 179
12:20	178
12:21	179
15:7	25
15:10	25
15:20–24	25
16	234
18:9–14	227, 230
19.40	207
19:41–44	101
21:26–28	140
22:14–20	104
22:19	124
22:24–27	160
22:66–71	140
24	124–26
24:13–35	124–25
24:15–16	124
24:30–31	124–26
24:35	126
24:36	25

JOHN

1:1–5	201
1:1–3	152
1:4	202
1:14	54, 221
1:19–42	56–57
1:29–34	242
1:29	32, 109n13, 220, 242
1:31	56, 57
1:32–34	57
1:36	57
1:39	57
1:45–46	57
1:46	57
1:47	57
1:49–51	57
2	135, 162
2:1–11	58, 60
2:1–5	162
2:1–4	45
2:4	60, 64, 135
2:5	60
2:6–10	60
2:11	61
2:13–22	108
2:13	220
2:18–22	220
3:22–30	56

2:23–25	57, 58	19:25–27	65
4:19–26	220	19:25	44
5	61, 62	19:26–27	135
5:1–17	62	19:34	135
5:18	162	20	132
5:19–24	162	20:1–10	122
5:39–40	220	20:1–8	112n17
6	61, 62	20:11–18	122
6:4	220	20:17	163
6:14	62	20:19	132
6:15	62	20:24–25	130
6:25–40	62	20:26–29	130
6:41–69	62	20:26	132
6:52–66	62	20:30–31	61, 61n18, 62
6:68–69	62	21	132–33
7	220	21:1–3	132
7:1–39	177	21:5	133
7:30	177	21:9–13	132
8	220	21:14	132
8:12	202	21:15–19	133
9	61, 62		
10:28–30	113	ACTS	
11	61, 62, 94	1:1–11	143
11:1–44	177	1:1–2	143
11:2	94	1:1	125
11:16	131	1:2	143
11:45–53	62	1:4–11	141
12:1–8	92–95	1:4–5	44
12:1	94	1:6–11	140, 141
12:3	94	1:9	144
12:6	93	1:11	144
12:7	93	1:13–14	44
12:8	94	2	146, 220
12:9–11	94	2:1–4	141
12:23	61, 177	2:3–4	147
13–17	103–6	2:17	193
13:1	177, 220	2:22–36	118
13:1–5	104	2:42–47	144
13:6	104	2:41	146
13:8	104	2:42	124
13:12–17	105, 160	2:46	124
13:34	103	3	128–29
14–16	141	4	129
17	6	4:8–22	129
17:1	177	4:16–21	146
17:20–26	163	4:32–37	144
18:1–3	93	6:1–7	125
19:23–27	135	7:54–60	140, 235

ACTS (continued)

20:7	124
20:11	124
27:35	124

ROMANS

5:5	163
6:1–4	111
6:3	111
8	87–88, 119
8:15	163
8:16–17	87
8:17	87, 88
8:18	88
8:22	207
8:29	88
8:32	87
8:35–39	88
8:35	87
8:37–39	88

1 CORINTHIANS

1:18–31	42, 128
1:21–25	129
1:27	41
3	239
3:10–15	239
3:15	239
3:16–17	221
5:7	9, 109n13
10:31	12n22
11—14	160
11:1	189, 230
11:17–34	126, 160
11:27–34	160
12:26	75
13:12	221
15:9	230
15:17	118, 148
15:20	205–6
15:23	205–6
15:29	234n117

2 CORINTHIANS

8:9	79
10:5	245
11:23–29	88
12:8–10	224

GALATIANS

2:11–14	125
3:16	20
3:29	20
4:4–7	32
4:4–5	40, 153
4:4	177
5:19–26	206

EPHESIANS

4:1–16	140
4:8	79
4:30	147

PHILIPPIANS

1:21	90
1:23	90
1:24–26	90
3	71
3:1–6	90
3:7–16	90
3:7–8	90
3:10	71, 90, 91n23
3:12–21	232
3:12–14	230

COLOSSIANS

1	217
1:15–20	206, 217
1:15	53, 54
2:16–17	9, 246
2:16	245
2:17	9
3:1–4	140, 145, 235
3:4	145
3:14	xiii

1 TIMOTHY

2:4–5	182

HEBREWS

1:1–3	140–41
4	220
4:15	53, 54

8	10	3:15	13
8:1–6	2	3:18	54
8:6	2		
8:8–13	146	**2 PETER**	
9–10	220		
9	108	1:4	157
9:27	235, 237	3:13–14	239
10:24–25	10, 18, 189, 191, 245		
10:25	189	**1 JOHN**	
11	188, 189, 221	1:9	208
11:39–40	17, 109, 221	2:2	32
12:1–2	11, 234, 235	5:3	170
12:1	187, 188, 189		
12:2	3	**REVELATION**	
		1:19–20	207
JAMES		5	224
1–2	77	5:6	109n13, 224
1:18	206	5:12	109, 109n13
1:27	120	6	234
4:6	227	7	234
5:16	208, 229	7:9–10	99
		21:2	192
1 PETER		21:5	153, 206
		21:22–25	119
1:10–12	17	21:22	108
2:5	189	22:13	249
2:9	3, 113, 117, 119, 167, 205	22:17	109, 206

NAME INDEX

Adam, Adolf, 2
Aquinas, *See* Thomas Aquinas, Saint
Athanasius, Saint, 158

Bainton, Roland, 159, 229n108
Balthasar, Hans Urs von, 196–97, 213
Barth, Karl, 153, 196
Baylis, Albert, 105
Benedict, Pope, 110, 216
Bigelow, Gordon, 15
Bonhoeffer, Dietrich, 58, 169–70
Breck, John, 186–87
Brooks, Philip, 21
Brueggemann, Walter, 72n1, 74, 180, 205n66
Buckley, Michael, 154–55
Burton, Tara Isabella, 238

Calhoun, Jimi, 224
Calvin, John, 43, 159
Caravaggio, 130
Carson, D.A., 61n18, 92–94, 156n9
Cavanaugh, William, 137n23, 166–67
Chesterton, G.K., 3, 216n86
Chrysostom, 115
Clapp, Rodney, xii, 135n20
Clement of Alexandria, 47–48, 201
Cone, James, 77, 79n16
Consolmagno, Guy, 212–13
Crosby, Cindy, 4

Dostoyevsky, Fyodor, 97–98

Eliade, Mircea, 10n19, 151–52n2
Elliot, Jim, 136

Enns, Peter, 203, 209n74
Erickson, Nancy, 209n75, 211
Esler, Philip Francis, 126

Farrow, Douglas, 141n30
Faulkner, William, 192
Faustina Kowalska, 121–22
Fee, Gordon, 77–78, 126n10, 160n18
Fox, Michael, 84–85
Francis, Pope, 74–75, 87, 189, 195–98
Francis of Assisi, Saint, 152, 189, 195, 209–10, 215–17, 231, 255
Frei, Hans, 7

Geist, Tania, 110–11
George, Timothy, 44n24
Gibbon, Edward, 36
Goldsworthy, Adrian, 26
Green, Emma, 37–38
Green, Joel, 23, 65
Gregory of Nazianzus, 32, 53–54
Gunton, Colin, 147, 153

Hardin, Jeff, 212–13
Harris, Max, 41
Harper, Brad, 6n12
Heschel, Abraham, 219n95
Hickman, Hoyt, 4
Hopko, Thomas, 119

Irenaeus, Saint, 31, 143, 158, 201
Irving-Stonebraker, Sara, 131

Jenkins, Philip, 36–37, 36n10
John of the Cross, Saint, 243n127

Name Index

John Paul II, Pope, 115, 191–92, 210, 236–39

Kateri Tekakwitha, Saint, 152, 215–17, 255
Kinkade, Thomas, 16
Kutz, Karl, 204

Lewis, C.S., 4, 131
Lincoln, Abraham, 138–39
Luther, Martin, 43, 158–59, 169, 226–29, 234

Matson, David Lertis, 124
McGowan, Andrew, 31, 34n7
Minear, Paul, 25
Morrow, Jeff, 203–4

Newbigin, Lesslie, 39, 154–55
Newman, John Henry, 7, 18n2
Nietzsche, Friedrich, 128–29

Oakley, Matt, 4
Origen of Alexandria, 31

Pease, Donald, 164
Pious XII, Pope, 185–86, 244
Prowse, Christopher, 175–76

Rah, Soong-Chan, 73–74
Rohr, Richard, 72n1

Sacks, Rabbi Jonathan, 51, 73
Saliers, Don, 4
Schweitzer, Albert, 67
Schwieterman, Edward, 213–14
Smith, James K. A., 10, 12n22, 246
Soulen, R. Kendall, 37
Steenwyk, Carrie, 72n1
Stookey, Laurence Hull, 4
Stuart, Douglas, 77–78

Teresa, Mother, 189–90
Taylor, Charles, 12n22, 13, 248–49
Tertullian, 31
Thomas Aquinas, Saint, 157–59, 178–79
Thomas, John Paul, 179
Tierney, Kendra, 4, 41n19

Van Gogh, Vincent, 201

Walton, John, 203, 205, 209, 211
Warhol, Andy, 177
Webber, Robert, 5, 12–13
Weber, Max, 79n14, 159, 212
Wesley, John, 231, 234
White, James, 4
Winthrop, John, 164
Wiseman, Jennifer, 212–13
Witvliet, John D., 72n1
Wright, N.T., 67–68, 91n23, 100–101, 103–5, 107–8, 112–13, 118–19, 132

SUBJECT INDEX

Advent, 4, 11, 15–28, 31–33, 39, 168, 192, 241, 246–49
Agape feast, 125, 160
All Saints' Day, 152, 226, 230–36, 255
All Souls' Day, 230–36, 255
American exceptionalism, 39, 164–66
American dream, 2, 8, 11, 20, 97, 189
Anglican (Church), 29, 31, 122, 157, 181, 233, 234n115
Apollinarianism, 53
Apostles' Creed, 44, 142
Ascension Sunday, 78–79, 140, 143–45, 247, 254
Ash Wednesday, 54, 71, 73–75, 77, 80, 87, 252–53
Atonement, Day of, 107–8, 208n71, 219–20

Baptism, 32, 40, 52–56, 63, 71, 81, 92, 162, 242
Beatitudes, 22
Biblical drama, 115–16
Black Friday, 11, 244, 246
Black history month, 77–79, 253

Chalcedonian Christology, 186
Chocolat, 88
Christ the King Sunday, 11, 47, 120, 151–52, 191, 232, 241, 244–47, 255
Christmas, 1, 3, 6, 13, 15–16, 23–24, 27, 29, 31–35, 37–39, 43, 47, 148, 168, 172, 244–45, 251–52
Christmastide, 11, 29–45, 47, 63, 151, 170, 175, 252

Chronos/Kairos, 175–77
Church, 3–13, 18, 21, 34, 41, 47, 52–54, 56, 60, 63, 66, 72–75, 78, 86, 91–92, 99–100, 103, 105, 107, 115, 117–20, 124–26, 128–33, 138, 141–46, 151, 157, 166–67, 188–95, 201, 206, 217–25, 230–34, 244–46, 248
Commodification, 39, 155, 197
Community, 6–8, 13, 17, 32, 37–38, 45, 78, 90, 105, 107, 115, 119, 126, 140–41, 143–45, 156, 169, 187–89, 216, 221, 225, 231, 238–39, 243, 245
Consumerism, 8, 39, 74, 96, 155, 244, 246n131
Corpus Christi, 152, 157, 255
Covenant (New), 2, 8, 10, 37, 79n16, 115, 119, 146, 157
Creation, 26, 51, 53–54, 67, 113, 118–20, 146–48, 152–53, 193, 195–97, 199–215, 217, 219, 243, 245
Cruciformity, 77, 79, 102, 128, 130, 167, 177, 225
Culture, 12, 15, 18, 71, 73, 78, 97, 100, 104, 135, 138, 177, 224

Depression, 35
Diachronic (time), 187, 188
Disability Awareness, 222–25
Discipleship, 48, 58, 131, 167, 169–70, 193
Divine Mercy Sunday, 121, 123, 254
Doubt, 45, 130–31, 157, 243n127

Easter, 6–7, 11, 39, 63, 71, 74, 77–80, 87–88, 92, 97, 103, 105, 108–13, 115–21, 140, 146–48, 151, 168, 172, 193
Eastertide, 11, 115–49, 151, 170, 172, 175
Ecology, 195, 210, 215–16
Ecumenical, 5, 6, 6n12, 44, 45, 155,
Emmanuel, 47, 52, 54–55, 156
Empire, 26, 97, 110, 113, 156
Environment, 212, 216
Environmentalism, 216
Ephesus, Council of, 44
Epiphanytide, 11, 47–69, 172
Eschatological future, 7, 67, 79, 166, 187, 191–92, 225
Eschatology, 9, 243
Eucharist, 6, 126, 157, 159–60, 192
Evangelical, 5–7, 20, 77–78

Faith, 11–13, 17–21, 42, 44–46, 58, 61, 64–65, 69, 78, 88, 91, 110–11, 117–18, 127–29, 131–33, 136, 155, 158–59, 163, 187, 189, 196–97, 206, 213, 219–23, 229–30, 232, 235, 238,39, 244
Father's Day, 3, 152, 161–63, 255
Feast of Circumcision, 40–43
Feast of Epiphany, 34, 47, 49–56, 61, 193
Feast of Fools, 41–43
Feast of Mercy, 104, 122
Feast of Tabernacles, 107, 152, 218
Feast of the Theophany, 53
Feast of Weeks, 8, 107, 115, 146, 218
Fellowship, 5, 71, 90, 125–26
Feminism, 83–85, 126n19
Festival of Booths, 8, 107
Festival of Sukkot, 8, 152, 218–21
Forty Days of Purpose, 80
Fourth of July, 3, 4, 148, 152, 164–67, 255
Free market, 39, 98
Freedom, 8, 26, 38, 97, 138, 164, 196, 229

Gettysburg, 137–38
Globalization, 75

Good Friday, 82, 97, 103, 105, 107–11, 113, 117–19, 248–49
Gospels, 25, 31–32, 66, 79, 84, 107–8, 112, 127, 132, 161–62, 242
Grace, 58, 94, 101, 115, 122, 158–59, 173, 182, 183, 196, 213, 226–28, 245

Halloween, 228–31, 233
Hanukkah, 36–39, 107, 219, 252
Haves/have-nots, 74, 77, 79, 125, 160
Heroism, 3
Holidays, 1, 3, 14–16, 24, 27, 36–39, 73, 108, 148, 161, 218–19
Holy Saturday, 11, 110–11, 113, 117
Holy Week, 9, 11, 14, 97–113, 115, 117, 119, 166
Homo liturgicus, 11, 204
Hope, 7, 31, 34–35, 69, 88, 111, 113, 131, 136, 142,167, 179, 187, 207, 241, 243

Identity, 1, 37, 45, 50, 56, 68, 78, 81, 94, 118, 140, 242
Imagination, 7, 12n22, 13, 131, 166
Incarnation, 10, 21, 54, 172, 175–76, 191

Kairos, 152, 166, 191
Kingdom, 18, 20, 25, 28, 65–67, 69, 78–79, 87, 101–3, 105, 119, 142, 147, 153, 163, 166, 169, 174, 191, 193, 220, 242–43

Lament, 73–75, 77, 79, 101, 138
Lent, 11, 56, 63, 66–69, 71–95, 100, 168
Liturgy, 2–3, 7, 9–10, 34, 73, 77–79, 115, 119, 138, 169, 180, 185, 188, 203–4, 241, 246
Logos, 152–53
Lord's Supper (Table), 5–6, 32, 104, 124–25, 157, 159–60, 166
Love, 9, 14, 18, 48, 64, 75, 82, 87–89, 91, 93–95, 97–98, 103–5, 133–36, 152, 155, 159–60, 163, 173, 177, 179, 181, 187, 191,

Subject Index

196–98, 200–201, 215–16, 226, 229, 231–32, 236, 237

Magnificat, 44–45, 65, 135, 183
Marginalization, 77, 127
Martyrdom, 3, 78–79, 88, 235
Mary, Blessed Virgin, 40–44, 181, 186–87
Mary, Mother of Jesus, *See Theotokos*
Maundy Thursday, 11, 97, 103–5, 112, 117, 157
Mercy, 121–23, 162, 174, 189–90, 222, 226–27
Messiah, 9, 17, 19–20, 22–23, 27, 31–32, 35, 50, 57, 62, 65, 99, 102, 117, 132, 146, 167, 183, 224, 242–43
Minority voices, 39, 164
Mosaic Law, 40
Mother's Day, 3, 134–36, 254

Nationalism, 38, 108, 137, 166, 229
Nihilism, 71
Ninety-five Theses, 228

Ordinary Time, 11, 47, 148–49, 151–247, 167–71, 172, 175, 179, 193, 200, 222, 227, 241, 248
Orthodox (Church), 34n5, 40, 119, 157, 185–87, 195, 229, 239

Palm Sunday, 11, 82, 92, 97, 99–102, 117, 253
Passover, 8–9, 37–39, 103–4, 107–10, 112–13, 115, 118–19, 146, 161, 218, 220
Patriotism, 166
Pax Romana, 25–26, 101
Pentecost, 13–14, 39, 47, 115, 118, 141, 143–44, 146–49, 151–52, 172, 175–76, 192–93, 218, 246, 254
Pilgrimage, 8–9, 50, 107–9, 161, 218–21, 249
Privatizaton, 3, 38, 108
Propaganda, 139
Protestant Reformation, 43, 152, 189, 226–29, 234

Protestants, 43–44, 158, 182–83, 186, 189, 226, 229–30, 232, 234, 237
Purgatory, 230, 234, 236–37, 239–40
Purim, 73–75, 83, 86, 219

Religion, 3, 10, 15, 28, 36, 38–39, 97, 101, 131, 137–38, 164, 196, 213, 245–46
Religious liberty, 36, 238n125
Repentance, 52–53, 74, 92, 229
Roman Catholic (Church), 6, 40, 43–44, 122, 157–58, 168, 179, 181–83, 185–86, 216, 228, 230, 233–36, 239
Rosh Hashanah, 219

Sabbath, 9, 62, 68, 162, 197, 205–6, 208, 219–21, 245–46
Sacred, 7, 10, 10n19, 12n22, 13–14, 108n12, 153, 161, 169n23, 176–77, 209, 212, 219n95, 235, 245, 246n131, 248
Sacrifice, 3, 42, 54, 85, 93–94, 103–5, 138, 141, 158, 208, 218, 232, 237, 242
Salvation, 3, 9, 27, 32, 35, 44, 48, 53–54, 65, 78, 108, 118, 126, 135–36, 142, 158–59, 182, 190, 192, 195, 220, 228–29, 237
Seasons, 11, 13, 39, 47, 73, 77, 81, 115, 141, 168, 172, 245, 249, 251
Secular, 1–4, 7–14, 12n22, 29, 38, 48, 115, 137, 151, 165, 235, 238–39, 244–49
Secular Humanism, 238
Secularization, 12n22, 13n24, 244
Signs, 25, 27, 57–58, 60–62, 121–22, 144, 193, 242–43
St. Paul's Cathedral, 137–38
Starry Night, 201
Story (narrative), 4, 8–9, 13, 13n26, 15, 21–22, 25, 3249, 63, 67–68, 73, 117–19, 125, 138, 195–96, 211, 219–20
Suffering, 9, 17–18, 66, 69, 71–76, 79, 83, 85, 87–88, 90–91, 111, 113, 119, 141, 144, 157, 173, 190, 208, 224

Sun of Righteousness, 47–48, 201
Synchronic (time), 187, 188

Temple, 2, 8, 10, 20, 34–36, 63–65, 68, 97, 100–101, 107–8, 119, 161, 167, 203–5, 219–21, 227
Temptations, 80–82, 112, 220
Thanksgiving, 1, 44, 244
Theosis, 159
Theotokos (Mary, Mother of Jesus), 3, 19–24, 26–27, 30, 32, 40–42, 43–45, 60, 64, 134–35, 161–62, 181–88, 190
Transfiguration, 47, 55–56, 66–69, 247
Trinity, 8, 53, 105, 147, 154–56, 182, 186
Trinity Sunday, 152, 154–57
Two Hands of God, 201

Vietnam Veterans Memorial, 137–38

Witness, 2, 6–11, 13, 21, 36, 38, 41, 50, 53, 74, 78n13, 90, 99, 115, 118, 125, 131–32, 135, 141–42, 146, 155, 181, 189–90, 204, 220, 232, 234–35, 245
World Day of Prayer, 195, 197, 199,
Worship, xi–xiii, 2, 6–14, 13n24, 21, 36–38, 41, 49–51, 53–54, 56, 68, 74, 99, 115, 118–19, 154n5, 159n16, 190, 204, 215, 217, 220, 234

Yasukuni Shrine, 137–38
Yom Kippur, 108, 219

Zion, 20, 21, 38

www.ingramcontent.com/pod-product-compliance
Lightning Source LLC
Chambersburg PA
CBHW030818230426
43667CB00008B/1278